CREATING THE CREATION MUSEUM

T0367040

Creating the Creation Museum

How Fundamentalist Beliefs Come to Life

Kathleen C. Oberlin

NEW YORK UNIVERSITY PRESS

New York

NEW YORK UNIVERSITY PRESS
New York
www.nyupress.org

References to internet websites (URLs) were accurate at the time of writing. Neither the author nor New York University Press is responsible for URLs that may have expired or changed since the manuscript was prepared.

Library of Congress Cataloging-in-Publication Data
Names: Oberlin, Kathleen Curry, author.
Title: Creating the Creation Museum : how fundamentalist beliefs come to life /
Kathleen C. Oberlin.
Description: New York : New York University Press, [2020] | Includes
bibliographical references and index.
Identifiers: LCCN 2020015057 (print) | LCCN 2020015058 (ebook) |
ISBN 9781479881642 (hardback) | ISBN 9781479805709 (paperback) |
ISBN 9781479897520 (ebook) | ISBN 9781479861811 (ebook)
Subjects: LCSH: Creation Museum (Petersburg, Ky.)—History. | Answers
in Genesis (Organization) | Museums—Social aspects—United States. |
Creationism—United States.
Classification: LCC BS651 .O26 2020 (print) | LCC BS651 (ebook) |
DDC 231.7/652074769363—dc23
LC record available at https://lccn.loc.gov/2020015057
LC ebook record available at https://lccn.loc.gov/2020015058

New York University Press books are printed on acid-free paper, and their binding materials are chosen for strength and durability. We strive to use environmentally responsible suppliers and materials to the greatest extent possible in publishing our books.

Manufactured in the United States of America

10 9 8 7 6 5 4 3 2 1

Also available as an ebook

CONTENTS

ABBREVIATIONS

Answers in Genesis   AIG

American Scientific Affiliation   ASA

American Association for the Advancement of Science   AAAS

Creation Research Society   CRS

Institute for Creation Research   ICR

Intelligent Design   ID

Museum of the Bible   MOTB

National Center for Science Education   NCSE

Old Earth Creationism   OEC

Social Movement Organization   SMO

Young Earth Creationism   YEC

Introduction

KEN HAM: People have been indoctrinated to believe that creationists cannot be scientists. I believe this is a case of secularists hijacking the word "science" . . . it doesn't matter whether you're an evolutionist or a creationist, you can be a great scientist . . . But I want you to also understand: molecules-to-man evolution belief has nothing to do with developing technology. You see, when we're talking about origins, we're talking about the past. We weren't there. We can't observe that . . . Here at the Creation Museum, we make no apologies about the fact that our origins, or historical science, is based on the Biblical account.

BILL NYE: There is no distinction made between historical science and observational science. These are constructs unique to Mr. Ham. We don't normally have these anywhere in the world except here [the Creation Museum]. Natural laws that applied in the past, apply now . . . Mr. Ham and his followers have this remarkable view of a worldwide flood that somehow influenced everything we observe in nature. A 500-foot wooden boat, eight zookeepers for 14,000 individual animals, every land plant in the world underwater for a year? I ask us all, "is that really reasonable?" . . . Billions of people in the world are deeply religious . . . But these same people do not embrace the extraordinary view that the Earth is somehow only 6,000 years old. That is unique, and here's my concern . . . what makes the United States a world leader is our technology, innovation, our new ideas. If we continue to eschew science, eschew the process, and try to divide our science into observational science and historical science, we won't move forward and embrace natural laws. We will not make discoveries. We will not invent and innovate and stay ahead.[1]

—Excerpts from opening statements at the Ken Ham vs.
  Bill Nye debate

On February 4, 2014, Bill Nye met with Ken Ham to film a public debate at the Creation Museum in Petersburg, Kentucky. The crowd swelled in the 1,000-seat Legacy Hall auditorium, selling out the $25-per-seat event. Seventy members of the press attended to cover the event, including a moderator from CNN. Meanwhile, thousands of people on the internet livestreamed the debate that lasted for more than two hours. Many supporters even hosted viewing parties in churches, community centers, and schools. C-SPAN would later air the debate in its entirety and the YouTube video boasts more than seven million views and counting.[2] Why all the fuss? Bill Nye "the Science Guy" is a popular science educator in the United States and a familiar face in the media since his television show debuted in the 1990s. Ken Ham is the founder of Answers in Genesis (AiG), the organization that built the Creation Museum, and has long been a leader and featured spokesperson for the creationist movement. The stakes for this debate felt high. Since the late 1980s, creation-evolution debates had faded to scarcity after prominent scientists such as Stephen Jay Gould questioned their utility for convincing the public, and questions loomed about whether they were merely providing a platform for creationists to gain more exposure. And, now, once again, well-known scientists such as Richard Dawkins and Neil deGrasse Tyson lamented both Bill Nye's involvement and the fact that he agreed to holding the event on AiG's turf. Would giving AiG this platform only aid the organization in its goal to persuade the audience that if one views both the Bible (a close, literal reading) and the natural world (observational, real-world data) as sources of authority, then the Earth appears to be less than 10,000 years old?[3]

There was no declared winner of the debate. Nonetheless, the public had somewhere to go—in-person and virtually—to learn more about Ken Ham's creation scientists and why Bill Nye was so concerned about this fringe group's impact on the future of the United States. "Prepare to Believe" is the slogan that greets visitors throughout the Creation Museum. Indeed, this event did prepare many audience members to believe and very much alarmed others; regardless, the debate seized the public's attention about a subject that many thought was largely settled decades before.

The typical story about the creationist movement centers on battles in the courtroom, like the Scopes Trial. *Creating the Creation Museum* is grounded in a new setting: a museum.[4] When visitors walk into the Creation Museum, they see a place organized like a museum and act accordingly. Since its opening in 2007, museum-goers wait in line, purchase their $30 general admission tickets, and proceed to walk through the more than 70,000-square-foot building.[5] In May 2017, on its tenth anniversary, the museum reached an attendance milestone tallying more than three million visitors. AiG continues to reach the public and spread its message regardless of any court decision.

Early on, some observers claimed that the museum was an anomaly that simply popped up as a quirky tourist destination; it would quickly fall into the cultural dustbin.[6] For them, the level of professionalism and the scale of the Creation Museum would come as a surprise. Indeed, it is not kitsch.[7] Media skeptics and political pundits suggested that the museum failed to engage the broader public because it did not mount a serious attack on the evolutionary science routinely depicted in natural history museums: Sites like these pose no threat to the authority of mainstream science since they are not taken seriously by many visitors.[8] These naysayers see in AiG an organization that is more interested in proselytizing and making money for its charismatic leader, Ken Ham, than legitimating its movement and securing a broader platform for creation science.[9]

While AiG's position stands in stark contrast to what many people in the United States believe, the overall credibility of creationism within the public sphere has not subsided. Survey trends from 1982 to 2017 suggest anywhere from 38% to 46% of those living in the United States believe that God created man within the last 10,000 years.[10] A recent National Science Foundation report concluded, "Many people know basic facts about evolution and science without believing in human evolution."[11] Understanding how these trends endure has remained unclear, despite the public's relatively consistent levels of trust in science as an institution and steady levels of science education knowledge, albeit comparatively low with regard to other industrialized countries.[12]

Scholars who focus on movement efforts in educational or political venues also find the persistence of creationist beliefs puzzling given their continual failure to significantly influence curricula or legislation. Why did AiG focus its ambitions exclusively on constructing a museum instead of adopting more conventional political tactics such as mass demonstrations, persuading political elites, or launching policy initiatives? The answer, in part, is that AiG's strategy has been to redirect the movement's attention back to reaching the popular masses rather than institutional insiders. And, AiG persisted in that strategy.

I show how the Creation Museum helps to solve a piece of the puzzle as it reflects the movement's broader efforts to shift from failed tactics to focus on social change by way of reigniting a culture war using its own site. The Creation Museum is not representative or typical. But I argue that when studying social movement activity, this uniqueness is an asset. While political debates and school board scuffles may garner some attention, maintaining a large-scale museum is precisely the kind of "unusual" social movement tactic positioned to attract sustained attention in a broader cultural context.

Why study this kind of museum? The case of the Creation Museum provides an opportunity to examine an attempt by a social movement not only to foster social change but also to investigate the places where that social change occurs, and how the locations they create matter. I explore how the Creation Museum is an unexpected social movement site, but one that becomes understandable if we analyze how creationists used it to physically ground their claims, better positioning them to secure cultural authority over time. My focus is on AiG and the Creation Museum because they reflect an attempt to target a public mouthpiece of the scientific establishment: the natural history museum, one of science's premier long-standing cultural institutions.[13] As historian of science Sophie Forgan (2005) suggests, "Architecture is designed to appeal first to the emotions and then to the intellect" (581). By linking scientific practices to religious and sociocultural political claims based on the literal interpretation of the Bible, AiG attempts to inculcate creation science to families and communities that feel as though they had been forced unnecessarily to reject mainstream science due to its secularity. Sites such as the Creation Museum seek to solidify supporters' commitments while reaching a leery yet primed broader audience who feel their perspectives are often marginalized. By empirically unpacking AiG's efforts, we gain insight into why some religious members of the public feel sidelined in society and how a group like AiG may offer alternative solutions that resonate with the disenchanted members of the public even if they do not fully support that group.

In *Creating the Creation Museum*, I argue that the impact of the museum does not hinge on the accuracy or credibility of its scientific claims, as many scholars, media critics, and political pundits would suggest. Instead, what AiG seeks by creating a physical site like the Creation Museum is the ability to engage plausibility politics—broadening what we, as an audience, perceive as possible if not reasonable and amplifying the stakes if we allow those ideas to circulate. In so doing, they draw from a well-worn creationist tradition.

Creationist Movement Background

Although the roots of Protestant evangelicalism in the United States date back to the early 1800s, the origins of the Young Earth Creationist (YEC) movement are based in the infamous Scopes Trial of 1925. The teacher John Scopes was found to be in violation of Tennessee's Butler Act, which passed that same year and prohibited evolution from being taught in the classroom statewide. The trial catapulted the nation into a public debate regarding the content and role of science in education and in American culture. As historian George Marsden (1980) documents, "Fundamentalists shared with the discontented intellectuals of the 1920s, if little else, a sense of the profound spiritual and cultural crisis of the twentieth century . . . Modernism and the theory of evolution, they were convinced, had caused the catastrophe by undermining the Biblical foundations of American civilization" (3). After the trial, the antievolution movement retreated as much of the American public ridiculed it as narrow-minded and behind the times.[14]

Throughout the worldwide turbulence of war during the 1930s and 1940s, antievolutionists emphasized cooperation and the spread of the gospel by forging new alliances increasingly through Christian associations of scientists.[15] By the 1960s, driven by strong fundamentalist convictions and creationist beliefs, Henry Morris and John Whitcomb Jr. published *The Genesis Flood* (1961), signaling a break from the more cooperatively minded evangelicals who were less unanimous in their views on evolution. Morris unequivocally became known as the founding father of the YEC movement. In 1963, YEC emerged as a distinct movement when Morris, along with nine other devout YEC adherents, formed the Creation Research Society. As opposed to earlier movement efforts in which the members lacked prestigious credentials—an enormous liability during the Scopes Trial decades before—five of the ten founding members of the Creation Research Society earned a doctoral degree in the biological sciences at mainstream universities and, as a prerequisite to becoming members, all of them were required to hold such credentials.[16]

Many within the movement regarded the period from the mid-1970s to the 1980s as the "Decade of Creation," evident in the following headline printed by the movement's publication *Acts & Fact*: "Scientific Establishment Alarmed at Creationism Rise."[17] The presidential election of a self-proclaimed evangelical, Jimmy Carter, in 1976, coupled with Jerry Falwell's advancement of the Moral Majority in 1979, an evangelical political action group with whom more than 40% of the American population was familiar, solidified the base in the 1980s to propel this new brand of evangelicalism to the mainstream.[18] And, fundamentalist factions such as young earth creationists were more than willing to go along. The movement received significant attention when newly elected President Ronald Reagan claimed in the September 1980 issue of *Science* that he had doubts about evolution and saw no reason for it to be taken as infallible; he suggested that there was a need to teach the theory of creation as well.[19] Predictably, media interest in young earth creationism grew considerably afterward. Whether the publicity itself was supportive or critical, members framed it as a success because any publicity shed light on the movement and broadened its recognition.

The 1987 decision in *Edwards v. Aguillard* forced creationists to distance their religious arguments from science due to concerns over the separation of Church and State in public schools. This judicial defeat was a significant blow to the YEC movement, and its members looked for strategies beyond the educational sphere. In turn, Intelligent Design proponents began to develop a distinct religious and scientific worldview. In keeping with old earth creationism's more conventional theory that the Earth is billions of years old, Intelligent Design was more palatable for a wider audience since its only religious reference was a general supernatural force: "A quarter of U.S. adults (25%) say evolution was guided by a supreme being."[20] Intelligent Design's tactical sophistication, its support from some prestigious academics at secular universities, and its broader appeal sustained legal and political battles from the late 1980s to the present: The publication of a controversial Intelligent Design textbook *Of Pandas and People* (1989), the founding of the think tank Discovery Institute (1991), and court battles like the prominent *Kitzmiller v. Dover* case (2005), in which Intelligent Design advocates unsuccessfully pushed for schools to adopt their curriculum, received substantial nationwide coverage.[21]

Even though scholars of creationism have documented the wide variety of tactics creationists employed throughout the twentieth century, examinations of the movement itself remain relatively narrow in scope. Research on movement efforts is generally confined to the domains of education and legislation, and to a lesser extent, politics.[22] Educational studies examine reform efforts primarily at the state and local levels and related to biology textbooks and the class time devoted to creationist curricula.[23] Legislative reviews focus on laws, policies, and legal strategies by antievolutionists who seek to shape how the courts define academic freedom or interpret freedom of religion in the Constitution.[24] Toumey (1994) broadly identifies the inclusion/exclusion of creationism in public school science curricula as the ultimate litmus test for success. Binder's (2002) focus on schools as a primary source of institutional power (not the state's courts or legislation) led her to conclude that political power needs to be disentangled from presumed institutional power to explain success. That is, Binder found that even when creationists had political clout across the cases she analyzed, they were resoundingly unsuccessful in sustained influence and integration into the public school curricula. Eve and Harrold (1990) and Lienesch (2007) mention creationists' more modest success at the grassroots level to influence local school boards and community members. Otherwise, the movement is largely seen as a persistent yet steady failure.

In terms of the future of the creationist movement, these scholars anticipated that the movement would endure but that the influence creationists will wield in the future would be limited.[25] With this body of scholarship defining the contextual parameters of creationists' efforts, other activities fell out of scholarly view, including the movement's other targets, its various types of tactics, or even the different outcomes it intended. In turn, I raise the empirical question in this book: To what extent were these parameters just a reflection of the movement—

perhaps all of the movement's efforts simply focused on schools or courtrooms—or the analytical blinders of the literature?[26]

I will show that movement strategies began to shift toward creating cultural venues in the 1980s, a move largely overlooked in scholarship on creationism. The Creation Museum is not the first or only development. In the late 1970s, the YEC movement opened a small creation museum in California. As recently as July 2016, AiG opened the Ark Encounter—a "life-sized Noah's Ark experience built according to the dimensions given in the Bible"[27]—just 45 miles southeast of the Creation Museum. This large-scale, multimillion-dollar site expands a platform for AiG to advance its ideological goals in varied sites, emphasizing education, entertainment, and tourism while receiving media coverage and solidifying creationism's continued relevance.

Locating Social Movements

Social movements are organized groups of people who cannot find or are denied access to conventional, institutionalized pathways to advocate for a cause.[28] While these groups differ vastly in their goals, most commonly, the target is the State. After all, as scholarship shows, the State is one of the few institutions that can enact swift—and often violent—repression.[29] Yet some movements circumvent the powerful State apparatus—including all of its economic, legal, and political functions—and target broader culture and society directly. Scholars increasingly point to how various institutions, ranging from educational systems to heteronormative family formations, serve as sites of power. Any of these types of institutions potentially are subject to resistance from challenger movements.

Researchers have hotly debated the role of culture in social movement activity. Some argue that culture is instrumental for shaping movement interests that mobilize action, inform how to choose tactics and targets, and influence the goal for change.[30] For others, culture recedes in importance. The "contentious politics" or "political process" perspectives, for instance, assert that the paramount goal for social movements is political participation or expanded rights via policy change (e.g., the Civil Rights Movement and Labor Movements were born out of legal and political exclusions).[31] Scholars working in this tradition consider cultural change as an insufficient goal and instead highlight legal and electoral contexts, giving much less attention to other apolitical factors that may affect participants' perceptions of opportunities and constraints, let alone how they may pursue alternative movement outcomes. To address this divergence, Armstrong and Bernstein (2008) developed a multi-institutional framework to consider the importance of conventional political opportunities and legislative influence matter as well as the factors that shape meaning-making across contexts. The advantage of this approach is that it does not isolate culture from spheres of influence such as politics, resources, and other "structural" elements.[32]

Social and cultural studies of science and technology scholars (science studies, for short) dovetail quite closely with social movement theorists in their emphasis on collective actors wrestling with and seeking to alter powerful institutions. This may include scientists mobilizing to challenge the institutions within which they work (and which are largely funded by the State) or laypeople co-opting scientific methods to challenge prevailing expertise. Science-oriented social movements often question the structure of federal government funding for research; the regulation of our bodies, food, and environment; or expansion of medical treatment options available—but generally they leave untouched the authority of science itself.[33] Scholars rarely examine how social movements seek to unequivocally challenge core scientific worldviews.[34]

Yet creationists have different ambitions. Historically, institutions such as museums have combined scientific accuracy and credibility with leisure activity. In the nineteenth century, natural history museums drew from the growing authority of the scientific method to create provocative spectacles for the masses.[35] To this day, museums leverage both science and popular passions, as demonstrated by contemporary efforts to infuse interactive technologies into museum exhibits ranging from dinosaurs to robots. Creationists target the natural history museum as the juncture where everyday people engage with scientific information and the look and feel of science. How it is conveyed, or the "symbols of science," to borrow Christopher Toumey's turn of phrase, matters.[36]

In this book, I broaden the scholarly horizon of what qualifies as social movement activity, beyond street demonstrations advocating for political representation and boycotts linked to calls for policy reform. I identify crucial sites of movement activity that otherwise would be set aside. I trace a wider range of creationists' movement efforts, without being restricted to different institutionalized outcomes more closely tied to the State, such as court cases, federal science education curricula, or electoral politics. It is not to suggest that resources, political context, and other known factors do not matter. Instead, I argue that for too long, the focus has been on educational and legal challenges at the expense of understanding how the movement's other milestones and tactics compare in achieving a long-standing movement goal: advancing the cultural authority of creation science.

Institution-Building

Social movements often find ways to innovate to meet desired goals and out of perceived logistical necessity. Movements carving out their own spaces frequently occurs during contestation when collective actors become more organized; mass demonstrations in the streets turn into less ephemeral bureaucratic structures.[37] Conflict and power struggles crop up as institutions combine contradictory rules that decide how things are done, who has authority, and what becomes common sense.[38] Movements build their own institutions, "institution-building," to create alternative sites and organizations in which movement participants may cultivate their own perspectives.[39] As social movement scholars Polletta and Jasper (2001) explain, "institutions removed from the physical and ideological control of those in power . . . supply the solidary incentives that encourage movement participation, but they also represent a 'free space' in which people can develop counterhegemonic ideas and oppositional identities" (288). Movements developing their own institutions, creating "free spaces," or adopting different organizational forms grows from an older line of work situated at the nexus of social movements and formal organizations rejecting the idea that models for organizing action were generic and unchanging.[40] This innovative way of organizing underscores how institutions can be challenged as they are both durable *and* subject to change.[41]

Many movements seek to establish a platform from which to demonstrate their organizational efficacy and to put their ideological beliefs into action.[42] One without the other is not sufficient. The most prominent example of developing an existing institutional resource is the black church in the 1950s and 1960s Civil Rights Movement.[43] The black Christian church was a product of slavery, and later segregation. Often excluded from worship at white churches, African Americans created churches where they could congregate outside of the immediate surveillance of whites. In turn, they developed their own ideas, practices, and rituals separate from the dominant group. The black church was a community institutional resource from which the Civil Rights Movement grew, providing adherents with a collective identity, purpose, strategy, and physical location to orchestrate movement tactics. In this instance, the institution laid the groundwork for later movement activity.

Comparatively, the different phases of the US women's movement were all about creating new institutions as an explicit rallying point for collective action via bookstores, health clinics, and feminist collectives.[44] The bureaucratic, organizational structure of established institutions was challenged by feminist collectives' egalitarian and consensus-driven model of organization. Alondra Nelson (2013) finds a similar process at work in her historical analysis of the Black Panther Party in the 1960s. The movement decided to build and sustain a network of community health clinics to address white-dominated medical establishment's long-standing practices of discrimination, poor treatment, and biased perceptions of African Americans' well-being, which were rooted in nineteenth- and early twentieth-century eugenicist theories of biological and moral racial inferiority.

However, institution-building is not just a practice of the political left or an occurrence in just the United States. Through a cross-national analysis, Davis and Robinson (2012) illuminated how various religiously orthodox communities use institution-building to "bypass the state," building parallel facilities to augment deficient secular social institutions. They found, in Egypt, Israel, Italy, and the United States, that such groups sought to influence law, challenge modernity's differentiation between the religious and the secular, and sacralize society. The various movements (a) had a broad set of goals rather than a single one (i.e., to sacralize society); (b) were ideologically rigid rather than flexible in their close interpretation of religious texts; and (c) were exclusive rather than connected with other movements, thus building the group's distinctive identity.[45] All of these factors are typically regarded as *obstacles* in conventional social movement literature. Yet the evangelical movement in the United States has long capitalized on these very features as well. Precedent dates back to the 1880s, when the establishment of Christian colleges, conferences, and publications became important for subsequent mobilization.[46] Lienesch (2007) argues, "even before it could give birth to what eventually became a full-fledged fundamentalist movement—activists had to turn from creating identities to building institutions" (33). By building the Creation Museum, AiG extends a long-standing fundamentalist tradition of stoking a sense of embattlement over moral authority by building its own institutions—universities, publishing houses, theme parks, non-profit clearinghouses—to counter the secular mainstream.

The existence of alternative sites is frequently documented in the literature, but often the analytical leverage is underspecified. These sites are typically nested into the history of the movement itself where they serve as descriptive markers of the internal movement culture.[47] In effect, they are treated as simply a stepping stone for political action—or in the case of the Black church in the Civil Rights Movement, as an important precursor.[48] The focus is typically on what the new institution or organization does for the broader movement in terms of political mobilization and strategy against an unresponsive political environment or repressive regime.[49]

Yet counter-institutions often target both the material and symbolic qualities of how authority operates within and outside the State.[50] Put another way, how people engage with a movement's claims is not just in terms of its political ideas, but also the aesthetics that bolster those claims and institutionally anchor them; examining materiality reveals the move from the political abstract (a sense of another way to govern or, in this case, another path for knowledge production) into something concrete for individuals to access.[51] The Creation Museum is not a house of kitsch objects to be ogled, and it is not simply a collection of arguments for rhetorical provocation. Like all museums' artifacts and related narratives, the Creation Museum's items and ideas are connected to actors who created them to accomplish a desired outcome. Social movements do not simply protest in the street or agitate for their day in court to persuade followers that they have something to offer. Often social movements need physical locations, a place to organize themselves and engage with the public; it is an obvious but often overlooked component.[52] Studies of how physical sites created by movements themselves work are rare in the literature.[53]

To describe how a social movement creates a place—a physical space from which to bolster its efforts for the long haul—I draw from Gieryn's (2000) definition of place: a unique geographic site that combines the natural world and the built environment and that affords meaning. While at first pass it may seem obvious that some material-forms (objects / places) command respect, and others do not, much research speaks to how epistemic credibility, or "the lie detectors of intellectual claims," is not intrinsically known but rather constructed.[54] Movements physically grounding their claims can challenge directly the presumption of the status quo's exclusive rights to the broader public to make authoritative arguments or offer alternatives. And, while this is not the only way to shore up plausibility for movement claims, frequently it is how social movements acquire it for their own institutions. Credibility rests on not only what is promised to adherents or on how it is packaged but also where it is delivered.

Focusing on a physical location could be perceived as almost "retro." After all, a brick-and-mortar building is a resource-intensive endeavor for social movement organizations, an old tactic rooted in the 1960s and 1970s. And while the rise of online activism, e-mobilization, and other forms of digital protest are increasing, the assumption that organizations and offline activism are no longer needed is shortsighted. Instead, a set of empirical questions emerges about how people are organizing online. While scholars should not presume social movement organizations always matter, it is important to investigate how organizations change and adapt (or fail) to the shifting use of technology and efforts to effect change in the twenty-first century.[55] Many social movement organizations now maintain websites and use social media in their efforts, which points to the significance of social movement organizations for long-term success (rather than a short-lived, targeted campaign), particularly for right-wing reformist groups.[56] If a movement's target is primarily to foment cultural change, then creating a place may be exactly what the movement needs to solidify the base and reach the masses to effect change across multiple institutions over time.

Many movements have sites, but only some of these appear to work. Why these sites emerge, how they operate, and what role they play in the movement are important questions with which to grapple. The answers to these questions illuminate how spin-off efforts emerge, how movement actors shift resources around to sustain the movement over time, and what all of this signifies for the movement's ability to acquire authority within and outside of the political arena. Examining where those efforts occur matters for answering questions of movement efficacy. Otherwise, we lose analytical insight into a key component of how some movements successfully maintain these spaces to persist and stretch what seems plausible, while others falter.

Plausibility Politics

What does it mean to make something plausible or "appearing worthy of belief"?[57] In an era of alternative facts, fake news, and a lack of trust in governing institutions, many across the United States are open to hearing other accounts, circulating questionable information, and forming third parties because they appear reasonable. Discussions about believability and trust seem to be everywhere:

- A 2014 General Social Survey found only 7% of Americans say they have a great deal of confidence in the press.[58] In that same year, a report on Political Polarization and Media Habits indicated political conservatives are more likely to distrust a variety of media sources. Yet across political affiliations, trust is bifurcated, "Fox News is the most distrusted source among consistent liberals (81% distrust), while MSNBC is the most distrusted source among consistent conservatives (75%)."[59]
- The plausibility of the 2016 presidential candidate, Donald Trump, came into question as a *Wall Street Journal* reporter notes widespread perceptions of Trump's "brash and unpredictable behavior" and wonders, "Yet the first and maybe final issue is the most basic one: Will Mr. Trump pass the plausibility test?"[60] Apparently, Trump did for many as he went on to receive 80% of the white evangelical vote and became president.[61]
- Psychologists Dan Kahan and Keith Stanovich published an article titled "Rationality and Belief in Human Evolution," and according to *Business Insider*, "It turns out that high CRT scores [Cognitive Reflection Test, a series of questions in which an intuitive answer is different from

the correct answer] most strongly predict that people will stick to their cultural beliefs about evolution. So very secular students with high CRT scores were likely to accept evolution, and very religious students with high CRT scores were likely to reject the science . . . people with highly developed mental tools for turning over and examining ideas are more skilled at explaining to themselves why they shouldn't—or should— accept a verifiable scientific claim."[62]

Plausibility politics is enacted in public across a variety of institutional settings, as evidenced in the examples above. It is the process of disentangling accuracy from reasonableness, and the opening is leveraged by a group to advance its point of view. For many, this feels new. For seasoned political pundits and historians, it does not. It is a dynamic as old as the institutions and representatives entrusted to govern society. Yet it is not just media outlets, politicians, or scientists who attempt to persuade the public of their claims. Social movements seek to carve out a sense of plausibility for their own arguments as well. Being able to closely examine how this unfolds in a particular location helps us better understand how groups fight to stretch and expand what we, as a public, find plausible and later credible.[63]

The cultural authority of science, or the likelihood that a belief or standpoint will be perceived as legitimate, is buttressed by a network of museums designed and built on the premise that secular, scientific worldviews are "right."[64] For example, more than half of Americans have gone to an informal science venue (park, zoo, science/technology museum) in the last year. And, while only 12% regularly get their science news from science and technology centers or museums, more than 54% of respondents indicate these centers and museums get the science facts right most of the time, which is more than any other source of information, including government agencies or news outlets.[65] So, the consequences are significant for popular opinions about science when a museum uses similar displays and objects to convince visitors of the plausibility of an alternative worldview. To understand not only how a movement creates a site and how supporters come to regard it as a museum, but also how skeptics contest, we must examine what it is about museums as places that groups such as AiG can wield for their purpose.[66]

Museums as Sites of Plausibility Politics

It is public perception that science-oriented museums wrestle in the world of truth and observable natural facts. Conversely, art museums, history centers, and heritage sites are the institutions that must wade into socially and culturally contingent history and critically engage with its past steeped in colonial legacies and overall elitism.[67] Science museums share this intertwined past, yet the institution of science often is left intact because the knowledge it contains is perceived as objective. While contemporary science museums' interactive exhibits may encourage more informal engagement, they are still bound up in the same long-standing authority of science. Research typically focuses on past controversies, after which most science-oriented museums sought to avoid confrontation altogether.[68]

Nevertheless, museums entangle various actors (e.g., visitors, trustees, museum professionals, city leaders), and they are social institutions through which value is classified and conferred onto some art, history, and science—but most important—denied to others.[69] The notion that "museums are in revolt" is wedded to groups who historically have been forced or otherwise relegated to outside the mainstream museum world's moral universe, such as indigenous communities, ethnic minorities, sexual minorities, variously able-bodied groups, and women.[70] Increasingly, these groups may champion their perspective in national exhibits, lobby for new museums under the Smithsonian Institution, or locally, push for more diverse representation.[71] Researchers involved in both policy development and professional museum management frequently implore museums to be socially responsible and inclusive to a broader number of groups.[72]

While a commitment to pluralism informs these new approaches and mandates for museums in the twenty-first century, what remains unspoken is that only some groups and communities are perceived as legitimate in their claims for increased (or any) representation. Fiona Cameron (2007) points to a normative undercurrent feeding board members and other museum professionals' decisions as they "still tend to define moral projects around contentious topics as lessons according to one dominant moral universal . . . and avoiding moral panic by curating topics according to a certain moral angle" (335).[73] I argue that

AiG's claim of being a different kind of science-oriented museum is possible, in part, due to the museum world's broad and unspecified use of concepts such as pluralism or inclusion without explicit discussion as to who qualifies as marginalized or who is envisioned as the broader community to which museums should reach out.

Plausibility is as much a political act as it is rooted in shared conventions for evidence (e.g., tangible observations of real-world activity). And, even though science museums are often perceived as neutral institutions by the broader public, in many ways this is what AiG skillfully challenges. AiG and its counter-museum is neither explicitly excluded nor addressed in mission statements or other museum-world commentary as a group potentially seeking inclusion. AiG capitalizes on the implicit assumption that inclusivity necessarily equates to representation of systemically marginalized groups.[74] While the white evangelicals who overwhelmingly comprise AiG are not historically marginalized based on their identity, the organization argues that its viewpoints are summarily dismissed because they do not fit into secularized normative expectations for science museums—and thus are marginalized ideologically.

AiG hopes to expose the secular bias they see as pervasive in contemporary American culture by offering the public a chance, literally and physically, to see their side. In doing so, they renew a familiar fundamentalist strategy dating back to the Scopes Trial: connecting social and moral decline to the advent of secular inquiry and evolutionary theory.[75] This coincides with popular perceptions among the public that the institution of science is inherently secular and that scientists are largely irreligious and antagonistic toward religious traditions. Despite historical patterns that suggest otherwise, these public perceptions have persisted strongly throughout the contemporary era.[76]

Ironically, then, AiG indirectly draws from a long line of work within the social sciences and philosophy that examines the moral, religious, and social foundations upon which science as an institution developed (i.e., how knowledge is constructed, as scientific findings do not simply emerge from the natural world intact).[77] AiG argues that while an emphasis on scientific observation and falsification is compelling, it contends that over time scientists have corroded the institution so much so that sociocultural conventions only privilege decontextualized, secular explanations. According to AiG, this bias is evident in the lack of debate regarding the origins of the universe and human evolution (e.g., the competing theories regarding how the cosmos formed, how life on Earth began, or why the fossil record of our evolutionary ancestry is incomplete and does not contain more evidence of intermediate species).[78] And while many may doubt the validity of AiG's claims and the soundness of its research, does this make it less plausible to others who have been primed to feel their viewpoint is no longer centered in the mainstream?

Creationism has ebbed and flowed in its prominence within the United States; however, the social movement's Protestant, white, male, elite roots are deeply embedded into our core social institutions, ranging from education and science to politics and religion.[79] So why is AiG able to make any public headway with its claims of marginalization? Why do prominent museum reviewers and critics discuss the Creation Museum so feverishly?[80] AiG and its alternative worldview resonate with members of the public who persistently seek to resurrect a conservative status quo across multiple institutions. For example, the Public Religion Research Institute reports that "[a]lmost half of Americans say discrimination against Christians is as big of a problem as discrimination against other groups, including blacks and minorities. Three-quarters of Republicans and Trump supporters said this, and so did nearly eight out of 10 white evangelical Protestants."[81] Franklin Graham, the son of prominent evangelist Reverend Billy Graham, tapped into this sentiment of embattlement and persecution when he proclaimed in the *New York Times*, "In my lifetime, he [Trump] has supported the Christian faith more than any president that I know . . . That doesn't mean he is the greatest example of the Christian faith, and neither am I, but he defends the faith."[82] AiG's approach reflects this sense of embattlement across the United States as many people who have long enjoyed majority status—whether it is rooted in their religious affiliation, race, gender, or economic status—feel that their position has become challenged. Given this context, they sympathize with AiG regardless of how ahistorical its claims of marginalization and embattlement may be.

Without explicit attention to and articulation of who is envisioned as legitimate or not in their demand for inclusion in the museum world and the broader cultural context, science-oriented museums are vulnerable to challenges on multiple fronts under the auspice of pluralism. The Creation Museum threatens to destabilize the common belief that only one type of secular institution can make claims about Earth's age or about human origins. AiG repositions itself to produce long-lasting effects on the public's perception of who can make scientific claims and what plausibility looks like.

The Structure of This Book

Creating the Creation Museum will sustain a sociological argument about the Creation Museum in relation to the broader creationist movement and interrogate the political implications of each. I examine the means by which this movement adapts over time, withstanding widespread academic and broader mainstream cultural challenges. By building its own museum, AiG has a site from which to curate the credibility of its claims and organizational prowess to a frustrated public. Meaning-making cannot be reduced to how movement actors talk about their choices or perspectives but must include what they do in action.[83] To understand how AiG's use of the museum-form to convey its own cultural authority comes with risks (e.g., it may not be persuasive enough to work), I show that it is important to analyze how it engages in plausibility politics.

After a walk-through of the Creation Museum in chapter 1, I unpack the underlying question that animates the book—why creationists built a museum—by considering three aspects of the institution that scholarly literature often treats separately: (1) why oppositional sites like the Creation Museum emerge, (2) how they work, and (3) to what extent are they effective for sustaining a group's point of view in the broader public sphere? I address these questions by drawing from a unique historical dataset of more than one thousand internal documents from creationist organizations, more than three years of on-site ethnographic fieldwork at the Creation Museum, where I was granted rare internal access to AiG's leadership, and an analysis of media coverage from various sources.

In chapter 2, I trace historically why internal movement dynamics led AiG to focus on the museum as a tactic. AiG could have built a college or a research center to reach and influence a broader public, among other movement strategies. In light of these available alternatives, I show how the museum emerged over time when young earth creationists shifted the focus of the movement away from old earth creationism, advanced effective leaders who reassessed previous movement actions, and adapted to the sociocultural as well as political environment of the 1970s and 1980s. In chapters 3 and 4, I examine how the built environment of the Creation Museum fundamentally shapes visitors' perception of AiG's credibility and the plausibility of its controversial claims. Unpacking the materiality of a contested site affords a close-up understanding of how a group attempts to make ideas and objects credible; what techniques does AiG use and how does it accomplish a plausible "look and feel"? These chapters underscore the political intentionality behind curatorial choices, aimed to teach museum visitors how to "read" every object and experience in the Creation Museum. In chapter 5, I explore what audiences think about the Creation Museum through an external media analysis that traces its impact on actors and organizations both within and well beyond the movement. I argue the museum attracted attention because of its ability to connect temporarily bombastic mobilization efforts with its non-disruptive character. I show how a media source's stance toward the museum's mission coincides with how effective or ineffective it finds its visitor experience, a connection that may at first seem politically counterintuitive.

In the end, *Creating the Creation Museum* is about plausibility politics in unexpected places—and about who gets believed and how they go about doing it. This book shows that tracing the process of how a group creates a place affords a deeper understanding of how, despite all odds, it can attract broader interest and sustain members through its own site. When movement activity comes as a surprise, institutions across the State, society, or culture are often ill-equipped to wrestle with its demands. Students of social movements, regardless of their political and social positioning, want to be better situated to anticipate challengers. I also hope this book proves useful for readers interested in broader questions about how sites created by movements figure into the current rise of populism within the United States, and increasingly across the world.

1

A Walk through the Creation Museum

> It's a hot day in July; the sun is beaming down. The line is long on the inside of the building. I'm waiting to purchase my ticket for the day and next to me I overhear a father in his mid-thirties excitedly declare to his son, who appears to be about 10 years old, "This is the greatest country in the world and because of that, now you are going to learn more about the greatest story."[1]
> —Field Notes, July 12, 2013

What is the greatest story, and who is telling it? For this father, it is the account of human origins in the biblical book of Genesis. The father and son are having this conversation outside of a museum, of all places, but it is not just any museum. The Creation Museum is just off the highway in Petersburg, Kentucky. It is less than three miles from the Ohio River, which snakes through Indiana, Ohio, and Kentucky where they butt up against one another. About twenty-five miles from downtown Cincinnati, the museum is not deep in the eastern Kentucky foothills or squarely in the Bible Belt as some reviews may imply, conjuring up the state's known religiosity and long-standing ties to evangelicalism.[2] At the same time, it is not on one of the "elite coasts" or in Colorado Springs, an epicenter of evangelical activity. In fact, the Creation Museum's location is strategic: It is less than ten miles away from an accessible international airport, within two-thirds of a day's drive for most people living in the United States, and stands right at the edge of the Bible Belt. The museum's founders factored in these points carefully and cite them often.[3] Coal power plants and casinos are nearby in Lawrenceburg, Indiana; the smokestack would billow into the air each day as I drove across the I-275 Bridge to the museum for fieldwork. Most mornings, while eating the complimentary breakfast at the Comfort Inn where I stayed, I would be among museum visitors, typically older

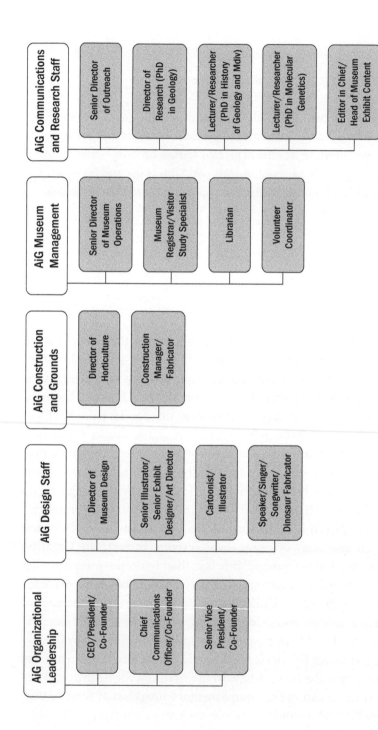

Figure 1.1. AiG Interviewee Organization Chart (n = 18)

couples or families with young children, excitedly preparing for their day's trip.

Tours and walk-throughs of the museum abound. AiG has an impressive website and an array of books about the museum.[4] Increasingly, academic books and journals feature the Creation Museum in their pages.[5] There is even an entire book dedicated to examining each of the museum's fifty-one rooms, containing approximately 160 to 180 exhibits along with four theaters and a planetarium.[6] In this trip around the museum, I focus on the broad strokes of how visitors are introduced to creationism, what is most surprising or unusual, and I unpack AiG's presentation of it. In effect, I examine how we, as visitors, are "Prepare[d] to Believe," not only in the exhibits but also in the bookstore, the cafes, and the outdoor grounds. Later, I provide a rare tour of the private, adjacent 25,000-square-foot AiG headquarters, which is out of view behind secured doorways. Throughout the chapter, I draw from primary data from fieldwork, including exhibit materials (both text and imagery), movement publications, internal AiG documents, and interviews with key movement actors to usher along our journey through the Creation Museum, see figure 1.1.

"We're Taking Dinosaurs Back"

The turn onto Bullittsburg Church Road unveils a commonplace rural landscape: a concrete mix supplier shop to the right and a tattered red barn on the left. Two stegosauruses greet visitors at the wrought iron gate marking the entrance to the Creation Museum a half mile up the road (figure 1.2). Upon entering the parking lot, security (a combination of off-duty and retired police officers) typically directs traffic and guides visitors to where they should park cars, church vans, and buses.[7] The building's front façade welcomes visitors with semi-opaque floor-to-ceiling glass panes (just enough to see visitors lining up inside) punctuated by large, light stone columns. Walking through the entrance, ceilings soar more than forty feet high. Brown, rough-cut-looking stone is punctuated by glass cases with pictures of "Dragon Legends" and other seemingly fantastical suggestions piquing visitors' interest about what lies around the corner.[8] Beyond the ticketing area, a green screen photo opportunity is provided by FotoFx, a contractor, and backdrop options include the ever-popular T. Rex attacking

Figure 1.2. Creation Museum, Front Entrance Gate. All photos taken by author from July 2010 to September 2017 unless noted otherwise.

"unsuspecting" visitors; staff often instruct people to act surprised and to "Have fun with it."[9]

Once inside the Main Hall, visitors encounter a fossil cast replica of a sizeable Mastodon, an extinct mammal that looks like a mammoth (figure 1.3). As AiG comments in the audio tour, the purpose of this large and imposing creature in the Main Hall is key to its mission: "[The fossil] turned out to be one of the largest and most complete mastodon skeletons ever found . . . Again, this is to help people understand that we are dealing with real things here. This is not just about fairy tales . . . And that's why they're [mastodons] there, just to challenge people."[10] Presenting its claims as boldly but as plausibly as possible, AiG showcases live "Darwin's Finches" encased in the middle of the large room. This move foreshadows that the organization does not shy away from taking on the progenitor of evolutionary theory in later exhibits.

Center stage in the Main Hall are two figures of young children looking over a pond where garfish and turtles swim; this scene is used to support AiG's argument that animals in the fossil record are currently living and not necessarily "millions of years old" (figure 1.4). Meanwhile, in the background, an animatronic young tyrannosaurus sways and roars beside the children. In *Behind the Scenes* (2008), AiG emphasized, "From concept to reality, photos of this single exhibit have appeared in countless newspapers and magazines worldwide as symbolic of the Creation Museum."[11] And this was intentional. When I asked the director of museum operations about the museum's media attention, he sighed. "Whatever write-up you get," he said. "They're meant to be negative critiques . . . It's almost like a canned phrase, 'They believe that dinosaurs and people lived together.' It's really worked out well for us. It's a hot button issue that people like to get on and complain about, but you always get credit for having really good-looking exhibits."[12] Before moving forward with the tour, it is important to unpack why dinosaurs are so important both for AiG as a YEC organization and for the museum as an institution.

AiG placed front and center a theory that it knew would provoke controversy: the possible coexistence of humans and dinosaurs. As it asserts, "dinosaurs lived at the same time as people, not separated by eons of time. If we accept God's Word, beginning with Genesis, as being true and authoritative, then we can explain dinosaurs and make sense of the world we observe around us."[13] Mainstream cultural and scientific com-

Figure 1.3. Mastodon in the Main Hall

Figure 1.4. Children and Young Tyrannosaurus

munities deem AiG's claim of coexistence as absurd. However, it is not surprising to the cynical visitor to find dinosaurs throughout the Creation Museum. From these visitors' perspective, AiG is simply another example of a long line of religious organizations trying to make money from its impressionable followers. Any science museum visitor expects dinosaurs, and with its profits driven by ticket sales and merchandise, AiG understands and leverages its visitors' expectations and seeks to meet them. Kids love seeing dinosaurs, and adults will pay for it.

Yet this approach also sparks controversy internally among movement sympathizers. Christians familiar with the history and cultural context of fundamentalism may be surprised to see dinosaurs so heavily featured. In the early twentieth century, many creationists objected to including dinosaurs as a part of a literal interpretation of the Bible, and often perceived them as an evolutionist trope to be avoided. They were also wary of dinosaur fossils given the notorious cases of fabricated creatures.[14] Later, when fossilized footprints, like those at the Paluxy River in 1945, were quickly and unequivocally understood among the mainstream scientific community as merely two different types of non-human animals' footprints, doubts lingered for creationists.[15] Perhaps it could be evidence of human and dinosaur coexistence? Eventually creationists would concede that the footprints were simply two animals, but nevertheless these kinds of discussions over the presence and timing of dinosaurs alongside humans were brought to the forefront for young earth creationism. It was an issue they could no longer ignore. During this same time in the mid-twentieth century, rifts began to solidify between old earth creationists and young earth creationists. Old earth creationists, many of whom would later go on to support tenets of Intelligent Design, maintained that a supernatural force (often perceived as God) created the world, and dinosaurs became extinct long ago, prior to humans. Conversely, YEC focused more closely on the Bible as the main chronicle of the world's events, so it needed to give credence to the suggestion that man and dinosaur could have lived at the same time since the Book of Genesis's Garden of Eden, where all creatures began.[16]

Other visitors' perspectives fall somewhere in between on the presence of dinosaurs in the Creation Museum—surprised but interested to see dinosaurs featured in everything from the front gate to the Garden of Eden. AiG knew it needed to face the question of dinosaurs head on, without wavering, as the topic builds controversy and notoriety among the cynics, interest and acquiescence among hard-core believers, and clarity for the undecided, including many Christians.

Commercializing the dinosaur theme and connecting the dinosaurs to the dragon legends introduced in the entrance, the Dragon Hall Bookstore is directly adjacent to the Main Hall. A large dragon-like creature is crouched above the main entry. Inside the store, the Old English Beowulf character guards the entrance; Saint George stands above the back door. Stained-glass windows and a large chandelier hang over the cashier's desk, creating a medieval setting (figure 1.5). But why dragons? What is the museum's connection to this medieval theme? As AiG provocatively suggests, "Dragons were considered real creatures until relatively recently. They appear in oral stories, art, and literature from cultures around the world, and some historians even describe them. Dragons represent the collective, though exaggerated, memory of dinosaurs before that word was invented in 1841 to describe their remains."[17] Specifically, AiG uses the story of Saint George and the Dragon as an example of how dragon legends point to a plausible connection of people living during the same time as dinosaurs. "Legend states that strong of faith and therefore fearless, he [St. George] battled the beast to save a king's daughter, and then offered to kill the beast if the townspeople would convert to Christianity."[18] As AiG acknowledges, dragon myths and legends are regarded by most as fantastical (and here even as an allegory for religious conversion). But it also cites mainstream scientific discussions that suggest some physical characteristics commonly associated with dragon legends do exist in the biological world, just not in any one known creature.[19]

Figure 1.5a-c. Dragon Hall Bookstore

Figure 1.5a-c. continued

The ability to weave doubt about dragons into answers largely perceived as myths is a key rhetorical strategy developed throughout the
museum. Perhaps it is not as far-fetched as once previously imagined. If
something we often label as a fairytale can be reasonably reconceived as
having some basis in the biological world via mainstream science, AiG
argues, then who is to say that dragon legends are not people's description of dinosaurs that lived among them in medieval Europe or during other eras in China, Africa, or the Middle East? According to AiG,
the creatures described by these cultures across history simply were not
called "dinosaurs" yet. All of this work serves AiG's purpose to show

Figure 1.6. Answers in Genesis Bumper Sticker, AiG publication

the public how perspectives are contingent on historical and cultural context. However, it always returns to the Bible for a resolution: "But the most compelling case for real historical dragon-human interaction is found in Genesis: land animals were created on Day Six of Creation Week, as was Adam, and so dinosaurs (also known as dragons) were made alongside man."[20]

Ultimately, why does it matter for AiG that individuals reconsider the historical plausibility of dinosaurs and humans living at the same time? Dinosaurs capture the hearts and minds of children everywhere and have remained the crown jewel for any natural history museum since the late nineteenth century.[21] AiG capitalizes on this history in a bumper sticker. The sticker portrays a road with signs for preeminent natural history museums accompanied by dinosaurs and other icons well-known to children (e.g., Mickey Mouse and Elmo); meanwhile, pointing across the road at a dinosaur billboard for the Creation Museum, a person exclaims, "You're using dinosaurs to attract and influence children! You can't do that!" (figure 1.6). The real challenge, and potential gain for AiG, is to question how visitors understand dinosaurs in evolutionary theory compared to YEC accounts. And the beloved creatures are front and center. AiG proclaims on another bumper sticker, "We're Taking Dinosaurs Back," with a depiction of Ken Ham carrying a T. Rex size dinosaur on his back (figure 1.6). Rather than distance themselves from dinosaurs, the museum actively broadcasts them on its billboards across the country, discusses them in television ads, and sells an array of dinosaur bumper stickers, signs, t-shirts, and toys in the bookstore.

Main Hall

A typical tour of the museum begins in the Main Hall. It is an opportunity for AiG to preview many of its core arguments up front, like the presence of dinosaurs in a young Earth. It also serves as a central location to showcase multimedia experiences like the Stargazer's Planetarium and the Special Effects (SFX) Theater along with more traditional wall-mounted, glass-enclosed exhibits.

The Planetarium feels familiar to any experienced museum visitor. The custom-made carpet is a cerulean sky with streams of yellow stars and galaxies woven across it. About eighty reclining chairs (which push back almost 45 degrees) allow the audience members to immerse themselves in the whirling constellations above their heads in the 30-foot-wide dome (figure 1.7). More than a million visitors have opted for the additional ticket ($7.95) to watch the 23-minute-long "Created Cosmos" presentation or a similar show.[22] As Creation Museum materials persuade: "This planetarium show will give you a better understanding of the immensity of the universe and the power of the One who created it."[23] Technologically, the show is strikingly similar to many at planetariums nationwide;

Figure 1.7. Stargazer's Planetarium

it impresses even ardent critics such as the National Center for Science Education, who in its museum review states, "Overall, the special effects were better than one would expect for such a small planetarium ... Other than religious statements and odd references to 'secular scientists' most of this could have passed for a good planetarium show."[24]

The Special Effects Theater has floor-to-ceiling video screens and seats up to two hundred people.[25] Featured speakers lecture at noon and 3:00 p.m. daily during the peak season, which is spring and summer and around the December holidays. Otherwise, the 30-minute special effects film, *Men in White* (2007), airs five to eight times throughout the day. On the stage, Wendy is an animatronic figure, a young white girl with blonde hair, staring into a campfire (depicted on the theater screen that she faces, back toward the audience) and contemplating, "some of the most important questions of life: what is the truth about where we came from? Is there meaning? Is there really a God, or did this all just happen by chance? If there really is a Creator, what does that mean for us personally?"[26] This prompts the fast-talking, sleek video production to begin. When watching it in the auditorium, seats vibrate, water spits out of each chair back, and lights pulsate. The film features angels Gabe and Mike (playing off the biblical angels Gabriel and Michael), who are personified by two white men in their thirties wearing white t-shirts, overalls, and wraparound sunglasses. It is designed to appeal to eight- to twelve-year-olds as it combines Wendy's existential questions with sophomoric-style humor from Gabe and Mike, who are hip, sarcastic, and deeply critical of the way evolution is taught in public schools. For instance, during my frequent visits, kids in the crowd frequently chuckled out loud when Gabe and Mike complained about silly teachers "lecturing on and on" in the classroom about human evolution and yet were rapt with attention when the "Men in White" discussed how each person was created by God and "not by chance."

While people wait on busy days to gain access to the Planetarium or the Special Effects Theater, many examine the glass exhibit cases in the surrounding hallways. Visitors see smaller vertebrate fossils and mineral crystal collections shimmering purple and green; AiG uses these to demonstrate how objects remain largely unchanged since their creation.[27] Another nearby exhibit displays an entire fossilized crab in a long, winding trail highlighting its last movement before it died. For the average visitor, the size and shape of the fossil may be noticeable, and they may find the information about how fast it was preserved interesting because it remained intact, but otherwise this exhibit is unremarkable. But here, according to AiG's director of research, Andrew Snelling, who has a PhD in geology, is one of the most noteworthy objects featured in the entire museum. As Dr. Snelling recounted to me:

> [The fossilized crab] emphasizes the quality of what's here. Dr. David Raup . . . he was arguably one of the leading paleontologists of the 20th century [formerly a University of Chicago paleontologist and the chair of geology and dean of sciences at the Field Museum]. The quality of his work, there's no question around. He was invited down here before the museum opened [2006]. He stood at that exhibit and almost cried. He said, "I've seen fossilized horseshoe crabs before, I've seen the trails, but I've never seen the trail ending with the actual fossil." That is a world-class exhibit, in that specimen. That in itself says that what's presented here in terms of the quality of the materials is equal to that of other museums. That's interesting because a guy like that . . . he acknowledged that it was well done, great to see, and made available to the public, as well, rather than locked away.[28]

These traditional glass case exhibits showcase to visitors, and perhaps more important, to scientific professionals, that the Creation Museum is "museum-enough," even if some details are not fully known to the casual visitor. The presentation appears very conventional, and museum-goers see the same kinds of objects and fossils that they—or even a well-known scientist—would expect from any museum.

Different Starting Points

After walking through the Main Hall foyer, Canyon Hall's sandstone-like grooved hallway is straight ahead. A video describes how the Grand Canyon could have formed in a short period of time by water. The audio overhead ponders aloud: "a long time and a little bit of water?" or "a lot of water and a little bit of time?" Images of the 1980s Mount St. Helen's volcanic eruption are nestled into a small observation shelter. According to AiG, both of these features underscore past and present examples of natural phenomena (floods and volcanic eruptions) and their effects

Figure 1.8. Paleontological Dig Site, southwestern landscape

on topography. This exhibit foreshadows an in-depth investigation later in the lower-level Flood Geology Room that underscores how dramatic changes in the natural world point to a younger Earth than commonly understood. The "knee-high museum" juts off to the right and is a low, eight-foot-long tunnel where glow-in-the-dark creatures lurk, to be touched and ogled by kids passing through.

Everyone reunites in a room that continues the rough-cut stone aesthetic. Fossil display cases along the wall include signs that state, "The evidence is in the present, but what happened in the past?" A mock Southwestern paleontological dig site anchors the room (figure 1.8). In this reenactment, two life-size male scientist figures, one identified as "an evolutionist" and the other a creationist, work on excavating an Utahraptor skeleton from desert soil. Overhead in a video, a white creationist and an Asian evolutionist—whose physical features are replicated in the figures—discuss how both scientists are trying to make sense of what they find. As the narrator states in the video:

> The skeleton exists in the present. They're trying to understand it in relation to the past . . . The origins issue is different than talking about building technology that puts man on the moon. We want those who come

here to start to think through the issue of origins—that it's different than talking about the present. We all agree on what we have in the present. The difference is how you connect the present to the past.[29]

This message, that all scientists start with the same evidence and fossils, sets up the next exhibit room.

Once they enter the Starting Points Room, visitors' paths become heavily guided in both content and direction as they funnel through the heart of the museum. This exhibit feels the most similar to a conventional museum with its hardwood floors, overhead track lighting, and white drywall serving as the backdrop for large placards. Two dichotomous worldviews are plainly displayed: one commonly seen in any natural history museum (Man's Word/Human Reason/Evolution), and another (God's Word/Creation) to which visitors may need an introduction. Here, on display is the distinct creation science approach of weaving a literal biblical interpretation with scientific language and expectations for evidence in the natural world. For example, the *Creation Museum Souvenir Guide* reads, "There is an element of faith at work in every interpretation of scientific evidence. Rocks and fossils don't come with tags on them, telling us how old they are."[30]

Working around the room, the first placard titled "Human Reason" is depicted with an image of stacked, well-aged books ranging from Plato to Charles Darwin and Steven Hawking. A quote by René Descartes looms above, "I think, therefore I am." This stands in contrast to "God's Word" on the right as shown by a single large scroll and the text, "God said, I am that I am" (figure 1.9). The rest of the exhibit continues this stark dichotomy as it explores the universe and its formation; plants and animals; sedimentary layers of rocks; humans and apes like Lucy, the famous Australopithecus and common hominin ancestor in an evolutionary tree; and a fossilized Utahraptor previously featured in the dig site, brought into the flesh to underscore how creationists explain dinosaur fossils. Comparative timelines sketch out how all of this fits either into a millions-of-years evolutionary chronology or into the less-than-10,000 years that creationists deduce from God's Word (i.e., the Bible).

The transition to the next set of rooms is an important one for AiG. It has already set up the foundation for YEC in a way that looks and feels like a natural history museum, with its sparse white walls and crisp

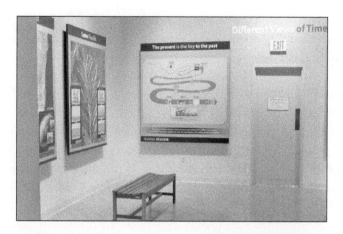

Figure 1.9a-b. Different Starting Points Room

sequential visuals. So, it is a quick shift to move squarely into religious history in the Biblical Authority and Biblical Relevance Rooms. Faux stone walls and human figures evoke the ancient past and underscore AiG's conviction for "biblical inerrancy," which is essential not only for YEC but also for its members' identity as conservative Christians with roots in Protestant evangelicalism. This viewpoint insists on the impossibility of scriptural error; any mistakes in our understanding of the Bible are a result of human fallibility. Biblical literalism, then, is the subsequent approach for how to go about interpreting the Bible, which is treated as an account of what actually happened, and through exegesis one can account for any literary devices used. For instance, biblical literalists view the resurrection of Jesus Christ as a historical event that happened, whereas non-literalists may view this account in the Bible as simply a spiritual metaphor for resurrection. Biblical interpretation has long been a divisive point among fundamentalists and later evangelicals, but for AiG, biblical literalism has helped to establish an underlying coherence among groups of believers otherwise historically prone to schisms.[31]

In the Biblical Authority Room, biblical figures such as Moses, David, Isaiah, and Paul serve as witnesses to the sacredness of the text and God's Word (figure 1.10). On an adjacent wall, scrolls declare that "God's Word has Triumphed against every Attack" and describe a series of historical events that challenged the veracity of God's Word as communicated in the Bible through "Attempts to Question," "Attempts to Destroy," "Attempts to Discredit," "Attempts to Criticize," "Attempts to Poison," and "Attempts to Replace." For AiG, this onslaught began in the very beginning, with the serpent in the Garden of Eden, but it stretches the narrative across time, outlining a wide range of these attempts from the Romans to the Enlightenment. According to AiG, when humans place more importance on the traditions of the church than on the biblical text itself, attacks persistently emerge. The present-day attack, AiG emphasizes, is outside of the church: "Secular museums all around the world teach evolution and 'millions of years.' That teaching saturates our world. And what we want people to understand is 'millions of years' is THE attack. It's the 'Genesis Three [Adam and Eve] Attack' of this era of history."[32]

The Biblical Relevance Room provides further context. Martin Luther is in a brown wool habit nailing his ninety-five theses to the wall,

Figure 1.10. Biblical Authority Room

beginning the Reformation and calling attention back to God's Word. To make the depiction of this historical scene more authentic, artifacts of the Bible are presented within glass, temperature-controlled cases. Beside the case is a replica of the well-known fifteenth-century Gutenberg press, which made copies of the Bible increasingly available throughout the Enlightenment era. A sweeping timeline is hung next to the press. Martin Luther, the starting point, represents the "Scripture Alone" era (sola scriptura), and the timeline slopes in a downward trend across the sixteenth century to "Scripture Questioned," which features Galileo using science to investigate the Bible and Francis Bacon suggesting the Bible was no longer needed to understand the natural world. Lesser-known historical figures loom large for creationists on the timeline, such as those who troubled the literal interpretation of six 24-hour days of creation by favoring the idea that the biblical days in Genesis actually represent thousands of years. The timeline leads visitors to conclude with "Scripture Abandoned." The signature historical moment that symbolizes the preceding two rooms' crescendo is depicted in a montage of Scopes Trial imagery from the 1920s. Technically, creationists won the trial and the Tennessean law against teaching evolution was upheld, but the perception of illegitimacy and eventual reversal of that decision is hailed as a cultural blow that still lingers over the creationist movement. The Scopes Trial is portrayed as the beginning of a cultural crisis in America, which led to a range of societal ills such as abortion, divorce, and even racism.

Visitors turn the corner from the historical context of Martin Luther and the Scopes Trial and are dramatically confronted by the present day: "Today Man Decides Truth [scratched out text is replaced with graffiti text] Whatever." This blend of relativistic nihilism is upstaged by red lighting, a blaring ambulance siren, and a darkened corridor full of recent headlines plastered across dirty brick walls, including "Is God Dead?" and "Up from the Apes" and "The Decline of Christian America" (figure 1.11). Public life in the church is juxtaposed by private interactions in the home. In a church scene, the pastor preaches that followers should reinterpret Genesis to fit into the modern, more realistic

Figure 1.11a-b. Scripture Abandoned Corridor

millions-of-years timeline. Symbolized by a giant wrecking ball labeled "millions of years" on the side of the church exterior, this kind of internal attack among believers underscores that if God's Word is not taken as truthful (biblical inerrancy), then destruction ensues. A video monitor embedded into the side of a pew captures a dysfunctional family of parents and teenage children. Span across to the other side of the room and the same family appears through three different peepholes into their home, creating a voyeuristic feel. The windows into the home capture the teenage girl talking to her friend about how to "get rid" of her unexpected pregnancy. In another bedroom, two brothers play violent video games, look at pornography online, and do drugs. Meanwhile, the mother, unaware of her children's activity, is in the kitchen gossiping about the pastor's wife to her friend, all the while her husband is on the couch tuned out in front of the TV.

In step with AiG's worldview, the problems in the contemporary era are forcefully narrated—and the solution is offered as the audience transitions into a tunnel: "As dark as things appear, God's Word gives us the foundation to rebuild. The place to start is . . . at the beginning, six thousand years ago (emphasis in the original museum plaque)." Visitors walk through the time tunnel, which is lit only by small white lights, making it so dark that it is hard to see one's own hand. At the same time, a voice reads passages from the first biblical book, Genesis, and the audience is ushered into the Six Days Theater. Long, carpeted benches offer the first place to sit in the museum since the Special Effects Theater; a four-minute video explores Genesis and the days of creation across three large screens that form an almost 100-degree viewing experience.

Upon emerging from the dark tunnel and theater, the Wonders of Creation Room signals a feeling of new beginnings. Billowing white sails hang from the ceiling; large white stucco pillars and bright lighting greet visitors. Large images (3 feet by 3 feet) of the "physical world" (the sun, the solar system), "living world" (DNA structure, animals, and plants), and the "human world" encircle the room, and a loop of short videos describes these feats of design. AiG beckons the audience to feel wonder and awe, so they begin to question how all of these creatures came into being. Strategically, the museum guides visitors toward AiG's intended premise that all of creation did not just evolve but was designed by God, including humans. As visitors exit the Wonders of

Creation Room, a historical narrative frames the walk through the rest of the museum.

Until this point, AiG invites visitors to consider multiple perspectives, what it frames as "Different Starting Points." Moving forward, the seven Cs, a mnemonic device created by AiG founder Ken Ham, orients the broader narrative of the Creation Museum. The seven Cs is a chronological walk through biblical time: "Creation, Corruption, Catastrophe, and Confusion—that's the geological, biological, astronomical, anthropological history that's foundational to the rest of the Bible. And then we have Christ, Cross and Consummation, the gospel that's based in that history."[33] The first four are what creation scientists, followers with advanced degrees in science, examine in their research in which they claim empirical evidence brings these past events to life. The final three—the gospel—are ideas with which many Christian visitors are more intimately familiar, even though they may not be strict creationists. A central goal of the Creation Museum is to bridge a reading of the Bible as a historical timeline that can be examined using some scientific standards for data and observations. The seven Cs guide the rest of the exhibits at the Creation Museum.

Moving through Biblical Time

While walking through a lush, habitat-style environment in the first C (Creation), visitors experience a replica of the Garden of Eden (figure 1.12). It is full of life-size animal figures, including dinosaurs, tropical foliage, and the serene sounds of a waterfall tumbling around Adam and Eve as they gaze at one another. AiG's decision about which kind of forbidden fruit to place on the Tree of Life was an important one. It is not the iconic apple, as many would expect, but rather what appears to be a mashup between a pomegranate and a mango, as the exact kind of fruit is unknown.[34] While visitors stroll through, they hear overhead: "The Lord God brought certain animals to Adam, and he gave names to all cattle, and to the bird of the air, and to every beast of the field."[35] Accompanying signs provide both the biblical passage and AiG's plain-spoken interpretation, including its significance. Two placards read, "How Many Were There [animals]?" and "What Did They Look Like?" These reference common questions about the plausibility of Adam naming all

Figure 1.12a-b. Garden of Eden

living creatures so quickly and how these animals relate to contemporary descendants. According to AiG, the answer can be found in "created
kinds" or "biblical kinds," which is roughly equivalent to the "family"
level in conventional biological classification systems. It claims Adam
only named general groups of animals, not every single species. This is
a topic I return to later in the petting zoo.[36] The idyllic garden scene is

only disrupted once a visitor notices the lurking serpent encroaching upon the biblical lovers.

The second C (Corruption) brings visitors to a loud, dark gray space where they see the immediate implications of a corrupted world: the aftermath of Adam and Eve's sin, eating the forbidden fruit. Addressing the common question that troubles many—"Why is there suffering?"— AiG works backward from the present era of atomic bombs, genocide, and drug addiction to the past when all things negative, harmful, and difficult in the world began. According to an exhibit placard, "[b]ecause of man's rebellion against His word, God cursed the creation." Museum guests turn the corner and walk past an animal sacrifice scene signaling the shift since Adam and Eve were vegetarian before the Fall. The audience witnesses "Cosmic Pain" that stems from God's curse, which is marked by violence, disease, and natural disaster. The biblical figures Cain and Abel, who were Adam and Eve's children, are examples of how the curse affects the very core of a family. AiG recounts the familiar story—since God favored Abel and his offerings more than Cain's, Cain killed Abel out of jealousy. Two muscular male figures depict this bloody scene. Opposite of this is a forthright discussion of incest under the exhibit placard title "Where Did Cain Get His Wife?" A series of follow-up bullet points argue:

> The farther back in history one goes (back towards the Fall of Adam), the less of a problem mutations in the human population would be. At the time of Adam and Eve's children, there would have been very few mutations in the human genome—thus close relatives could marry, and provided it was one man for one woman (the biblical doctrine of marriage), there was nothing wrong with close relatives marrying in early biblical history.

Here, AiG seeks to make their rationale accomplish two tasks. First, it addresses a common question it receives from those challenging its adherence to the Bible and relies on general scientific language related to genetics to support its claim. Second, AiG drives home its insistence on heterosexual marriage, a theme that underlies much of its framing of homosexuality as a cultural crisis.

Moving forward, visitors meet Methuselah, the longest living descendant of Adam and Eve. According to AiG, since humans lived longer in the beginning owing to fewer genetic mutations, Methuselah did not die until he was more than nine hundred years old. He sits next to a scroll from the book of Genesis detailing the shared genealogy of human civilization. Methuselah serves as the marker of time and the transition into the next exhibit on the Ark and the Great Flood: the third C (Catastrophe). Visitors are submerged in a cross-section of Noah's Ark, recreated out of wood. AiG claims their replica is only 1% of the original ark in scale. Animatronic people discuss and act out different engineering approaches to build this kind of structure. Male carpenters discuss mechanisms for keeping planks in place. They wonder aloud why others are not taking Noah seriously about the impending flood and the need to be ready. Meanwhile, women weave baskets in preparation for feeding and caring for those aboard the ship, both humans and animals (figure 1.13).

After walking through Noah's Ark and witnessing the destruction caused by the Great Flood in the Voyage Room, visitors turn the corner and return to what feels like a conventional science museum exhibit. Dim track lighting glows overhead, large visuals are plastered across the walls, and a combination of dioramas and videos urge visitors to ask questions. As AiG signals in its guide book: "In this area, we wanted to show that real science supports the Bible, and when it comes to mechanisms for the Flood, much research has been done by creation scientists."[37] The 1980s volcanic eruption of Mount St. Helens in Washington State is a familiar example that creation scientists use to underscore the idea that "[a] small catastrophe in the present helps us understand a huge catastrophe in the past," as stated on an exhibit placard. For AiG, this event yields useful observational data recent enough that many visitors may have been alive to remember. This stands in stark contrast to the Great Flood, as described in the Bible, which the Creation Museum claims happened thousands of years ago. In the exhibit, creation scientists outline in several videos how they distinguish between local (observed) and global (inferred) phenomena. Based on empirical *observation* of real-world activity such as Mount St. Helens' quick destruction of the surrounding area within hours and *inference*, which is based on conjecture tied to scientific theories, AiG suggests it is plausible to infer that broader destruction would

Figure 1.13a-b. Noah's Ark Room

be possible on the regional and global levels if an event like the global flood occurred. A worldwide flood would have eroded the topography in weeks. But for AiG, inference is also rooted in biblical accounts. In short, the exhibit outlines in detail AiG's interpretation that much destruction is possible in a short time—a vital argument for a group who asserts that Earth is less than 10,000 years old.

Figure 1.14. Flood Geology Room, Natural Selection Exhibit

To wrestle with a more familiar topic in the mainstream scientific community, the museum curators have roped off a separate area of the Flood Geology exhibit with a large sign that reads, "Natural Selection is not Evolution" (figure 1.14). In the accompanying placard, AiG concedes that natural selection via microevolution, or change within species, is not only possible but probable:

> Natural selection is supported biblically and scientifically. It can be viewed as a God-ordained process that allows organisms to survive in a post-Fall world. Natural selection cannot (despite the common perception) be the mechanism for molecules-to-man evolution since it does not have the ability to create new genetic information (mutations cannot do this either). Natural selection allows limited variation within populations, preserves the viability of populations, and is, in fact, a great confirmation of the Bible's history.

The focus of this exhibit is how natural selection, while a central mechanism for evolutionary theory, is not synonymous with the theory. AiG uses familiar examples, such as antibiotic resistance, dogs as beloved pets, and lesser-known examples—such as the live blind cavefish on display in the exhibit—to unpack how mutation or variations suggest that organisms change naturally or artificially (i.e., through breeding) over time. But it is important to note, AiG disentangles all of this from cross-species or "molecule to man" evolutionary change—which they absolutely reject. This echoes their embrace of scientific ideas of genetic mutation (allowing early humans to mate and live longer) but not of evolution as scientifically conceived. The observable phenomena that readily occur in the present day are accepted and highlighted in this exhibit, but AiG positions as evolutionary theory any idea that extends beyond what is readily observable. The organization associates evolutionary theory with secularism and therefore doubts it because of its "different starting point."

The final section of the Flood Geology Room contains the newly installed Ebenezer exhibit, an Allosaurus. AiG uses Ebenezer to address the question of what happened to the dinosaurs during the Flood, when many of them died. After the Flood they died due to environmental change, competition for food, or possibly at the hands of humans. Visitors then pass through a series of transitional placards. The Ice Age section discusses how the Earth cooled shortly after the Flood, how continental drift took place, and how speciation variety rebounded in the animal and plant kingdoms after the Flood. By coupling the presentation of fossil casts with technical videos covering the feasibility of a global flood, AiG unabashedly displays an alternative explanation of human and natural history on a grand scale.

In the fourth C (Confusion), the Tower of Babel represents humans' disobedience of God's command to spread across the Earth and multiply the human race, so God introduced different languages to confuse and force dispersion. Differences arose between groups of people, and in the "Hall of Shame" AiG provides examples in a glass case where symbolic objects serve as "[p]ainful reminders of a history marked by abuse and racism" (figure 1.15). AiG points to Social Darwinism, rooted in a nineteenth-century interpretation of evolutionary theory that suggested certain groups of people were less fit for survival and should be eliminated, as what encouraged people to treat groups of human beings as inferior based on their race and other problematized cultural indicators. The oppression of Australian Aborigines, US chattel slavery, and

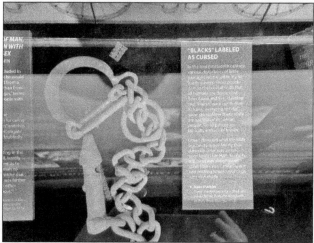

Figure 1.15a-c. Tower of Babel

the Holocaust are featured as examples of what happens when Darwin's work, particularly the *Descent of Man*, is upheld over the Bible. Again, AiG emphasizes that when people follow the Bible—unlike the dysfunctional family depicted earlier—peace and harmony return to human relations.

The first four Cs thread together the conceptual and physical museum walkthrough for visitors. The origins of humanity (Creation) signals the beginning. Then AiG chronicles the fallen world after the initial sin in the Garden of Eden and humanity's curse. As a result, much pain, suffering, and hatred occur, which is showcased in Corruption (second C) and the many lost lives of the Great Flood, or Catastrophe (third C). Finally, Confusion (fourth C) stems from the Tower of Babel, and in many ways that event shapes the contemporary era, in which people yearn to address a long-standing sense of divisiveness.

AiG offers the final three Cs—the Gospel—as the solution to the world's brokenness: the fifth C (Christ), which is God's gift of Jesus Christ to humanity; the sixth C (Cross), which is the crucifixion of Jesus Christ; and the seventh C (Consummation), which is the wait for God's return for believers and the only C that has not yet occurred. From 2007 to 2016, this portion of the museum tour was presented in the Last Adam Theater, which screened an eponymously titled 15-minute film. AiG lays out the case for the Gospel and its presentation of it:

> The creator became a man, Jesus Christ, who obeyed God in everything, unlike the first man, Adam. Jesus, the messiah, died on a cross to pay the penalty for mankind's sin against God. He rose from the dead, providing life for all who trust in him. One day, at the consummation, the creator will remake his creation. He will cast out death and the disobedient, and dwell eternally with those who trust in him.[38]

This section is the most conventional evangelical aspect of the museum in terms of its explicit and urgent effort to fortify believers and evangelize to visitors who may be interested in this version of salvation. In 2017, AiG began to present this same material in a new exhibit via original artwork of Jesus Christ, his crucifixion, his resurrection, and his believers' salvation upon his return. This is the thematic climax of the entire museum and what every member of AiG's staff indicates is the most important. Fittingly, this concludes the formal walkthrough of the museum experience.

Other Attractions at the Creation Museum

After the walkthrough, visitors can view a variety of smaller stand-alone exhibits in the Palm Plaza on the lower level of the museum. Throughout the past decade, these exhibits have continued to shift. Typically there is a first-century chapel, a "Dinosaur Den" with a variety of large-scale dinosaur figures, Dr. Crawley's Insectorium, which features an interactive animatronic Dr. Arthur Pod in his laboratory, and a space for traveling exhibits. During the summer of 2017, the temporary exhibit was from the Museum of the Bible.[39]

Beyond the Palm Pizza pop-up food café, one walks through a brief but detailed "Answers Hall." This space includes a timeline of the AiG organization and Ken Ham's role in the broader creationist movement, followed by an appeal to donate to and support AiG. Visitors can either exit through the bookstore/gift shop via the two flights of stairs or take an elevator to the first-floor hallway where other on-site food options are just steps away: Noah's Coffee, Bruster's Ice Cream (the national chain), and Noah's Café, which is the largest cafeteria in the Creation Museum.

In 2012, AiG added Legacy Hall to serve as a stand-alone space for semi-public events (figure 1.16). It seats approximately one thousand people and is used for conferences, workshops, and special events that are distinct but connected to the museum's regular activities (e.g., a conference participant would attend a homeschool conference at the Legacy Hall and would receive complementary access to the museum. Most notably, the now infamous 2014 broadcast debate between Ken Ham and Bill Nye took place in Legacy Hall. While most of the special events are sponsored and run by AiG—ranging from educational workshops to Christmas Town, a replica of Bethlehem during the birth of Jesus—Legacy Hall is also available for rent to like-minded groups and even for private events such as weddings.

The Creation Museum is not limited to the building itself. The surrounding botanical garden and grounds provide ample opportunity to embark on a self-guided audio tour; a mile of paved walkways suitable

Figure 1.16. Legacy Hall

for strollers and wheelchairs weave throughout meticulously landscaped gardens. Opened in May 2008 on AiG's first anniversary, the gardens are maintained primarily by volunteer groundskeepers with oversight from an on-staff horticulturalist. More than six thousand plants reflect geographical climates far from the Ohio River area. In addition, a petting zoo is nestled in the back corner of the grounds; it is home to alpacas, wallabies, and most important, for AiG, a zonkey and a zorse. The combination of zebras with donkeys or horses showcases the plausibility of an important argument presented in the museum about speciation via biblical kinds (figure 1.17). As the audio tour describes, "[The animals in the petting zoo] show us that horses, zebras, and donkeys are members of what the Bible calls a kind. When God sent two of every kind of animal to Noah's Ark to be saved from the flood that means He only sent two of the horse kind—a boy and a girl. All the modern-day horses, zebras, and donkeys are descendants of those two horses."[40] While the $5.00 camel rides and the petting zoo are intended for children, the displays posted next to each animal stall match the same level of content and format provided in the museum exhibits, here referencing Adam naming the animals in the Garden of Eden.

Figure 1.17a-b. Petting Zoo

Behind the Scenes

AiG uses museum-industry standards without attempting to become enmeshed in the network of mainstream museums as it has never sought accreditation. As the director of research commented to me, AiG does not see accreditation as necessary given that the public already vets the museum: "People won't show up at the door unless it's worthwhile to come to and can stand up to scrutiny. In that sense, the public is probably the accrediting agency. [laughs] The same is true in the secular world. The scientific community will chide the curators and the developers if they haven't done a good job of presenting the models, and the interpretations, and the quality of the exhibits."[41] This type of rationale has long-standing roots in AiG's distrust of secular mainstream institutions; ultimately, the public is AiG's source of validation rather than the biased community of elite scientists.[42] However, logistically only a small percentage of museums operating are actually accredited, approximately 5%.[43] And AiG, as a non-profit organization, wants to assure visitors and benefactors that it is financially stable, so it is accredited by the Better Business Bureau. The parallel financial accrediting body, the Evangelical Council for Financial Accountability, commonly used by megachurches and other large evangelical institutions, also approves the museum.[44]

AiG not only connects research with public exhibition, but it also developed a formal Collections Management Policy document: "While the museum was not originally intended for the purpose of collecting objects, in accomplishing its mission it has undertaken the care of many objects and considers the proper care and documentation of its collections essential."[45] This is customary practice in the museum world, where an explicit set of standards for quality is upheld in maintaining fossils and other collections. A volunteer with a background in biology, not museum management, developed this policy. Later, she sought additional training to become the museum registrar/visitor study specialist, as there is no curator at the Creation Museum. She convinced AiG leadership that it was vital for her to attend a Smithsonian Institution workshop for museum planners. Her rationale for attending was clear, "if people don't know how to do things in a museum then they [the objects] wouldn't be properly regarded . . . I wanted to make sure it was a real museum."[46] She also belongs to the Visitor Studies Association and mentioned that although conference attendees may mock her affiliation with the Creation Museum online and in blogs: "during the workshops and professional meetings people are nice face-to-face" (ibid.). She indicated that they have no reciprocity with other institutions/museums, but they do lend items to institutions "with similar missions."

Along with AiG, the museum registrar/visitor study specialist is aware that both museum professionals and research scientists receive the museum with skepticism. Nonetheless, AiG is a non-profit organization that runs a museum on its own terms, according to its own standards that it shares with the evangelical community, all the while borrowing from established museum-industry practices and conventions to strengthen the plausibility of its exhibits. Behind-the-scenes access shows us how AiG does it.

Locating the AiG Organization

The private areas of the museum allow AiG to display the movement's message out front while keeping its other efforts away from the public view. In the early days of its design, the publicly accessible museum was slotted to sit beside the private organizational headquarters, which is now approximately 25,000 square feet. It is not accessible to the public nor is it mentioned on maps of the museum. Typically, it is not featured in any promotional materials for the Creation Museum either. The casual visitor to the museum is largely unaware that an area even exists next to the exhibits. The entrance is an electronically secured doorway without any signage beyond a "staff only" sign (figure 1.18). In keeping with the layout of many natural history museums, the separation between exhibition and research spaces, or the public and the private, is frequently unannounced.

The AiG headquarters houses an office space with an internal core of sixteen staff cubicles. Organizational leaders and on-site PhD creation scientists occupy formal offices along the outer ring, with one-way windows that look onto the botanical garden. Other spaces include a large conference room called "the war room," an on-site technical production team (to run a sound booth), an extensive website design team, and an internal archive and library complete with rolling stacks (figure 1.18).

Figure 1.18a-b. AiG Organizational Headquarters Doorway; Museum "War Room" Sign

With the familiar taupe cubicles, water cooler dynamics, and a professional yet casual atmosphere, AiG's headquarters looks and feels like any other office in the United States (figure 1.19).[47] Inside jokes punctuate their work; one day during fieldwork, I noted the bathroom down the hall was closed, and the sign on the door stated, "we live in a fallen world"—a riff-off of the curse (due to Adam and Eve's sin) that AiG depicts so gravely in the museum.[48]

When I interviewed Ken Ham, one of the first topics that came up was rather mundane and unexpected: maintenance. Something familiar to any leader, founder, or CEO is the daily upkeep and costs to ensure everything runs smoothly:

> And I think that that's one of the traps that Christians and non-Christians fall into—that you can't just talk about building something. The cost of maintaining just the electrical system, the air conditioning system, the restrooms, the equipment . . . The cost of maintenance is enormous. So, for this place we maintain it, and we're able to maintain it, but you've got to have the people coming in.[49]

While he notes that they are able to maintain the Creation Museum, the cost of operations is clearly something they considered when setting the price point and building up the infrastructure necessary to run it. This is an aspect they highlight to invested members in *Behind the Scenes* (2008): "The museum spends $60,000 annually just to replace projector bulbs."[50] It takes a lot to keep the Creation Museum open to the public more than 350 days a year.

Having a museum affords AiG an opportunity to attract staff and volunteers, to pursue fund-raising, and to engage in various forms of outreach. The benefits of an on-site, central location are outlined by a cartoonist / longtime illustrator at AiG:

> Before, when the ministry was just offices, you would hear about the speaker going out on the road, and some of the debating that would happen there. . . . [But] Now, I can come out of the AIG offices, into the museum, and I can see people looking at the displays and hear what they're thinking sometimes . . . You get all kinds. I've spoken to Christians that

Figure 1.19a-b. AiG Headquarters Office Area

were all excited about it. I've spoken to atheists that didn't like it at all, and everywhere in between. I really like the access to seeing the audience.[51]

The headquarters provides a logistical hub for the movement, as this staff member suggests. Physically linking the museum—a public attraction—with the headquarters allows the staff to interact not only with other creation scientists and fellow staff, but also with adherents and skeptics among the museum's visitors. Before the museum opened, this access was only available to traveling speakers.

With on-site organizational efforts occurring in the background, the museum can rein in its previously dispersed activities. When I asked the director of communications, one of the co-founders of AiG and of the Creation Museum, why they chose to build a museum, his reply suggests convenience, efficiency, education, and outreach:

> [W]e thought, "let's create a center that's convenient for people to get to, and we can teach people here" . . . Our speakers still give talks here at the museums. . . . [But] They're in their own home and beds that evening. We're reaching far more people with a centrally located facility than we could possibly do if we had even 30 speakers on our staff traveling around the country.[52]

A museum was not only well suited to attract public attention, particularly among youth, but also to serve two key logistical functions. It exposed substantial numbers of people to AiG's message. And movement speakers no longer needed to travel the circuit as frequently, giving lectures and meeting believers. Instead, the adherents would come to them at the museum. Beyond the desire to build and operate a professional attraction that draws a significantly larger audience than those who attend conferences, lectures, and seminars, the museum is also simply easier on the core members of AiG. Striking a balance between the quality of the outreach and the feasibility of reaching enough people is imperative. Increasingly, the emphasis is on growing the Creation Museum as a multi-purpose facility that holds the private AiG staff headquarters for AiG, the large auditorium of Legacy Hall, and the classrooms for small group presentations and demonstrations (approximately 25–50 people each). All of this underscores the museum's role for establishing cohesion into one place for AiG's mission and for its staff.

AiG has steadily grown since its inception in 1994; typically, there are approximately ten to fifteen board members and approximately one hundred people employed in full-time and part-time positions. These staff members are bolstered by a broad base of volunteers, which fluctuates greatly depending on the season and need. The volunteer coordinator indicates that for an average month they have approximately two hundred volunteer days a month, mostly from adults, "When someone would come for that day, that's a volunteer day . . . Most of them are not kids. Most are adults and some of those folks come one or two days a week from locally. Some folks come from long distance, and they'll come and spend a week or two here."[53] AiG also has hosted some volunteers in a nearby house while they work on-site.[54] Given that AiG emphasizes service—donating time, talents, and money to advance evangelical efforts—the level of volunteerism that the coordinator describes is not surprising. For example, I saw on one hot July day approximately fifty to seventy-five volunteers weeding the lush botanical gardens—and this is a common occurrence.[55]

What is most striking is how the museum becomes a rallying point for many adherents. Some of AiG's employed staff members initially started doing volunteer work, then decided to relocate their families to the area, and later joined the staff. Many adherents also donate valued items. The vast majority of items displayed in the museum are donated or on loan.[56] This is just one way the museum garners support and commitment from believers. The key is a physical connection between the movement headquarters and the museum: a multifaceted site for movement members to dedicate their energy through a general means (stuffing envelopes, greeting people, gardening), donating a very specific skill set (carpentry knowledge, an interest in museum operations), or lending a valuable object to the collection.

Espousing a populist ethos and a broad base of support, the director of communications contends that, as an organization, AiG lives off of volunteer work and small donations: "This museum was not built by a lot of rich people. Our average gift was about $130. Very, very broad base of support. . . . A strong organization is built on lots of general rank-and-file support."[57] What the museum appears to provide is an identifiable

Figure 1.20. AiG Off-Site Collection Storage

institution through which adherents attach themselves to AiG's mission and goals. This is reinforced by a religious ethos rooted in a sense of community and a culture of service with the goal of evangelizing.

Housing the YEC Ideology

In this backstage of the museum, the institution serves as the logistical hub for AiG's broader movement efforts. Yet it is not just a place to store fossils, corral movement leaders, and collect funding. The headquarters also acts as a space for knowledge production. This occurs through research and publication as well as preservation efforts that shape AiG's sense of where it fits into the broader creationist movement.

Research performed by museum staff members spans multiple disciplines, but all of it draws from and upholds both the Bible and the natural world as valuable sources of information. On-site research staff members examine fossils in the museum's collections, correspond with research collaborators, and arrange off-site research trips (figure 1.20). The director of research described his perspective on the museum's emphasis on research, "you have collections, but you do things with them [for instance] . . . museums can sponsor fossil excavations." He goes on to detail the process, "[by] preparing a fossil from the rock, and then exhibiting it, and then researching it, and then publishing what the fossil shows. A museum should be like a research institute, as well as communicating to the public."[58] His account captures the important work that is done on-site for the dissemination of research that informs both the museum's exhibits and the movement's publications for the broader public.

Publications for both scholarly and lay audiences further demonstrate how AiG's research informs movement initiatives. Technical publications aimed at YEC scholars include peer-reviewed, creation-oriented journals; this is a long-running movement strategy dating back to the mid-1960s. Yet often these publications relied upon membership in the organization and fee-based subscriptions. When AiG began the *Answers Research Journal* (ARJ) in 2008, it was the only YEC peer-reviewed journal to operate as an online, open-access journal available to download free of charge. It is perceived as a credible resource, especially for those whose visit to the museum may have sparked an interest.

Additionally, AiG publishes a lay audience magazine, *Answers* (launched in 2006, a spin-off from the original *Answers* newsletter started in 1994), which is described as a publication "to illustrate the importance of Genesis in building a creation-based worldview, and to equip readers with practical answers so they can confidently communicate the gospel and biblical authority with accuracy and graciousness."[59] *Answers* and *ARJ* are similar in message but strikingly distinct. *ARJ* is structured as a publication for any person seeking technical information. *Answers* is a popular publication focused on a down-to-earth, concrete treatment of questions and challenges that surface in broader society, particularly in relation to YEC apologetics. Both are associated with AiG via the website and the museum bookstore, as the organization sells and advertises them there when visitors check out. This explains how *Answers* boasted a circulation of more than 70,000 subscribers in 2014, up from approximately 30,000 when it launched in 2006.[60] For AiG, knowledge production and dissemination for both audiences is the goal, as opposed to reaching only a technical and scholarly audience. Given the connections between the journal and the Creation Museum, AiG can support such efforts since the requisite infrastructure is largely provided on-site at the headquarters. Website production teams, editorial staff, artists and fabrication teams, and research staff are all set up to produce the journal alongside many other books, videos, presentations, and exhibit materials.

Meanwhile, other staff members work to document and archive AiG's history and role in the creationist movement. A longtime staff archivist and librarian identified the primary functioning of these spaces at AiG headquarters: "For the archives, and what I hope would be a special collections room, it definitely would be a history of the creation-evolution controversy."[61] Many movement materials were published through small Christian-owned publishing houses that may no longer be in operation. Collecting and archiving such books and primary documents is vital for verification and for tracing the movement's development. Even AiG's founder, Ken Ham, admits that the organization has fine-tuned its arguments over time: "it wouldn't have been good to build the Creation Museum thirty years ago. I would say the message has matured a lot since then. We've got a lot more answers. I think that we're more articulate. I think we understand the issues more. I mean at every stage in your life you think . . . people think they know it all [laughs]."[62] Especially when it comes to the museum, AiG prioritizes improving on what it has done previously—whether it is to strengthen an argument against external critique, to rouse interest, or to resolve doubts about creation science. Knowledge production takes shape on-site in the museum headquarters, serving the museum and the organization simultaneously.

Where did this forceful, unequivocal YEC museum come from? How did AiG position itself to open such a site in its pursuit to shore up plausibility for its alternative, politically charged claims for cultural authority? In the next chapter, I situate AiG's organizational efforts within a longer view of the creationist movement to unpack why it elected to build a museum at all when other options and strategies were available.

2

The Creationist Movement in the United States

Why did AIG seek cultural legitimacy by creating a museum for the masses rather than by pursuing political change in courts or by persuading influential movement elites? Other options were certainly available given the broader creationist movement's development of a multifaceted tactical repertoire.[1] It included establishing a Christian college/university, specifically a graduate school; developing a supporting research center that publishes peer-reviewed journals; or establishing a legal advocacy group. Considering these possible alternatives, I trace the configurations of strategies developed across the twentieth and twenty-first centuries and employed by YEC organizations. In this chapter, I show that AiG built the Creation Museum as a result of ideological fissures in the movement, shifting leadership, and reassessment of cultural institutions as another route for plausibility politics.

I approach organizational decisions as interactive episodes, linking social movement actors to others in the movement and to their opponents or targets.[2] Identifying the discrete episodes within the YEC movement across time highlights how these social movement organizations (SMOs) relate to each other and provides insights into the choice to build a museum. Scholars have not yet satisfactorily explained this type of outcome. The rise of AiG and its decision to build a museum surprised creationism scholars and other social movement researchers because of their narrower focus on political opportunities. They neglected the broader contextual focus and efforts to build an alternative institution, which was key for challenging the cultural authority of science outside of the domain of politics. As sociologist Robin Stryker (1996) suggests, "a historical narrative becomes a puzzle when extant theories prevent scholars from expecting that development" (314).

SMOs are longitudinal forms of social movements. An SMO emerges when it becomes a formal organization with a known location, group of participants, internal and external visibility, and a continuity of its mission as well as routines.[3] Steady scholarly interest centers on organizational aspects of social movements within their own internal dynamics and the positioning of a movement in a broader field of actors. This focus on the "social movement industry" points to how SMOs with relatively similar goals interact with one another or, as organizational studies scholars Soule and King (2008) put it: "many different organizations pursuing related but subtly different goals and drawing on different sets of tactics" (1596).[4] Actors make sense of claims by linking them to what already exists or is familiar. SMOs forge a collective identity built around perceived common injustices, shared interests, and identified external targets. Additionally, scholars have explored how SMOs develop an intelligible and persuasive message for their audiences in which novelty becomes deeply important.[5]

Most studies that consider cultural elements have centered on social movements located on the "left" end of the political spectrum, a trend dating back to the upheavals of the mid-1960s.[6] In their review, Gross, Medvetz, and Russell (2011) suggest that sociologists have largely avoided social movements grounded in conservative worldviews. Conservatism, as used in this context, combines at least three elements: *political* (maintenance of status quo or reversal of recent sociohistorical developments), *economic* (advocacy for a free market), and *moral* (social order without violence)—although the boundaries among these three analytic categories are fluid and often slippery (330). Generally, if scholars examine conservatism, their emphasis waivers from unpacking the extreme right-wing or Republican political parties (in the United States or cross-nationally) toward better understanding the historical social movements of the right.[7] For example, McVeigh (2009) uses the case of the Ku Klux Klan in the 1920s to underscore that the weakening of adherents' economic, political, and status-based "purchasing power" initially increased the movement's capacity to influence national politics, which it later lost with the erosion of its membership base.

In his century-long historical analysis of the politically and religiously conservative antievolutionism, Michael Lienesch (2007) directs attention toward failed efforts to change federal public policy, but also toward more successful state and local legal efforts. By framing the movement as an opposition to evolution—a scientific theory otherwise rarely challenged in mainstream American culture—creationist-related efforts

have persisted, albeit with mixed results when evaluating the sociopolitical dynamics and educational legislation. Instead, I focus on the YEC
context of the latter half of the twentieth century into the twenty-first
century to examine how and why a social movement organization chose
to use a unique physical site to realize its goal of cultural resonance and
legitimacy.[8]

To analyze the YEC context and to understand how SMOs in a field
relate to one another across time, I trace how YEC organizations split
from one another. [9] Social movement scholar Deborah Balser (1997)
argues:

> Factionalism refers to the conflict that develops between groups, belong-
> ing to the same organization, who formerly held common beliefs but who
> experience a growing divergence in their views and interests . . . (who)
> pursue different goals, strategies, and tactics, stemming from their di-
> verging interests. (200)

I show that creationism as a social movement experienced three episodes of factionalism from the 1960s to 2007. First, an *ideological* split
occurred between young earth and old earth creationism throughout
the 1960s. Second, a divergence in leadership catapulted the Institute
for Creation Research (ICR) to become the central social movement
organization from the 1970s through the 1990s. Third, AiG's adaptation of cultural institution-building, under the direction of Ken Ham,
developed the Creation Museum to influence public opinion about the
creationist movement from the 1990s to 2007. This sequence of episodes came to light when I analyzed archival materials from internal
creationist SMO newsletters (more than 1,000 newsletters across four
organizations).[10]

Put simply, the museum is a contingent outcome that warrants sociological explanation. Interestingly, other creation museums anticipated
the one eventually built in Kentucky, such as the California museum
operated by ICR from 1976 to 2008. The goal of this earlier museum
was not to advocate and entertain the masses with a multimedia experience but to use intimate spaces in which folk dioramas and local fossils
could convince scientifically trained believers and their families about
the truth of creation science. In this chapter, I showcase how movements

shift between multiple goals and targets over time and how different strategies emerged as the result of factionalism among SMOs. Only a social movement analysis that attends to the key role played by movement ideology, the efficacy and social skill of its leaders, and the possibility that multiple institutions could be sites for resistance has the tools to demonstrate that the Creation Museum was an inevitable outcome rather than a surprise.

Episode 1: Divergence in Ideology

American Scientific Affiliation and the Creation Research Society (1963–1971)

In the decades after the Scopes Trial, evangelical scientists debated the direction of the antievolution movement and in 1941 created the American Scientific Affiliation (ASA) to consider evidence for and against Darwinian evolutionary theory. Participants sought to appraise rather than refute evolution, avoiding confrontation with mainstream establishment scientists and distancing themselves from "extreme" creationism.[11]

In 1949, ASA began to publish a journal with editorials and articles, adding a lively newsletter ten years later. Their core activities included producing manuscripts for circulation among interested scientists and solidifying an emerging network of evangelical scientists. For leader Alton Everest, even though ASA recognized and appreciated the efforts of previous creationist organizations, he suggests that they were

> relatively ignorant of these other groups. For this reason their influence on ASA was negligible and it is only in retrospect that we can see how fortunate this was in the formation of the policy of the ASA . . . we consider it distinctly improper for the ASA to become so enamored by particular interpretations of these accounts that we shift our efforts from study to propaganda.[12]

Compared to earlier associations, which were narrowly defined or plagued with infighting, ASA's founders envisioned it to be a safe harbor for plurality. It was a place for Christian scientists to gather and debate rather than move to an extreme position that would rob them of the chance to influence secular science and the broader culture. It was all too aware of the movement's history. For example, in response to a member's request to have a more forceful discussion in the ASA newsletter, it wrote, "We must not forget, however, that one factor in the weakening of the impact of the Gospel on the world was the virtual disowning of intellectuals by fundamentalists during the past century. The ASA is part of a great swing back to a more balanced view of the place of the scholar in the overall Christian witness."[13] And, throughout the 1950s and early 1960s, ASA continued the focus on avoiding confrontation with mainstream science.[14]

With members of ASA steadfast in their commitment to multiple interpretations of the Bible and tolerant of diverse understandings of the relationship between being a Christian and a scientist, a fissure emerged. Beginning in the late 1950s, several pivotal events pushed those with a YEC perspective away from ASA. Bernard Ramm, an ASA member, published the *Christian View of Science and Scripture* (1954) to move evangelicals toward progressive creationism (i.e., creation was revealed but not necessarily performed within six literal days) and away from a YEC perspective that accepted the Bible as a source of scientific data and advocated flood geology theory. This move rallied YEC adherents.

Largely unknown to mainstream scientists at the turn of the twentieth century, antievolutionists long touted George McCready Price's flood geology theory published in *The New Geology* (1923). According to Price, the prolonged cataclysmic flood described in the Bible that Noah and his family faced destroyed not only all civilization, burying antediluvian fossils, but also Earth's topography, giving rise to the current geographic conditions. Interestingly, Price's work was used at the Scopes Trial by William Jennings Bryan, the evangelical lead prosecutor, to underscore the scientific evidence of creationism—a turn of events that inevitably angered Price due to Bryan's equivocation about the length of the days for the creation week.[15]

Henry Morris, who held a PhD in electrical engineering, was an ASA member who often presented papers at the annual conventions. John Whitcomb, a young theologian, heard Morris at the 1953 convention and was disappointed when Morris's work on flood geology was received poorly among fellow ASA members. Nonetheless, Morris and

Whitcomb began to correspond.[16] They got to work on publishing what would soon become the battle cry for the YEC movement: *The Genesis Flood* (1961) to counter Ramm's disparaging work on YEC and flood geology.[17]

Shortly after Morris and Whitcomb's publication of *The Genesis Flood*, Morris unequivocally became known as the founding father of the YEC movement. However, YEC's start as a distinct movement, in opposition to the ASA, emerged only in 1963. This is when Walter Lammerts, along with Morris and eight other devout YEC adherents, formed the Creation Research Society (CRS).[18] As opposed to past movement efforts, in which none of the members had prestigious credentials, five of the ten founding members of CRS had earned doctoral degrees in the biological sciences at "mainstream" universities.[19] Indeed, as a prerequisite, all of them were required to hold such credentials to be a voting member (as ASA also did).[20] They launched the *Creation Research Society Quarterly Journal* in July 1964, and page one of the first issue stated their precise ideological commitment to YEC: "Haec credimus [This we believe]: For in six days the Lord created heaven and earth, the sea, and all that in them is and rested on the seventh.—Exodus 20:11."[21]

Yet the battle lines between the ASA and CRS were clear long before the latter's formation in 1963. In a 1973 *Creation Research Society Quarterly Journal*, CRS would reflect on how they were edged out: "The American Scientific Affiliation was formed in 1941 . . . After a few years the statement of belief was liberalized in order to attract more members and the thrust against evolution was lessened."[22] Those who left the evangelical ASA due to its refusal to adhere explicitly to YEC tenets fomented an ideological break.

Lammerts was steadfast in his insistence that the association must adopt a strong position against evolution. This was clearly reflected in CRS's ideological positioning across the two organizational newsletters. In general, ASA gave little attention to ideological matters in contrast to CRS's active discussions. ASA focused instead on how to negotiate secular spaces. For both SMOs, following God's Word was important for the religious ideology. ASA, however, did not emphasize the Book of Genesis or literal interpretations of the Bible, but these were core tenets for CRS and the YEC movement.

While ASA concentrated on securing its future as an organization, CRS actively sought to establish a new collective identity. By focusing on how evolutionary bias persists in scientific and educational establishments, CRS conveyed a sense that they were embattled. Lammerts ensured that CRS's focus would be on textbooks for high school students in contrast to ASA's focus on college students. CRS perceived the Biological Sciences Curriculum Study (BSCS) of 1963, funded by the National Science Foundation, as a larger threat. BSCS represented a nationwide push for professional, hands-on, laboratory-focused high school biology textbooks. Previously, most textbooks were not updated for decades and did not mention evolution. BSCS "took responsibility for putting evolution back into high school biology," and it was successful.[23] Within the first year of publication, "approximately 50 percent of American high school students taking biology used BSCS books."[24]

CRS dove into its own attempts to steer high school biology classrooms toward an alternative: high-quality creationist textbooks, whose royalties would help to further establish the organization. In 1965, Lammerts noted that CRS needed to work on "challenging the evolutionary bias of the BSCS series now being adopted by many school boards," and the organization formed a Textbook Committee to work on CRS's own creationist competitor.[25] The committee piloted the book *Biology: A Search for Order in Complexity* in two high schools (one public and one private) in the fall of 1966, and in 1970, published through the well-known evangelical publishing house Zondervan.[26] As historian Ronald Numbers (2006) indicates, the book sold out its first printing, but this was largely due to its adoption in Christian schools. It was not widely adopted by public schools, and even in states where it was, like Indiana, it was later deemed unconstitutional due to its reliance on biblical creationism.[27] Nonetheless, royalties from the textbook helped to sustain CRS, and new memberships increased.[28]

When it came to protest events, ASA was more concerned with academic debates and petitions rather than CRS's protests or weekly radio platforms intended for popular audiences. Yet neither organization attempted to secure a broad base of laypersons, as both were professional societies requiring academic credentials for membership.

In many respects, ASA displays what conventional literature would expect of an established SMO; it was institutionalized with a broad base of support and resources, and it was more concerned with reaching external audiences than jockeying for position within the YEC movement. ASA was particularly interested in challenging external secular leaders and organizations—such as the American Association for the Advancement of Science and the American Institute for Biological Sciences—and in curbing the government's role in steering research away from biblical understandings.[29] ASA also directed its attention toward rival external religious leaders and organizations, whether distinguishing itself from Billy Graham or continuing a dialogue with Inter-Varsity Christian Fellowship and the National Association of Evangelicals.

Alternatively, CRS had a much narrower focus. It concentrated on challenging the BSCS textbook publications. CRS also wanted to harness the cultural upheaval of the 1960s to secure legislation that was more favorable to its cause. It attacked ACLU's activities as well as judicial actions such as the 1963 *Epperson v. Arkansas* case, in which the Supreme Court ruled that states could not prohibit the teaching of evolution. In contrast to ASA, CRS oriented itself toward improving its position by forming the YEC branch of the antievolution movement.

Ideological distinctions between ASA and CRS were reinforced by the differences between CRS's advancement of flood geology theory and ASA's sense of creation science, which highlighted the relevance of fossils, and the possible interactions between religion and science. Unsurprisingly, the scientific method was an emphasis for both SMOs. CRS, however, discussed the method more often in its attempts to bolster creation science via a Baconian view of scientific methods and emphasis on observation.[30] CRS framed its cultural crisis ideology as a response to what it called "secular humanism," which is a moral packaging in which the centrality of humans displaces the importance of the supernatural.[31] CRS argued that both religious and creation science evangelism would be the proper antidote, specifically in the public educational system. While ASA directed some of its attention to education and a broader cultural crisis, it did not explicitly attach it to secular humanism. This was, yet again, a salient difference, as YEC adherents continued to perceive secular humanism as the primary culprit for the widespread moral degradation in even more recent years.

The word "ideology" is often tied to how individuals share perspectives that allow them to make sense of a complex world.[32] Scholars suggest that an ideology's durability depends on how it contrasts with other ideologies (e.g., secularists versus creationists) and on its ability to ensure its viewpoints and solutions are not always in flux but rather are deeply held convictions.[33] As a result, ideological commitments emerge in social movements when adherents regard world events as incomprehensible or when social tides shift.[34] In effect, ideologies activate when groups seek to resurrect a status ante quo or to challenge conventions.[35]

For social movement scholars, it is vital to examine ideological production and negotiation, as they point to how movements choose among alternative courses of action.[36] The task is to focus on the *how* of social action (i.e., how collective groups use ideological explanations), which requires going beyond movement actors' ideas or declarations.[37] Too often, when scholars attempt to distinguish the role that ideology plays in movement mobilization and potentially factionalism, they reduce that role to an artificially simple and coherent set of ideas that necessarily unite members. This is most prominent in relation to individuals' beliefs regarding religious ideas and values.[38]

The factionalism between ASA and CRS was not just about a divergent set of interests rooted exclusively in internal organizational dynamics. Although that was a factor, the split was fundamentally tied to divergent ideological worldviews. Scholarly literature often perceives factionalism as the consequence of a change in resource allocation or organizational strategy due to shifting goals, but this episode underscores the need to consider the vital role of ideology as well. For CRS and ASA, the chasm grew from a difference in how central evolutionary theory should be to their core missions and identities.

Episode 2: Leaders at the Helm

Creation Research Society and the Institute of Creation Research (1972–1993)

The YEC movement is hierarchical in structure, so the leader of each SMO plays a pivotal role in the trajectory of the broader movement. The historical development of the creationist SMO leadership lineage is adaptive, at times conflict-oriented, in that every leader emerges internally. Each leader was a member in the SMO that was prominent during the preceding movement episode; then, each leader branched out to create their own SMO. How do leaders learn to be effective and capitalize on available resources, assess potential opportunities, or creatively devise alternative interpretations? Social movement and organizational studies scholar Marshall Ganz uses the term "strategic capacity" to examine a leader's intention and organizational action to secure desired movement outcomes.[39] Timing is essential because previous movement experiences with collaboration and competition are key to identifying opportunities. Success does not always hinge on the quantity of available resources, but rather on the ability to leverage existing assets across time. Ganz's theory of strategic capacity emphasizes why a particular organization is more likely to develop a series of effective tactics, giving less attention to the ultimate success itself (although this may happen, too). While environment and context are important for a social movement's development, understanding how leaders steer the movement's direction is a vital first step.[40] To do so, we must pay attention to creativity and novelty to understand more robustly how leaders become effective. I argue that a focus on creativity and novelty for effectiveness becomes particularly clear during "Episode 2" in Henry Morris's shift between CRS and ICR.

With CRS going strong in the late 1960s, its then-president, Henry Morris, devoted his energy to creationism as a social movement. Morris assumed leadership of CRS in 1967, which came after Lammerts stated that he was not interested in the position since he was consumed by editorial work at CRS's journal. Morris was technically the leader of CRS until 1973, yet his desire for a broader SMO motivated his move to San Diego in September 1970. There he co-founded Christian Heritage College (CHC) with Tim LaHaye, an increasingly well-known leader in the evangelical movement and a pastor of the Scott Memorial Baptist Church. Throughout these transitions, Morris was acutely aware of the movement's storied history with the mainstream media and educational institutions since the Scopes Trial in 1925. In response, he sought to pitch the new young earth creationist organization, Institute for Creation Research, as an entity committed to creation science or scientific creationism.[41] In his first "Director's Column" of ICR's newsletter, *Acts & Facts*, in 1972, Morris makes explicit ICR's new direction:

> The Institute for Creation Research is now the only creationist organization, so far as we know, which is controlled and operated by scientists

(The Creation Research Society is an association rather than an organization). Though each of the various creationist organizations can provide a valuable service, and the help of pastors and other laymen in this field is necessary, it is vital that the basic leadership and literature of the movement be provided by recognized scientists. Our ultimate effectiveness will depend upon scientific and educational acceptance, not upon political maneuvering, sales promotions, or emotional fund appeals.[42]

With that turn, ICR took control of the creationist movement and reached out to different audiences than those pursued by the more mainstream evangelical ASA or the YEC movement's CRS. ICR was the first YEC organization to have not just a headquarters, but also a college, a creation science research center, and organizational offices. ICR used these spaces to host seminars, summer institutes, and a weekly radio ministry called *Science, Scripture & Salvation*.[43] And, in 1977, ICR created a modest museum at CHC with dioramas and hands-on activities run by a scientist.

Although ICR adopted a three-pronged agenda to promote creation science through research, texts, and speaking events, it published little original research in the first decade and invested far more energy in missionary efforts.[44] ICR gained visibility by hosting more than a hundred academic debates between ICR scientists and faculty at universities (secular and Christian) throughout the United States and elsewhere. One notable debate was nationally televised from Liberty University, with Jerry Falwell as the moderator, featuring ICR's Duane Gish versus Russell Doolittle of University of California–San Diego. It was widely acknowledged in both secular and creationist circles alike that Gish's credentials, skills, and flourish were impressive.[45]

While both Lammerts and Morris were fervently committed to the YEC movement, Morris appreciated that a broader public (rather than exclusively credentialed scientists) needed to be aware of creation science to sustain and spread the movement. Lammerts, however, regarded Morris's move as a distraction.[46]

At first look, it may have seemed that Lammerts's perspective would hold more weight. After all, Morris's credentials—notably his family's religious background and scientific training—were not as sterling as Lammerts's. By movement standards, Morris's familial religious background lacked explicit ties to advocacy for biblical literalism, and he did not hold a PhD in biology or geology, the two most desirable disciplines in terms of credibility. But it appeared that a decade after the two men branched off to form CRS, a shift toward emphasizing organizational dynamics was most salient. Although an individual's credentials were paramount throughout the post-Scopes era, as evident in the very founding of CRS and its insistence on academic credentials, by Episode 2, the ability to couple a credible background with strategic capacity was more important.

One of Lammerts's strengths as a leader was rooted in his personal background as a respected scientist with degrees in biology, geology, and horticulture from such institutions as the University of California–Berkeley. On the other hand, Morris ranked high in his positioning and his efforts to shift toward diversifying the movement. This occurred via CHC, as he built the graduate program to foster and attract adherents and shape future leaders.

During this episode, CRS maintained a strong sense of collective identity based on a feeling of being embattled with and persecuted by evolutionists. While ICR also defined itself as being in battle against evolutionists, it moved to convey its professional credentials as an organization with broader goals and more updated tactics than CRS. First, Morris's positioning of ICR reflected his appreciation of the external context surrounding the movement. ICR worked hard to manage its appearance among both external secular and religious audiences, most notably with the addition of Jerry Falwell, who launched the widely known Moral Majority, a Christian right-wing political organization, in 1979. This development created an even broader network of well-positioned evangelicals to capitalize on the changing political tide of the late 1970s and 1980s.

Second, ICR positioned itself as a sophisticated social movement organization with a broad knowledge base capable of influencing legal and political debates. It did so while maintaining a safe distance from the daily battles in courts or school boards by providing advice:

> When a political approach is followed in a particular state or community, then I.C.R. suggests that a resolution be proposed, rather than a legislative bill or an administrative or judicial directive. A resolution

encourages, rather than compels, the teaching of creation, and so should not encounter the usual bitter opposition of the educational and scientific establishments. Also, if the resolution stresses (with documentation) that creation and evolution are both equally scientific and/or religious, and that fairness and constitutionality warrant an equitable treatment of both, then hopefully responsible officials will support it. Accordingly, I.C.R. has prepared the foregoing sample suggested resolution for consideration by state legislatures . . . With appropriate changes, it could also be modified to a form suitable for submission to state or local school boards, or to other bodies (e.g., to church denominational meetings, parent-teacher associations, museum advisory boards, or to other groups concerned with this problem).[47]

ICR was sophisticated when navigating the political arena, emphasizing equity rather than replacement. It aimed for a widespread yet skillfully framed influence (using provided templates) in churches, schools, and museums. ICR was quick to connect media coverage to legal efforts. Morris consistently cautioned against celebrating any judicial gains, given the historical lessons from the Scopes Trial.[48]

Nevertheless, ICR anticipated far in advance a tactical shift within the YEC movement. Its focus on the scale of the audience, regardless of how it framed its message, shone through:

Before what is probably creationism's largest audience to date (estimated at 20 million!) a testimony to the validity of the Bible and scientific creationism was given by John Morris on N.B.C.'s "Today" show on the morning of April 15 . . . The N.B.C. news team seemed somewhat skeptical but nevertheless interested and impressed by the interview.[49]

Yet, media coverage for the sake of exposure was not the goal in and of itself. ICR would begin to leverage public opinion polls to influence policy decision-making.[50] In 1982, ICR reported, "the Gallup Poll discovered that 44% of the American public agree with this statement: 'God created man pretty much in his present form at one time within the last 10,000 years.' . . . it is easy to understand why the evolutionary establishment is so viciously opposed to any attempt to give creation-science (or even a critique of evolution) a fair hearing."[51] This pattern bolstered

ICR's confidence that a sizeable proportion of the public was sympathetic to the organization's position. It just needed to reach them.

In contrast, CRS rarely engaged in these kinds of external battles. Its interest in politics narrowed to those members of Congress who shared their beliefs and the legal efforts of local groups when federal-level efforts failed. For instance, the *Edwards v. Aguillard* case (1987) banned the teaching of creation science because, the Supreme Court argued, it violated the First Amendment of the Constitution. This broader judicial setback provided an opportunity for CRS to restate and reorient its organizational purpose: "Even though the Creation Research Society is vitally concerned about this issue, it officially was not involved in the politico-legal maneuvers . . . Our mission is research and publication."[52] Instead, CRS maintained an exclusive focus on how scientific media such as *Science* covered creation science and evolution.[53] With Lammerts at the helm, CRS maintained its long-standing interest in flood geology theories, fossils, and the scientific method. Under Morris, ICR packaged its emphasis on creation science ideology into televised debates, visual aids, videos, radio programming, a college, and a small museum. CRS's detachment from the public sphere was central to ICR's ability to acquire visibility and power—within the movement as well as among the broader public.

Throughout the two decades that comprise Episode 2, the shifts between complementary—but increasingly distinct—SMOs became clear. This dovetailed with the direction of the YEC movement. More generally, Lammerts continued to publish CRS's peer-reviewed creation science research journal and maintained an active research committee. Gradually, CRS secured its own niche within the larger YEC movement. This underscored its positioning as an SMO that stemmed from the initial divergence between CRS and ICR's funding in 1972. CRS, under Lammerts's guidance despite shifts in leadership, advocated for narrowly defined boundaries and consistently projected its collective identity as a professional society. From the organization's founding, Lammerts's indefatigable agenda focused on the peer-reviewed journal and the kindergarten through twelfth-grade textbooks, advancing at the expense of other activities.

The dual focus on creation evangelism and creation science set the stage for the increasing role played by institution-building for the YEC movement; it was of vital importance to ICR but minimal or non-existent for CRS. In 1983, Morris highlighted the quality of CHC's and ICR's unique positioning: "The profession of Creationist Scientist [*sic*] is not for amateurs. It takes real scholarship to be a creationist scientist. The various fields of creation science are highly specialized and require advanced training."[54] CHC was the first explicit YEC institution of higher education, blending two important spheres of influence: the role of public science education outside of the K-12 classroom and the perceived broader public cultural crisis.

When ICR came under attack, Morris connected the dots as to how the role of the government and legislation could affect other movement goals. Such was the case in the late 1980s, during a conflict over CHC's continued push for accreditation:

> If a state can force not only public schools but even a private Christian school such as ICR to teach evolution as a scientific fact, and to relegate creationism to the status of a fringe cult, our religious, academic, and civil freedoms are in grave danger. If this effort succeeds, other Christian colleges and schools could soon be forced to teach all their science courses in an evolutionist context . . . If the scientific opposition to evolutionism is stifled at the graduate level this will almost certainly precipitate a domino effect—not only throughout Christian education, but eventually also in the church and all other Christian institutions. If the Bible can no longer be taken seriously when it deals with science and history, then its spiritual message will soon be completely dissipated.[55]

In this excerpt, Morris not only underscored the unique opportunity the CHC affords as a credible, professional Christian higher education institution, but also the potentially disastrous implications if they were denied accreditation. He used this as an illustration of the cultural crisis and the centrality of creation science within education as one vital step toward remedying the situation.[56]

As ICR eclipsed CRS to become the formative SMO for the YEC movement, so too did the movement's notion of what constituted effective leadership. Initially, the central crisis for the YEC movement—securing leaders with credibility and credentials—was accomplished during this time (what I call Episode 1). What superseded this by the start of the 1970s were leaders' abilities to combine their strategic capacity with personal characteristics that capitalized on the ideological and professional aspirations of the movement. This entailed a command of the movement's collective action repertoire, including past efforts, struggles, and methods for innovatively recovering from failures. While it was largely about the organizational dynamics between CRS and ICR, the role of multifaceted leadership (not just charisma) was paramount in understanding how the YEC movement persisted as the political, legislative, and social climate became increasingly hostile toward it in the late 1980s and early 1990s.

Episode 3: Museums and Institution-Building Take Center Stage

Institute for Creation Research and Answers in Genesis (1994–2007)

ICR focused on its graduate school as it faced accreditation challenges with the state of California in the late 1980s and early 1990s. As Morris sums up in 1995, "Suffice it to say that the Lord brought a wonderful victory out of what seemed for a while to be almost certain defeat. The final outcome was a federal judicial declaratory judgment that not only ICR, but also all Christian schools, were free to teach their courses according to their own judgment."[57] While ICR seemed well positioned to maintain its place as the leading social movement organization for the YEC movement, other members of the movement focused on shifting its direction yet again.

Ken Ham joined ICR in 1987, connecting his Australian network and the International Creation Science Foundation with Morris's US-based ICR. Ham had strong credentials stemming from his family's background; his father was a prominent minister in Australia advocating biblical literalism.[58] His educational background, however, is particularly noteworthy as Ham was the first YEC leader without an advanced degree.[59] Yet, as a high school biology teacher, Ham had a better grasp of the contemporary cultural landscape and the perceptions of the YEC movement among a variety of audiences. Consequently, Ham's affiliation with ICR positioned him to connect multiple organizations within the YEC movement and to develop personal cross-national ties—all within ten years of being an active member in the movement.

Ham, along with Mark Looy and Mike Zovath (two other ICR staff members), broke off from ICR in 1993 to form Answers in Genesis—at the time, called Creation Science Ministries—with the intention to recapture the public's interest in creationism. None of AiG's leaders had advanced natural science degrees, a stark contrast from ICR. Instead, AiG extended the movement's budding scientific credentials to emerge as a Christian apologetic ministry. As Ham noted in a published interview, "It became clear that ICR, the world's largest creation organization, had been looking for someone to develop a lay-person's program. Rather than going back to Australia, they asked if I would consider opening up an office in the eastern part of the U.S., where most Americans live."[60] AiG produced items such as the widely read *Creation* magazine (from Australia), music, videos, and a website.[61] It also hoped to grow by building its physical infrastructure, such as a headquarters and eventually a museum. Ham was the true inspiration behind this initiative, and he was the most senior movement activist. Looy's background was in communication and media relations, so he managed the public face of AiG. Mike Zovath was a former military operations officer and oversaw the eventual construction of the museum site.

Comparatively, ICR dug deeper into its repertoire, focusing on distributing creation-oriented books and continued general appeals for funding and paying less attention to expanding its physical infrastructure via CHC or the museum. ICR promoted its long-running series of debates (although Morris lamented evolutionists' increasing unwillingness) and radio programming. By emphasizing distinctiveness yet cooperation among the SMOs, above all else, ICR continued to promote a sense of professionalism for the movement. Even after Morris retired, his son John Morris, who assumed the head of the organization, stated:

> Through the years, we have tried to maintain a long-range focus. Solid scientific research, in-depth leadership preparations through the graduate school, debates on university campuses, thoughtful books which convince those in positions of influence—these are the methods which will win in the long run. Of course, we also hold seminars for laymen and produce materials for children. These are essential, but they are not the key elements in a victory strategy.[62]

Each SMO became increasingly divergent in terms of its tactics and strategies. While ICR purported to maintain a broad focus, in practice it concentrated on professional creation science (graduate education, seminars) while AiG was steadfast in creating a decidedly populist focus to the movement. ICR was well-resourced and had a history of active, professional organizational members. AiG focused on acquiring a solid base of volunteers that did not necessarily have professional credentials, which were required by both CRS and ICR in the three decades before. A split from ICR seemed inevitable with a sharp decline in the discussion of shared resources—organizational or otherwise—in their respective newsletters.

AiG focused on its newly forged collective identity and emphasized that it was heavily embattled by evolutionists and other more "compromising" Christians—anyone who was not committed to a close interpretation of the Bible, which echoes CRS's positioning in the 1960s and early 1970s.[63] For example, while AiG found itself positively aligned with Focus on the Family, it regarded Billy Graham or the National Association of Evangelicals as "compromising Christians" rather than allies.

AiG highlighted the cultural crisis that it perceived as rampant in the 1990s and signaled that at the core of this decay was the issue of secular humanism, which had long been a focus for the YEC movement from the mid-twentieth century onward:

> We certainly are in a battle . . . The humanists are very active in taking their false message to this world. Please pray that more of the church will get behind ministries like Answers in Genesis that are fighting these humanists in the "front trenches"—right at the foundational level of this battle. We need more soldiers, but we have already the best "artillery" in the universe: the Word of God. Also, let's spread *Creation* magazine far and wide, and continue to try to get it into libraries. Help us by showing AiG videos to the people the Lord gives us opportunity to influence. Let's be more zealous than the humanists.[64]

AiG recommends its own materials, magazines, and videos to evangelize both for the Bible and creation science. And, AiG most squarely targeted those groups who challenged their beliefs. It would stoke battles with the American Atheists, the American Humanist Association, and the

National Academy of Sciences. The National Academy of Sciences was an explicit concern as it published a book in the late 1990s attempting to infuse more explicit instruction on evolution into the classroom.[65]

AiG saw the evangelism of creation science as the antidote to secular humanism's encroachment on society. This positioning of creation science signals AiG's adoption of the concept from ICR in the previous episode and highlights how AiG prioritized it more. ICR focused on the need for intervention in the educational system to address the cultural crisis. AiG's framing underscores the value of tracing ideological worldviews as they often shift within a social movement organizational field; rarely does one SMO remain static in terms of the ideologies it champions.

Both organizations took a distant but wary approach toward politics, which struck a different tone in the 1990s compared to the more politically and religiously conservative tide of the late 1970s and 1980s. After a series of unfavorable judicial decisions at the national level, both ICR and AiG were reluctant to position themselves as politically active SMOs. Presumably, this was also complicated by the fact that as recognized 501(c)(3) non-profit organizations, they were legally constrained in their political advocacy as well.

The role of institution-building speaks to how a SMO leader and his organization seek to position themselves. The emphasis is less on persuading an elected official to support a ballot initiative and more on how a group seeks to harness a previously external, often constraining symbol, to aid their movement.[66] To that end, there are two key differences between ICR and AiG: the amount of coverage dedicated to alternative institution-building and the way each institution was positioned in relation to larger movement goals. With respect to internal coverage, ICR declares it is the first SMO to establish a creation museum:

> In recent years there have been numerous creation museums opened around the country and internationally, all inspired by the first such museum at ICR, which opened around 1975. . . . Creation museums now operate in dozens of locations in many states and several other countries. Some are "mom and pop" ministries, and some are extensive and well-equipped with fossil specimens and creation research discoveries.[67]

The ICR museum began as a small set of collections housed in a temporary office on the CHC campus. An enthusiastic curator, Karen Jensen, who later left to get her PhD at Loma Linda University, a Seventh Day Adventist school, maintained the museum.[68] Later, Gary and Mary Parker—a husband and wife team—began the project in earnest and the ICR museum opened to the public in 1977. They saw the museum through multiple iterations, including the move to a freestanding headquarters and museum building. They left in 1988; a few years later, they would go on to collaborate with AiG on its museum.[69]

However, while ICR saw itself as the root of the initiative in terms of museum-building, others in the movement did not discuss ICR in this context. The AiG literature on the Creation Museum makes no mention of the predecessor museum at ICR, probably to heighten the contrast between the two organizations. One way to explain this disconnect is that, first and foremost, ICR simply did not actively discuss or promote its own museum, even within its own publications. Throughout Episode 2 (1972–1993) and during Episode 3 (1994–2007), only sixteen of the thirty annual reports—comprehensive overviews of the most prominent activities from the previous year—mentioned the ICR museum. Surprisingly, these reports were quiet regarding the museum development during the first five years of its operation, and it was not featured until 1981. This trend of omission continued at multiple salient turning points.[70] For instance, when ICR discussed the departure of Ham to form AiG, it made no mention, complimentary or otherwise, of ICR's own museum-building efforts that coincided with AiG.[71] At the end of this episode, in 2007, when ICR outlined its relocation to Dallas as a means to expand and strengthen the graduate school, again it did not mention its museum or how the move would affect it.[72]

Nonetheless, during the early 1990s when the coverage of museum-building activities gained more prominence in ICR, the organization elaborated on the content and the supporters of the exhibits (e.g., donors). Most consistently, it highlighted the frequency and size of the tours given within the museum.[73] For instance, the 25,000 attendance mark after the reopening and expansion of the museum in 1992 signaled a great sign of success for ICR.[74] And, John Morris was acutely aware of the utility of the museum for media coverage: "Unfortunately, most ICR supporters have not been able to travel to San Diego to see the museum. T.V. interviews showing ICR scientists in the museum have served to whet the appetites of many to see the museum, but for most, that has not yet been possible."[75] Otherwise, the focus remained on advertising creationist tours of the Smithsonian National Museum of Natural History, offered by ICR. Yet, despite this renewed interest in the museum under John Morris's leadership in Episode 3, his fund-raising goal of an additional $1 million to support the museum never came to fruition.[76] Initial coverage of institution-building—museum-building, in this case—is vital for approaches to be successful, not only to clarify how it fits within the collective identity of a given SMO, but also for securing funding. ICR failed throughout and John Morris's efforts were too late.

Beyond the sheer volume of coverage of museum-building activities, AiG distinguished its approach from ICR's tactics by situating its efforts within an explicit trichotomous framework used in social movement analysis: a *diagnostic frame* (identifying the problem), a *prognostic frame* (suggesting the solution), and a *motivational frame* (figuring out how to implement that action and who should be involved).[77] AiG focused on shaping how individuals perceived cultural institutions and sought to connect these institutions to issues of moral decay. Specifically, AiG underscored the prominence of evolutionary theory in natural history museums, for instance, so that followers would question the perception of science and culture as benign. In this sense, AiG adopted museum-building to frame the YEC movement's long-running diagnosis of evolution and secular humanism as the roots of the cultural crisis. AiG positions the museum as a prognosis that will resonate with a wide number of public audiences given their familiarity and prominence of natural history museums. As Ken Ham states:

> Indeed, evolutionists absolutely hate it when AiG uses dinosaurs to proclaim the falsity of the idea of evolution and the truth of the history in Genesis. Nearly every secular reporter who visits the AiG Creation Museum (under construction west of Cincinnati) seems perplexed as to why we're including dinosaurs—and they often express amazement that we would even dare to do so. And so when their TV or newspaper report comes out, there it is again: a mocking statement about dinosaurs and humans together. Children and adults alike are fascinated by these crea-

> tures. Unfortunately, most people equate dinosaurs with millions of years and the evolution belief system. Dinosaurs have become almost icons for evolutionary teaching—they're treated as sacred "gods" that belong only to evolutionists for their purpose of indoctrinating generations in secular humanism.[78]

In other words, the motivational framing solution was AiG building its own alternative cultural institution. However, AiG anticipated the public's and the scientific community's scorn and disbelief. So, the organization used the dinosaur, an icon with cultural and scientific significance, in the Creation Museum to buttress its efforts to challenge the institution of science organizationally (in a museum) and ideologically (evolution as a pillar of secular humanism).[79]

A part of motivational framing for the endeavor was the need for a physical place—not just an argument or a book—for individuals to experience AiG's arguments for themselves. The Creation Museum for AiG was and continues to be salient to the movement. For twelve years AiG strove to position the museum as an alternative institution; it challenged how secular scholars portrayed science to the public and served as an important site for the battle against secular humanism.

Compare this to the often more narrow, technical discussion of evolutionary bias as displayed in natural history museums by Henry Morris and ICR. In 1979, the feature newsletter article he published outlined the perceived bias of the tax-funded museum:

> The federal government is, both constitutionally and legally, supposed to be neutral in its attitude toward various religions. Yet in its prestigious national museums, especially its Smithsonian Museum of Natural History, it openly seeks to indoctrinate its swarms of visitors (estimated at 17 million annually) in the religion of evolutionary humanism, naturalism and materialism.[80]

It is important to note that Morris never mentioned, let alone framed, the newly opened ICR Museum as the necessary alternative. He clearly laid out the diagnosis of the cultural crisis, yet over time he never points to his museum as the prognosis nor to ICR as the one to offer it in a motivational frame embedded within a museum.

Interestingly, however, in its materials, ICR generally discussed natural history museums more often than AiG did.[81] Meanwhile, AiG focused on asserting a unique positioning, often with less direct reference in its newsletter to natural history museums compared to ICR. AiG used the broader categorization of museums to identify how professionally the Creation Museum stands in comparison, exemplified by statements such as, "AiG expects it to be an incredible attraction for unbelievers"; or "We believe that the wonderful displays and talented people already available to us would make this a better museum than most secular ones!"[82] And, Ham paired prognostic framing with the motivational framing of museums as a key mechanism for protest. This stems from his earlier work with ICR, as he signals in articles like "Make Museums Count for Creation."[83]

Alternatively, John Morris published the article "Do Museums portray truth?" in the ICR newsletter series *Back to Genesis* the same year that Ken Ham left to form AiG.[84] This is not surprising given Morris's interest in redirecting the efforts of ICR. Morris appeared intent on highlighting the efforts of ICR to maintain its museum, seemingly adopting the prognostic framing that Ham had introduced to ICR years before. Despite John Morris's seemingly more explicit interest in the museum than his father Henry Morris, he kept on message with ICR's arguments regarding the answer to the issue of bias and societal decay, along with the credibility of creation science, when he states, "The Graduate School could be considered ICR's primary communication tool, but it only directly reaches a chosen few. The Outreach Division, on the other hand, reaches untold multitudes with the creation message."[85] As ICR moved forward on maintaining a broad focus on creationism, it was bolstered by a particular type of institution-building in the higher education arena. John Morris was unable to shift the deep-seated organizational and leadership capacity of Henry Morris, who always stated that the primary contribution of ICR was building the "first strictly creationist graduate school of science in the world."[86]

While the strategy of institution-building was a long-held approach among the YEC movement (and the Christian evangelical community in the United States and internationally writ large), AiG focused its energies on cultural tactics and used museum-building as its specialization. This contrasts with ICR, which consistently upheld CHC, and later the ICR graduate school in Dallas, as its primary goal. Furthermore, ICR supplemented this focus on educational alternative institutions with a non-stop schedule of conferences, lectures, and seminars pitched at adults while AiG ushered in a focus on engaging more youth with children-oriented events.

After Ham's departure and the rise of AiG, ICR never returned to a central position within larger movement discussions or received much attention from external media. I find that after a series of failed attempts by the broader movement to maneuver around closed legislative and political opportunities, Ham, as AiG's leader, sought to cultivate cultural resonance instead. He adapted and differentiated the audience for the YEC movement through the creation of an alternative cultural institution: a museum. The option to build an institution like a museum existed in the movement's repertoire. But, with the combination of Ham as the leader pulling on his diverse cross-cultural sociocultural ties and deep commitment to publicly promoting creation evangelism as the antidote to the cultural crisis fueled by secular humanism, AiG ushered in a newfound cultural resonance. AiG does not mention ICR's museum (in operation from 1977 to 2008) in any of its literature on the Creation Museum, clearly aiming to demonstrate that its distinct strategic choices were entirely its own.

* * *

Three decades after its inception, the YEC movement accumulated a tactical repertoire of both successful and failed tactics. As YEC faced federal judicial exclusion throughout the twentieth century, it redirected its efforts even farther away from explicit attempts at legal influence. The choice to build a museum illustrates this point. By focusing on political conditions only, much is lost to view. Scholars wedded to political process anticipated educational and legal approaches like those advocating Intelligent Design, but they would not be equipped to account for the rise of AiG and its cultural institution-building.[87] In keeping with what most social movement scholars would anticipate, no single framework or factor alone explains what led up to the innovative, distinctive Creation Museum. The need to turn toward evaluating various frameworks across the progression of the contemporary movement is warranted beyond conventional factors. I consider three themes within the social movement literature: ideology, the strategic capacity of leadership, and alternative institution-building. Beyond just adding more factors, I underscore how movements may shift focus over time to cultural targets.

Taking a bird's-eye view across the three episodes, it becomes clearer what we gain analytically when examining a range of factors in tandem. In Episode 1 (1963–1971), ASA relied on deep resources as the incumbent SMO while CRS appeared to be more innovative in its organizational tactics, which spurred the formation of the YEC branch. The shift hinges on the split over ideology. CRS advanced all of the ideologies that would come to shape the YEC movement while ASA suppressed them and did not address religion at all. ASA sought to avoid taking hardline positions and wanted to remain neutral when it came to the religion and science interface. CRS, which was also a professional society like ASA, struck out on a different path based on a specific set of ideological worldviews.

In Episode 2 (1972–1993), ICR not only garnered more resources and used a broader range of organizational tactics than CRS, but it was also more invested in its positioning vis-à-vis the broader external evangelical context. These differences are rooted in the split over strategic capacity between CRS's Walter Lammerts and ICR's Henry Morris. Under Lammerts's legacy, CRS remained narrow in organizational tactics and ideologically rigid in terms of religion. CRS was insulated from a lot of the broader external context, particularly other religious leaders and organizations, which were absent. Lammerts's personal credentials did not translate into strategic capacity when it came time to leverage his knowledge of the movement. Alternatively, Morris capitalized on his established collective action repertoire as well as varied cultivated ties with religious leaders and positioned ICR at the center of the movement, creating another split.

Finally, in Episode 3 (1994–2007), the divisions are not as distinct. But, tracing AiG's priorities demonstrates how the combination of material resources, layperson outreach, and active cultivation of a perceived cultural crisis among members were rooted in Ham's skillful reading of the movement's trajectory. He continued to nurture the sociocultural focus on alternative institution-building that ICR maintained in Episode 2 to engage with the broader external context, but Ham also assessed what had and had not worked historically and revised his

approach accordingly. AiG refused to emphasize creation science ideology at the expense of evangelical religious ideology or the perceived
cultural crisis. Instead, AiG, under Ham's leadership, re-coupled these
two ideologies (religious and cultural crisis) as CRS had done during
Episode 1.

AiG maintained a steady focus on media outlets. To attract attention, the organization tied its movement to a specific type of alternative
institution-building: a museum. Here, the differences in Ham's approach
are most stark as AiG focused on questioning existing institutions by
building a museum and engaging youth—the opposite of what ICR
emphasized with its focus on higher-education alternative institution-
building (i.e., not museums) and engagement with adults (i.e., not
youth). Ultimately, Ham brokered his own extensive familiarity with the
movement by combining what had worked in Australia and ICR, in a
new way. This led AiG to focus on building its own SMO, connected but
distinct from the YEC movement, and using the media-friendly, youth-
oriented Creation Museum. All this bolstered AiG's attempts to impart
cultural change via the YEC movement based on addressing the fostered
cultural crisis rather than a relatively exclusive focus on advancing creation science via science education like ICR.

What does rooting its efforts into a building afford AiG in its rally
cries against secularization? How does the organization compel visitors
to take its claims for a biblically informed creation science seriously?
In the next chapter, I unpack how AiG uses the built environment and
human sensory engagement to persuade its audience that it built a museum offering a plausible alternative worldview.

3

Enacting a Museum

> Well, from an impression standpoint, [we wanted] a "wow" every time
> you turn a corner. A museum building doesn't look that spectacular from
> the road. There's not much when you drive by on the freeway that you
> notice. When you pull into the parking lot, you say, "Wow, that's cool."
> "What do we do now?" "Well, go to the museum." That was part of the
> plan, the design of the whole place . . . One room looks like an environ-
> ment, and the next room looks like a museum. Like going to the cave and
> the dig site. That's an environment. Then you walk into the next room and
> it's our sanitized museum work.
> —Art Director/Senior Illustrator[1]

By intentionally crafting the "wow" factor, AiG strives to use every possible means to strengthen the plausibility of its argument because it
knows museums do more than display: they persuade. The positioning
of glass cases, the arrangement of objects, the lighting, and the draft-
ing of interpretive captions all build an authoritative narrative. These
familiar technologies of display make it difficult, possibly even counterintuitive, for the casual visitor to doubt that the artifacts are authentic
and the assertions true. Credibility is literally built in. If a museum's
authority over content can be disentangled from the museum-form,
then challengers can gain ground for their own worldview in the public
sphere by exacerbating the disconnect.

To understand how a fringe group can mold an institution into a
museum and convince enough people to perceive it as such, I examine
what it is about museums' institutional aesthetics and conventions that
a group like AiG leverages and mobilizes. What are the political implications of these kinds of sites? In other words, what does the museum-
form accomplish for AiG? This chapter aims to provide insight into how
a SMO builds a museum. I argue the curation of a place like a museum

is a strategy for legitimation, but it hinges on AiG's ability to engage our senses. An emphasis on materiality can deepen our understanding of what factors make a sensory environment plausible. It is not just the museum's content that visitors can *see* that must be credible, but also what they hear, touch, smell, and even eat at the Creation Museum. The form and feel of the building matters as much as the activity that occurs there. It is about how the experience makes visitors feel that informs the extent to which they will "Prepare to Believe."

Scholars point to a renewed emphasis on what people do with their beliefs, resources, and values. Often referred to as the "practice turn," this approach came to the forefront for sociologists by the end of the twentieth century.[2] But a focus on "doing" had long characterized science and technology studies through which scholars traced where and how scientific credibility was produced and reproduced in a variety of sites—houses, labs, and field sites.[3] Historically, museums relied on their ability to amass collections of objects. In the nineteenth century, as they began to use objects to inform research, display arguments, and attract visitors, museums harnessed the power they now embody. Objects are profoundly relational in nature, thereby groupings, progression, and order matter a great deal for how arguments and sense-making are communicated to museum attendees.[4] As historian Steven Conn (1998) skillfully notes in his examination of museums across the United States during the Victorian era, museums were institutions in which to display "objects invested with knowledge" (9). The salience of objects for natural history museums increased the stakes, as no single fossil or specimen could demonstrate an ongoing evolutionary process. Traveling collections, constructed out of newly produced scientific facts about nature and society, continued to gather cultural authority for what became increasingly regarded as secular science. Effectively, museums began to "do" science. Natural history museums took on legitimating and policing functions and made the visible and publicly accessible case for science as credible, useful, and authoritative.[5]

By moving the young earth perspective out of the church and into a museum, AiG exposes in a physical, public site the tensions between religion and science as two sources of legitimation and belief—but not explicitly so. The Creation Museum cannot appear to be a church: Its visual code must be read as a museum rather than as a sacred space to sustain the appearance that creation science is a legitimate rival to scientific evolutionary theories depicted in natural history museums. But how does AiG accomplish this balance? The Creation Museum operates as a site where AiG inserts a view of human origins that counters the dominant evolutionary theories into spaces that traditionally house mainstream science. To understand whether visitors "buy" the message and label AiG's alternative space as a museum, I must first unpack just how the organization tried to achieve this effect.

Studying a Social Movement's Museum

Using the museum-form to advance movement goals is not unique to creationists. Groups—who range dramatically in their political leaning and approach from Hezbollah with their Museum for Resistance Tourism in Lebanon (c. 2010) to the 1960s- and 1970s-era Black Museum movement—use the museum-form to reach a broader public audience.[6] Studying how a group works through the cognitive choices to create a museum helps elucidate what types of sites may result from social movement activity. To take seriously how the architecture of buildings and the objects inside relate to the social construction of cultural authority and knowledge requires an understanding of the site and the materials used to articulate the vision behind the project.

As cultural anthropologist Birgit Meyer (2010) underscores in her work on the role of sensations influencing believers' perception of their relationship with God among Pentecostals, "Aesthetics is not outside of power structures but enmeshed with them" (754). Being attuned to how groups activate multisensory engagement and wield material culture, including auditory cues, color palette selections, lighting choices, and the spatial arrangement of each room, underscores how movement actors are directing visitors to "read" the physical structure.[7] Nonetheless, AiG's use of the museum-form to convey its own cultural authority comes with risks, i.e., it may not work or be persuasive because sites can be disruptive and unruly, and audiences conditional in their interpretation.[8]

Despite my sustained focus on the physicality of the site, the importance of the built environment rests on the ideas and arguments it inscribes in its materialized form. Individuals and groups jockey to have their design choices adopted and others thrown out.[9] Sociologist Thomas Gieryn (2002) suggests, "We mold buildings, they mold us, we mold them anew . . . Buildings evoke endless narratives, not always consonant with those heard earlier as people and powers were enlisted and aligned to move dreams toward reality" (65). It is precisely because of these negotiations that scholars who study buildings and physical sites caution against a too literal reading. Just as one does not want to extrapolate recklessly from an isolated survey response, one does not want to "over-read" a physical building as the direct result of a single, coherent plan.[10] To negotiate this balance, it is important to consider both what stakeholders discuss during the design process and the audience's eventual "read" of the finished building that the creators create.

For this chapter, I rely on primary data from fieldwork observations attuned both to the built environment and visitors as well as interviews with key AiG movement stakeholders.[11] Throughout multiple years, during prolonged on-site visits, I have witnessed a wide range of audience engagement. There are older couples who carefully read all that is posted, listen to each video, and occasionally pose hushed questions to one another. Groups of teenagers from a youth ministry only focus on the highlights in each room, joking about some of the exhibits, such as pointing to the Lucy figure (an early hominid used to defend evolutionist theories) and suggesting to a friend, "Hey, that's you!" But later, they closely engage with the exhibit on natural selection and sincerely wonder aloud about who their dog descended from. Parents attempt to capture their young children's attention with anything they can look at or touch, but often, these children literally pull the adults through exhibits without spending much time or attention to read anything. And finally, a ten-year-old child symbolizes the telltale sign of museum fatigue by sighing and whining, "I'm tired. Where are the chairs? I want to sit down," while siblings excitedly chat and imitate the mechanics of the roaring animatronic dinosaur.[12]

During these numerous visits to the Creation Museum, I focused on how its content and presentational style engaged visitors' senses, distinct from how any one member of the public experienced the museum. For this chapter, I adopt a typical museum-goer experience, tracing what I encountered, how I was able to navigate the space, and what demanded my attention. In later chapters, I will systematically examine public reactions to the Creation Museum.

The Look and Feel of a Museum

AiG needs to appeal to multiple audiences (e.g., the general public as well as professionals) while emphasizing both content and form. It is introducing the public to a set of alternative ideas via a familiar museum-form. And, while most museum professionals and educators are frustrated by the Creation Museum, the design and professionalism of AiG's museum-form compels these critics to take it seriously as a concern, if nothing else. I argue that AiG achieves a balance through *purposeful decisions* (i.e., AiG's justification) and *inference* (i.e., conclusions visitors make while walking through based upon prior experiences and presumptions).[13] Not everything is reducible to the movement strategy. We, as an audience, readily justify to ourselves, often unknowingly, why we find some kinds of buildings and their contents professional and authoritative, while others we do not.[14] It starts with money.

AiG ensured that the Creation Museum was fully funded prior to opening its doors because it sought to dispel the sentiment that "oddball museums typically don't have much money."[15] Responding to a question about the museum-form, the art director/senior illustrator commented to me:

> We know what quality is. If you look at all the sculptures and stuff like that and all of our figures, we are hiring . . . the top bracket of the best of the best in the industry . . . Then, you have the stuff that you have to do, that it needs to look like a museum, it can't look like Disneyland. You can notice the difference if you come to our place, versus going to an amusement park. Our stuff is meant to look real versus fantasy . . . That's really what we [the art and design team] were hired to do. It isn't my job to convince somebody to be a Creationist. My job is to make the message more enjoyable, to present it well, to open the person's eyes to the possibility that there's some legitimacy to this.[16]

Tying the museum's perceived credibility to the quality of the design and layout of the museum itself suggests that AiG does not necessarily privilege content (creation science arguments and exhibits) over form (the built environment).

This is purposeful, as AiG makes clear in a 2010 promotional video clip featuring a conversation between Ken Ham, CEO/founder, and Mark Looy, the head of communications: "Christians deserve a high-quality and professional museum. This type of thing is not just reserved for secular crowds."[17] This sentiment was echoed during a subsequent interview I had with Mike Zovath (head of operations), who remarked, "Christian museums are often b-level. [We] break that mold as we are high tech."[18] While the Creation Museum is intended as an attraction, it is also designed to educate and persuade. This is evident in the art director's distinction between "real versus fantasy." The form matters because AiG wants people to regard the Creation Museum as a serious institution and not as a theme park. AiG seeks to persuade visitors to thoughtfully engage with the arguments it presents, or, at the very least, walk away with lingering questions. The museum is not just an attraction where one can escape reality. Rather, it is a high-tech, modern site intentionally built to encourage visitors to reflect on what they believe, why they believe it, and to establish the plausibility of creation science.

The negotiations between purposeful efficacy for AiG and inferred professionalism by the audience can be found in every facet of the museum. A central example is evident before even stepping into the building. The museum's structural style evokes many other institutions, periods, and ideas. Its front entrance has columns that extend the full height of the portico (figure 3.1). These reference the classical façades of many well-known turn-of-the-twentieth-century natural history museums, such as the Field Museum in Chicago or the Roosevelt entrance to the American Museum of Natural History in New York. The space between the columns is filled with dark brown glass, rendering the entrance hall invisible from the outside. This type of glass is typical of some recent laboratory buildings as well as many new megachurches affiliated with evangelicalism, a replication that calls attention to how many contemporary built environments are multilayered themselves.[19] Meanwhile, visitors can readily highlight and infer other references in the architecture. Edward Rothstein, for example, comments in his *New York Times* museum review, "The entrance gates here are topped with

Figure 3.1. Creation Museum, Building Façade

metallic Stegosauruses . . . It could be like any other natural history museum, luring families with the promise of immense fossils and dinosaur adventures."[20]

More evidence of AiG's purposeful decisions and reliance on audience inference is noticeable in the museum structure's nod to the local region and ancient history. The reinforced concrete sides of the building are clad with material that was crafted on-site to give the appearance of rough-cut limestone. This evokes both the nearby quarries of Kentucky and Ohio as well as ancient building structures (figure 3.2). Beyond situating the museum in a time-honored tradition and evoking the feeling of a well-worn institution, these design decisions incorporate a naturalistic feel in the building that is important for conveying AiG's creationist message. For instance, the first room after the museum's Main Hall is a corridor carved out of this stone-like material and designed to look like the Grand Canyon (figure 3.3). This design connects to AiG's argument that the canyon could have been formed in less than 10,000 years. It also reflects industry conventions. The decision to use a type of "fake rock" is not unique to the Creation Museum. As the construction manager/fabricator commented to me, perlite is a common industrial mineral used in many buildings because of its light weight and its low cost; it is dramatically cheaper than covering a building with real stone in terms of materials and labor.[21]

Figure 3.2. Perlite Building Features

Figure 3.3. Grand Canyon Hallway

Moving inside the museum, an overview of the floor plan reveals that the Creation Museum's structure and narrative guide visitors past artifacts and through dioramas along a winding S-shaped path, see figure 3.4. The rationale for this does not explicitly coincide with AiG's ideological goals: a literal, linear walkthrough of the Bible. A driving factor was the director of museum design's aesthetic background, influenced by his time working for Dream Makers in Japan, which fostered his preference for gardens with structured pathways.

But the biggest factor was that the building's foundation had already been set when he joined AiG. As he notes:

> I tried to develop something that, that felt natural because I was working with an existing building, and it wasn't just a box. It was a physical space that had some major constraints in it, you know, the lobby being one of them. Because it was just this lobby that just kind of funneled down to this long neck, and then finally opened up into the mezzanine, and it was open air. That was kind of a crazy thing. One of the first things that I did was, I made a model for them. They'd never even seen what the thing was going to look like.[22]

AiG's straightforward vision was realized into a winding, curved path that yielded a chronological narrative, but not without a twist, literally.

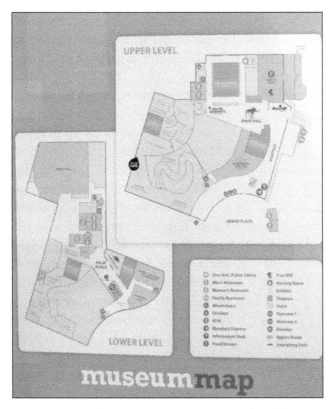

Figure 3.4. S-Shaped Structure, Creation Museum Floor Plan

In addition to AiG's purposeful decisions being driven by the mission and logistical necessities, it also designed with symbolism in mind, as AiG writes: "Many guests don't realize they are descending gradually as they walk down the Creation Walk . . . This descent mirrors mankind's descent from the Garden of Eden to God's judgment at the Flood."[23] These structural realities coincided with AiG's desire for the audience to infer the standard chronological path historically used to display evolution in museums.[24] As Darwin's theory of evolution began to take hold in the late 1800s, so did the now-familiar linear museum routes, which moved sequentially from one room to the next. Cultural sociologist Tony Bennett (1995) has underscored the impact of this transition: "The museum visit thus functioned and was experienced as a form of organized walking through evolutionary time" (186). The content and theories undergirding an exhibit often shaped the physical layout of the museum.[25] The Creation Museum might infer the flow or form of mainstream natural history museums, but it adapts these to explicitly demonstrate linear parallels between biblical accounts and scientific evidence. In turn, the space itself becomes an echo of nineteenth-century approaches to museums.[26]

While the content of the exhibits in the Creation Museum references other-worldly factors, its design and the narrative style are strikingly similar to many contemporary natural history museum exhibits, such as in Chicago at the Field Museum's *Evolving Planet* (figure 3.5). In that exhibit, there is also a meandering yet chronological path, but one that spans millions of years using the standard geological timescale: "The story told in this exhibition has taken four billion years to unfold. You can explore it in about an hour."[27] Museum reviewers often criticize the Creation Museum's winding path as narrowly confining visitors' movement and as rigidly outdated. Comparatively, reviewers of the Field Museum's exhibit simply referred to it as "the tried and true walk through time."[28] While museum professionals may critique the heavily guided walk-through-time pathways, it is a familiar form that audiences anticipate in a natural history museum when presenting the history of the Earth and human origins.

The look and feel of the exhibit matter for authenticity; the Field Museum professionals know and appreciate this just as much as those of the Creation Museum. However, one central twist is that AiG reverses

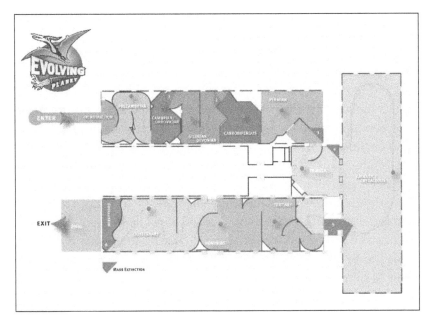

Figure 3.5. Field Museum, Evolving Planet Exhibit Overview. Field Museum Publication

the flow of the S-shaped curve since it foregrounds controversy and debate in its very first exhibit while natural history museums like the Field Museum wade through millions of years before arriving at human origins and our common ancestors. For the rest of the chapter, I compare the Creation Museum to the Field Museum, focusing on the Evolving Planet exhibit since it is a permanent, core exhibit.[29] This provides the opportunity to assess the extent to which AiG is unique or unusual in its presentation and how it adapts museum conventions to engage with its contemporaries.

Five Senses Engaged

Valorizing sight in the hierarchy of the senses is nothing new to Western European societies. While the seventeenth and eighteenth centuries were more multisensory, by the nineteenth century the rise of a scientific, empirical worldview eschewed knowledge gained through senses beyond sight. This announced a shift away from "touch" initially prioritized by eighteenth-century scientists who believed it was a better way to confirm and validate observations.[30] And, this change dovetailed with a push for the secularization of institutions as opposed to the long-standing intermingled spheres of science and religion. In effect, the aristocratic curiosity cabinet that mixed earthly and other-worldly items of the seventeenth century slowly transformed into museums, functioning as institutions for scientific exhibition, research, and teaching by the nineteenth century.[31] But equally significant was the transition of the audience from fellow elites to the mainstream public. The demographic shift in museum-goers dramatically changed the forms of acceptable engagement with the objects on display. Elites had acquired the collections and supported the museums. To them, the rest of the public needed to be trained in how to act, how to look, when to speak, and where to sit in a museum.[32]

Only recently has museum culture leaned toward the interactive again.[33] Ironically, then, the contemporary focus on multisensory engagement with an abundance of videos to watch as well as screens and objects with which to interact has an enduring historical precedent. Museums simply employ different technology to maintain the public's interest (and elites' funding). To unpack how one's multiple senses shape the perception of plausibility, I examine how the Creation Museum experience is structured through all five senses. What did I see and how was I directed to move? When and where did I hear audio cues? What could I touch and how did I interact with a given exhibit? What could I smell when I walked through the main building? What was available to taste, including the food on-site?

Sight

In museums, our experience is most often driven by what we see—and as audiences, we are trained to prioritize.[34] But even our sight and ability to find our way are guided by a built environment's direction. We are led down a path by the placement of walls and railings, directed by posted sequential exhibit signs that guide us around a large room clockwise. Or, we are invited to explore, moving from one exhibit to another at our own pace. In that sense, just seeing something is not the full extent of materiality. Rather, it is about how material-forms propel our movement and engage or estrange us.

AiG relies heavily on the museum practice of orienting visitors through their sight line. Beginning in the "Starting Points Room," and throughout the museum, the visual and verbal narrative is explicitly and consistently shaped by a dichotomy presented between "God's Word" (based on a close reading of the New King James Version of the Bible) and "Man's Word" (used interchangeably with "Human Reason"). A sign in the Starting Points Room reads: "Same Facts, Same World, Different Starting Points Leads to Different Views" as depicted by opposing time scales. As the PhD creation scientist on staff, Georgia Purdom, remarked to me:

> I would say the majority of the scientific community would look on our starting point as being the real issue. They might say it's our science. But it's really not, because we've produced very good science. I have a Ph.D. from Ohio State. I have been published in secular journals. There's no question about the science. The problem is our starting point.[35]

She draws on common hallmarks for credibility within academia, such as publications in peer-reviewed secular journals, along with her credentials from a well-respected public research institution to confer external validation. She goes on to frame the issue of "starting points" as simply a debate about the underlying assumptions of scientific arguments. This move repositions AiG into a space to talk about how its alternative view should be debated and not simply shut down or ignored by secular scientists as irrelevant. By prominently laying out this frame in black signs and placards with bold white text at the start of the museum, AiG implores the audience to see that scientific evidence is not necessarily contrary to a biblically informed perspective. Civilization, AiG argues, could have developed via a series of trees to form an "orchard" or distinct lines of species. Thereby humans were created in the image of God rather than related to other species that were formed from the more familiar singular evolutionary tree of life based upon a common ancestor (see figure 3.6 for how AiG depicts this side by side).

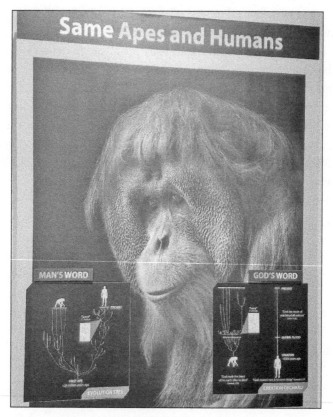

Figure 3.6. Starting Points Room

Ham, the primary visionary behind the Creation Museum, draws from his background as a high school biology teacher in his explanation of how the museum presents its logic:

I like to teach step by step, building on each step so that kids can understand it logically. When I go to a museum, to me it's confusing, because you go and you've got the hall of mammals, and you've got this, and you've got that [room] . . . in evolution they might give you this timeline through millions of years and Big Bang, but the way kids think and the way adults think, they find it hard to hang what they believe on something. And where do you put it? Whereas, when you do something chronological . . . I tell people I like to present the Christian Gospel the way God does it in the Bible by starting at the beginning like a murder mystery . . . And the other thing I wanted to do was teach people how to think critically about science. I mean I was doing that way back when I was a teacher. Kids, you can pour this together in a laboratory and it changes color . . . [But] when you're talking about [human] origins you weren't there. That's different. You can't see it . . . And so I taught them how to separate out the observational science from historical science.[36]

Visitors walk through time, just in a different timescale than they are accustomed to in other museums. As Ham outlines, AiG establishes a chronological approach to weave together the two sources of authority (the Bible and natural world) in a series of displays accessible to adults and children alike. This is AiG's primary strategy for encouraging visitors to square their religious beliefs with the creation science presented in juxtaposition to secular, mainstream science. AiG has curated a conflict between God's Word and Man's Word and has forcefully distinguished between "historical science" and "observational science." While observational science may be a familiar principle for how contemporary science is commonly understood based on a combination of observations, falsifiability of claims, and replication of research—historical science is AiG's assertion that all scientists interpret data beyond what they can observe.[37] This informs Ham's central argument behind the frame—"same evidence, different starting points"—in which the starting point is either biblical or secular and rooted in evolutionary theory.[38]

AiG frequently uses this argument to frame what the organization perceives as missing from public education: a transparent discussion of scientists' working assumptions and underlying worldview that informs how they interpret the data. The museum explicitly confronts these perceived assumptions at the beginning of the museum walkthrough. In the display, two school-aged children figures talk to each other (signaled by callout conversation bubbles), and one declares, "Come on. Let me show you the rest," while the other kid remarks, "I never heard this before in school" (figure 3.7). This appears to resonate with many visitors I have seen over the years, particularly those attending with children.[39]

On one visit, a dad with four children around twelve years old (two appear to be his, two are his children's friends) walks through the Starting Points Room. One of his kids turns and says, "But the Earth is old, right, Dad?" In response, he pulls them all aside and says, "Let me teach

Figure 3.7. School-Age "Visitors"

you something." They proceed to talk about teachers and what it's like to be in school. And the father asserts, "They [teachers] believe in an old Earth because they believe in evolution and don't believe in Adam and Eve or the Great Flood." The kids exasperatedly roll their eyes and say, "Yeah, but this is real!" and he counters, "Yeah, but you don't have to *tell* her that necessarily when you're in class." At this point, one of the kids who was not his child chimed in with enthusiasm, "But I already did!" And they all laugh while the father shakes his head, saying, "That's one way to do it."[40] This back-and-forth negotiation between kids' sense of certainty about their beliefs and their doubts about how to talk about it in public is couched in a shared, cultivated understanding. The kids' comments attest that they know creationist arguments are not welcome

in the public school classroom (and presumably in many other mainstream institutions) even if they do not always fully abide by the understanding. The decision about whether to confront the teacher points
to the broader discussion among creationists regarding strategies for
dealing with the mainstream. Members and supporters of AiG would
most likely use this anecdotal observation as evidence for the need to
simply maneuver around the public school system either in the form of
homeschooling or private religious schooling given (largely) failed legal
efforts to shape public school curriculum.

Comparatively, the Field Museum makes no mention of different starting points or challenging viewpoints in its visuals; it presents
evidence for evolutionary change over millions of years exclusively. It
also does not mention how this may fit with any other explanation for
human origins (historically or contemporarily), which most commonly
have roots in religious traditions. As a challenger, AiG uses this typical
natural history context to reinforce its visual juxtaposition over "starting points." It taps into audiences' inference, their presumption, that any
alternative explanations for human origins would not be present in a
natural history museum or science center because it is secular. Plausibility is politicized to the extent that the audience find some claims
more credible the more they adhere to what visitors expect to see in a
museum. Moving forward, the use of sound powerfully ushers visitors
from one "C" to the next so that they experience how AiG unfolds its
starting point argument through more than just sight.

Hearing

The aural experience of a museum matters for understanding how a
space is constructed to influence visitors' perceptions and feelings during their experience. Historically, patrons listened to collection owners
describe the wonders of their curiosity cabinets.[41] Later, a museum
docent lectured visitors as they walked the hallways of the nine-
teenth- and twentieth-century museums. However, what most clearly
distinguishes the twenty-first-century museum is the sheer frequency
and variation of audio cues that fall outside of formal guidance.

Upon entering the Creation Museum, I was met with a cacophony
of sounds. An animatronic Sauropod sways and roars loudly. Over-

head, speakers announce when the next talk will be given in the Special Effects Theater. Ambient background noises—a mix of the official museum soundtrack and visitors' voices—fill the nooks and crannies of corridors and transitional pathways. The soundtrack includes a blend of acoustic guitar, ambling river streams, and fluttering piano keys.[42] It is available for purchase onsite at the Dragon Hall Bookstore. Self-guided audio tours are available. The roaring dinosaurs, logistical cues for onsite attractions, the soundtrack for sale, and additional exhibit audio all offer a first impression of what a credible, contemporary science museum should sound like.[43] It is never silent.

Throughout the main exhibits, narration drifts from black cone-shaped speakers approximately eight inches in diameter discreetly dangling from the ceiling or embedded in the drywall. Moving from the tropical Garden of Eden, I stroll toward a gray, narrow hallway that resembles well-worn concrete. I am confronted by a dilapidated door full of hollowed out scratches, including the phrase "The World's Not Safe Anymore" jaggedly etched into it. This sentiment is amplified by a jarring and noticeably louder series of noises: babies wailing, wolves howling, glass shattering, and sirens blaring. As visitors, we are no longer in a safe, tranquil space as we enter Corruption, the second C. Here the aural effect is one of discomfort.

The root of this unease, "Cosmic Pain," results from Adam and Eve's original sin of eating fruit from the forbidden Tree of the Knowledge of Good and Evil. Large black and white photos (approximately four feet by six feet) cover the wall to depict human suffering ranging from mass graves and painful childbirth to natural disasters and drug use (figure 3.8). It is quite loud and difficult to absorb the information in this space, as AiG notes in its behind-the-scenes book: "Designers wanted to make it dark and shocking, while at the same time taking into account that children would be viewing. Much thought went into how much blood to show and how graphic the images should be," but apparently their careful consideration was not enough.[44] I noticed many visitors still pick up the pace to move to the next exhibit. For instance, one family rushed out with their young children (three kids under the age of ten), who were covering their ears and were visibly distraught.[45] This design reflects purposeful decisions AiG made to underscore its message of pain as captured in the text above the large photos: "All of creation suffers from

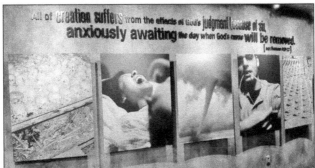

Figure 3.8a-b. Corruption

the effects of God's judgment because of sin, anxiously awaiting the day when God's curse will be removed [with a suggestion to read the book of Romans for follow up]." While there are a few placards in this exhibit, it is the audio cues that force visitors to take in the imagery and move swiftly. It is not a place to linger. The message of pain and suffering is quickly and dramatically imparted.

Upon turning the corner, I am ushered back into a familiar space full of earth tones, painted landscapes on the walls, and wide, carpeted pathways. A large animatronic Utahraptor greets us as it moves and rumbles a slow roar—even its eyelids flutter. On one occasion, a few children noticed the eyelids and commented, "SO life-like! It creeps me out!"[46] This transition in and out of the Corruption exhibit points to how effective audio cues are for signifying dramatic events and driving home a key argument.

Comparatively, in Field Museum's Evolving Planet exhibit, the formation of our planet is brought to life on a large projector. But it is the sounds that capture visitors' imagination: the bubbling up of lava and the thunderous meteorites crashing into the barren landscape underscore how foreign (and uninhabitable) the Earth at that time would have been. As the exhibit's audio emphasizes, "The early earth was a very different place."

However, at other times in both the Creation Museum and the Field Museum, the audio transition is a complicated blend of multiple soundtracks competing for visitors' aural attention. At the Creation Museum, the Wonders of Creation exhibit plays three different films with narration running simultaneously in the room that is only 500 to 700 approximate square feet. It is difficult to parse out what is being said without standing or sitting directly in front of the screen and reading the closed captions.[47] The Greening section of the Field Museum's Evolving Planet exhibit is where Earth becomes hospitable on land. Meanwhile large dinosaurs wait for visitors in the next room. During this transition, I hear both the small interactive video of an interview with a paleontologist and the booming noises of meteorites in the video presentation around the bend signaling the halfway point with a statistic on the wall stating: "You've just walked through 94% of the history of life on Earth."[48] Credibility is not always about the most effective choice but rather the mere inference of similar practices. As a visitor familiar with the museum experience, I anticipated a lot of information to be presented both visually and aurally. And sometimes, it even came from multiple exhibits at the same time. Increasingly, visitors like myself also expect digital technology to complement the traditional museum conventions of looking and listening. We anticipate the ability to touch and engage with objects and screens as well.

Touch

Children's museums and science centers were among the first to reverse the hands-off trend and include interaction as a salient feature of their programming. Importantly, they were positioned as a counterpart to traditional museums in the second half of the twentieth century.[49] Further reintroduction of interactivity was ushered in with the now widespread use of digital, haptic tools, which enables museum-goers to "feel" the exhibit and experience its argument through their fingertips. This return to previous conventions also points to the complicated entanglement of religious ideas and scientific practices that defined much of the 1800s, as Classen (2007) notes in her historical review of museum practices: "Touch had an advantage over sight in that it was understood to be the sense of certainty, an association symbolically grounded in the biblical tale of Thomas, who needed to touch the risen Christ to believe in his reality" (900). However, by the mid-1800s, touching objects on display was increasingly discouraged. This trend coincided with other manners shifting outside of the museum walls, such as the taboo of eating with one's hands in Western societies, which was common at the time. The ebb and flow of normative behavior highlights how museums operate at the nexus of the ways we understand the world, what we believe about it, and how we are trained to conduct ourselves within it.

AiG made purposeful decisions to interactively engage their audience. The team incorporated multimedia digital technology in the planetarium shows, created interactive seats that vibrate and spray water during the Great Flood in the Special Effects Theater, and developed hands-on flip boards to reveal answers about what dinosaurs ate in the Dinosaur Den. Yet AiG also hopes audiences will readily draw from their expectations for what conventional museums offer as well. Visitors absorb new, unusual content via the familiar museum-form and technology used to communicate the alternative message. The organization also seeks to poke fun at past conventions. Signs are scattered throughout the exhibits declaring, "Thou Shall Not Touch," a playful take on both biblical languages in the Ten Commandments and the long-standing rule of not touching anything in a museum. Another sign is more to the point: "Do Not Pet the Raptor. He's not friendly and neither are the costs to repair him."[50] This humor punctuates an otherwise somber exhibit following the second C (Corruption) on pain and suffering. The tongue-in-cheek reminder suggests that it is not permitted yet underscores the real-world context of museum maintenance and cost. It reaffirms that the Creation Museum, like other mainstream museums, also contains expensive objects in need of protection.

Given that multisensory engagement is the revitalized currency for the museum experience, AiG strategically provides markers of their competence in understanding this contemporary museum world. As the director of museum design explained to me, "Everybody has grown up on Disneyland and MTV and, nobody really wants to read very much . . . so we really needed to use the tools that were available in this day and age like videos and special effects theater . . . more experiential than anything else."[51] The issue of text versus interactive features hits a particular nerve within the museum world. Many venues wrestle to find a balance between maintaining their "museum-ness" and engaging in the twenty-first-century entertainment and social media landscape to demonstrate their relevance. The museum director went on to explain how he draws from entertainment "to be able to tell the story" using all available tools:

> I've been to just about every museum that you can think of . . . in the United States, I mean every major one that's worth anything at all . . . And the more I got into it, the more I found that they were theme park design people, involved in the museums, because they were trying to tell stories . . . I mean people are trying to find a way to engage, the audience, you know, to get them to come. And in some cases, they're making it more fun and less teaching.[52]

His comments reflect how the Creation Museum is an example of how technology used within museums may purposefully be divorced from the museum's main mission to educate. Instead, the emphasis becomes more about reaching the audience "where they are." Often described as a more democratic approach within the museum world, the focus on interactivity highlights that visitors want to move and choose how they engage with the information, and most important, research suggests that individuals stay longer near an exhibit if interaction is involved.[53]

With this focus on engagement in mind, AiG indicates its awareness of how powerful interactivity may be for the visitor: "An effective museum cannot be solely an attractive building with artifacts and text-heavy signs on the walls. In general, people do not read most of those signs and learn very little in such an environment. To effectively present a message, it must be designed and developed as 'edu-tainment.'"[54] AiG uses this edu-tainment approach to its advantage; it shares its argument and worldview with a broader audience who may vary in its interest about creationism but wants to be entertained regardless.

A prime example of how the Creation Museum uses interactive exhibit features to engage visitors is in Noah's Ark and the Voyage Room—under Catastrophe, the third C. Scale models of the ark are broken down into detail through a series of placards to engage me and more curious visitors with questions such as "What constitutes a cubit [a measurement noted in a biblical story of Noah]?" To reinforce the display, a touch screen quiz is embedded on the inside of the wooden structure. It asks visitors to consider how Noah's Ark might have been built and tests their knowledge of the biblical measurements (figure 3.9).

Moving through the exhibit, I gradually walk down a path into what feels like the inside of the ship. The ceiling lowers and all sides are wood-planked in the Voyage Room. Here the focus is on the biblical significance of Noah heeding God's call and why so many people would not get on the ship because they lacked faith. In the center of this lower section there is a table with large puzzle pieces on it with which a smaller child could play. Next to it is a seat at a table with a desktop computer inviting older children and adults to wrestle with the plausibility of AiG's arguments by engaging with a complicated set of questions (rated easy, medium, or hard) to determine just how Noah and his family survived. Surrounding the table are dioramas of people, the unsaved, clinging to large boulders and cliffs as the flood waters rise. Everything and everyone not already on the Ark drowns. An animatronic Noah and his family

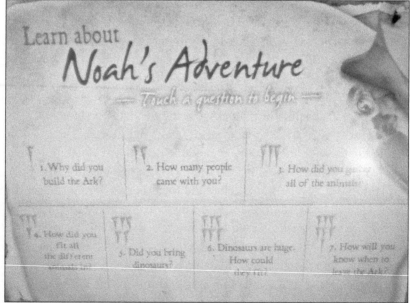

Figure 3.9a-b. Noah's Ark Exhibit, Interactive Touch Screen

Figure 3.10. Ark Drawer Pullout

are nestled in an interior portion of the ship. A detailed touch screen activates Noah to talk to you, prompted by the question you selected such as "Dinosaurs are huge, how could they fit?" or "How will you know when to leave the Ark?" As AiG notes in the Creation Museum Souvenir Guide, "Children of all ages love talking to Noah in the Voyage Room."[55] Finally, near the end of this exhibit, AiG faces the practical but messy question of how Noah and his family dealt with all of the waste that the animals would have produced while on board for an extended period of time. A drawer with a large rope handle suggests you should pull it out and find out how wooden slotted drawers stuffed with hay could safely store the excrement (figure 3.10).

This portion of the exhibit, as stated in the audio tour, is where the museum creators provide me and fellow visitors a preview of what to expect at the Ark Encounter, AiG's companion site, which is a theme-park attraction more than forty miles away. The interactive features highlight AiG's desire for museum-goers to really engage with the content rather than just pass by. Importantly, this is where the organization evangelizes to visitors about the prospect of salvation and following God's call. The audience engages with this explicit message but readily infers that much of this exhibit feels like any other museum in terms of the range of interactive options such as touch screens, puzzles, animatronic figures, and pullout drawers. AiG's desire to include touch as a central element of this exhibit coincides with both contemporary tools and the long-standing nineteenth-century approach to draw together multiple spheres of natural and supernatural knowledge. This attempt to thread the past and the present through touch is not unique to creationists.

In the Field Museum's Evolving Planet exhibit, evolution is the mechanism that explains how Earth developed over billions of years to form the world we know today. It is evident in what visitors read, hear, and touch. "Evolution: How It Works & How We Know" is a central video series throughout the entire exhibit, captured on consoles that have the same look and operate by the user pressing a red button for the narration to begin. A few of these videos are informal behind-the-scenes discussions featuring a Field Museum research scientist (e.g., paleontologists, paleobotanists, and anthropologists) talking about their research process. Some animated videos underscore a central argument related to that part of the planet's timeline, such as phylogeny, or the study of how organisms and species are related to one another: "How do we know where mammals came from?" In the second exhibit area, "Oceans," the featured video is a "Step-by-Step Guide to Becoming a Fossil." It walks through the four primary steps for how a living creature becomes a fossil. After watching time-lapsed layers of the ocean floor settle and then dry up, the final step concludes, "If your luck holds out then you might get spotted by a fossil hunter and wind up in a museum collection where a scientist can study you to learn about evolution."[56]

Other interactive features involve more participation, such as answering "Which three of these plants and animals do you think lived with Dimetrodon [a prehistoric group of animals]?" or visitors learn how to pronounce the complicated names of dinosaurs. Tactile engagement includes touching replicas of teeth, hip sockets, and large bones to learn

Figure 3.11a-b. Interactive Features in Evolving Planet

how to distinguish dinosaurs' features and to be impressed with their sheer size. For example, visitors can stand in a large Apatosaurus footprint to measure how many of their own footprints could fit inside it. One can also drive a plunger into a tar pit to see how disastrous it was for saber-toothed tigers during the Ice Age (figure 3.11). Overall, while the Evolving Planet as an exhibit is larger and more elaborate than any singular exhibit in the Creation Museum, the multiple types of interactive technology deployed and the range of touchable objects model what a twenty-first-century museum should feel like for the public. But the Field Museum never loses sight of its mission, which is to educate and engage with the public to provide a better sense of our "Evolving Planet." And here, the pairing of a strong organizational mission with professional, up-to-date interactive tools is what AiG claims to similarly accomplish with its own mission to evangelize at the center. Or, to put it another way, their own starting point.

Smell and Taste

The remaining two senses are perhaps the ones least associated with contemporary museums: smell and taste. In the late 1700s, the smell of decaying items on display would combine with coal smoke and soot from the fires used to heat patrons' homes, which would linger on their clothing.[57] Later in the 1800s, the odor of chemicals and processes used to preserve items, such as formaldehyde, would permeate the museum environment. With the increase in number of members from the public who started attending museums, body odor and fragrances began to comingle with the items on display. Technological advances and cultural norms now make these kinds of aromas a thing of the past, but in their place is an institutional ambiance of central heating/cooling systems and at times stale air.[58]

Much of the Creation Museum smells like any other institution: largely unnoticeable to a typical visitor except for a few exhibits that use water as a feature. The musty smell of cool running water creates an aroma of a well-hydrated room. This is used to reinforce how lovingly Adam and Eve gazed at one other while standing beside a waterfall in the Garden of Eden. Later, throughout the exhibits in the Flood Geology Room on the lower level, the sound of large water droplets falling into an echoing pool of water is punctuated with informational videos in which creation scientists suggest the feasibility and power of a worldwide flood. Cool blues and greens depicting seafloors or waterways stand in contrast to arid red-hued canyons outlining subsequent erosion models after the Flood receded.

In the Tower of Babel Room, museum-goers enter what feels like an ancient courtyard; winged statues resemble Mesopotamian figures and water spills from two ram friezes. Visitors read about why God dispersed people who shared a universal ancestry from Adam and Eve. AiG contends that the Tower of Babel story in the Bible has been misinterpreted by Christians in the past: "We are all descendants of Adam and Eve, so there is only one race of people . . . When they mapped the human genome [mainstream scientists] confirmed there's only one biological race."[59] Meanwhile visitors hear and smell water trickling in the background. This provides a soothing element to an otherwise purposefully provocative room that discusses chattel slavery in the United States and Social Darwinism as instances when the belief in a shared ancestry was lost. Smell serves as a reminder to sit and reflect on the significance of the exhibit. It is a background sense, more subtly engaged, and it blurs the line between AiG's purpose and the audience's inference. Many water features like this can be found throughout natural history museums (and in many other museums and monuments). The dampness of the Greening exhibit, which focuses on the beginning of land life in the Evolving Planet at the Field Museum, evokes an underlying feeling of reflection, too.

But smell is not only regulated to the exhibits or objects in a museum. Food and eating meals have been a part of museum visits since the inception of the museum itself.[60] As one walks through the final Cs (Christ, Cross, and Consummation), AiG dramatizes the significance of Jesus Christ's crucifixion and his eventual return for believers. It is clear that the central arc of the museum's chronological walkthrough has concluded. But what equally signals the end is the smell of food: The sweet aroma of homemade fudge from Uncle Leroy's stand wafts through the air near the Legacy Hall foyer (a large auditorium for special events) and in Palm Plaza (a large room with separate off-shoot exhibits), "Palm Pizza" is on the menu. Other food options on-site include Noah's Coffee and Bruster's Ice Cream kiosk, along with Noah's Café,

Figure 3.12. Noah's Café

which is the main dining hall located off the Main Hall entrance. Noah's Café feels like any contemporary museum dining space in the United States; sandwiches range from $5.00 to $7.00 and include vegetarian and gluten-free options (figure 3.12). The café mirrors the Noah's Ark exhibit with rattan ceilings and murals of the Ark Encounter on the back wall. Museum-goers may also bring their own food, but must eat it in the lower lobby by Palm Plaza or picnic outdoors in the botanical garden by the retention pond. From the Creation Museum's geographic location, the closest external restaurants and fast-food options are more than a fifteen-minute drive away, thus implicitly discouraging visitors from readily leaving.

Compare this to the Field Museum's Explorer Café, which is a similarly family-oriented dining space with long wooden benches and bright lime green accents, located on the building's lower level (sandwiches range from $6.00 to $9.00). And, while the Field Bistro on the main floor has beautiful views of the Chicago skyline, the fully stocked bar offering specialty beer and wine suggests this space is for an adult crowd (no alcohol is permitted or offered on-site at the Creation Museum). Interestingly, the serving utensils and plates are compostable at the Field Museum's cafes, which signal the institutional commitment to sustainable practices. This is not an emphasis at the Creation Museum given its complicated stance on sustainability and the role of humans in climate change. Nevertheless, the Creation Museum has increasingly adopted more conservation practices, such as having water fountains with the option for visitors to fill their own water bottles.[61]

AiG's ideological purpose anchors the design process. The Creation Museum borrows the look and feel of natural environments, sequential signage filled with facts and examples, and interactive technology, mirroring other twentieth- and twenty-first-century natural history museums. Yet the overall chronological timeline is infused with biblical content. It encourages audiences to fill in the gaps, to infer the similarity as well as the distinction of the Creation Museum when compared to other institutions. While AiG adapts similar display strategies in its exhibits, they inject starkly different content. For instance, the Starting Points and Flood Geology exhibits deliberately mimic the *form* of other natural history museums' exhibits, despite directly opposing their *content*. Comparatively, the Noah's Ark exhibit introduces different content orthogonal to a contemporary science museum as it is from a biblical rather than secular source, but it is housed within an up-to-date interactive atmosphere.

Ultimately, the importance of familiarity for authenticity in science museums is paramount, as science writer Steven Allison-Bunnell (1998) argues, "if what goes on in the museum is to be classified as modern science, then it must look like what everybody knows science looks like" (83). The Creation Museum is a result of AiG's decision to construct the museum with enough similar "markers of museum-ness" for visitors to perceive it as a museum yet also allow for AiG to push against the foundational evolutionary, millions-of-years timescale underpinning most natural history museums. Despite its vastly different ideology and mission, the Creation Museum wrestles with similar challenges any museum faces: how to present a credible narrative through its structural, visual, aural, and technological design. AiG underwent many adaptations until it settled upon the current version.

An Alternate Look and Feel: How the Creation Museum Could Have Been

When an institution like the Creation Museum operates for more than a decade, it is tempting for scholars to take for granted the initial decisions that shaped it, as if there were no other possibilities considered. But, of course, AiG's leaders made many choices about their vision and how to realize it. These decisions could have been different and produced an alternative set of sensory experiences.

The process of enacting the museum took more than twelve years, marred by local zoning battles and funding constraints.[62] During this time period, AiG circulated regular updates via the *Answers* newsletter as it identified fund-raising goals and sculpted its mission statement to reach lay audiences more effectively. Here is where AiG honed not only its message but also its aesthetic. Potential names for the museum were considered: Answers in Genesis Museum, Nature Works: Creating Natural Magic, Natural History Discovery Center, Creation History Discovery Center, Creation Exploration Museum, and eventually the Creation Museum. Evident in these choices, AiG waivered over whether the name should be closely tied to the organization or more explicitly connected to natural history traditions, science centers, or exploratoriums across the world. While the vision to build a museum had existed for a long time, the importance of it being referred to as a museum was up for debate. And so were the logos. They were sketched by hand on the back of hotel napkins as well as digitally created. Images of picks and axes evoked a field site, sunshine beamed down from the sky, swirling galaxies floated, and a range of animals that were not dinosaurs—butterflies, snails, and fish—were featured on various options (figure 3.13). The choice to showcase dinosaurs was not determined until much later.

Groundbreaking ceremonies occurred in 2001. But the shape of the building varied over the years, and building was slow. AiG relied on donations (both monetary and in-kind) to amass the necessary resources to move forward. For instance, it provided tours during construction: "Charter memberships turned out to be a great source of support. With the membership package, members were given the opportunity to attend several Behind the Scenes tours during the construction of the museum."[63] AiG finally opened the Creation Museum in May 2007, a full six years later.

Initially, the front façade was supposed to be open instead of the enclosed portico it is now. A large globe was set in the middle of a fountain with water washing over it, presumably to evoke a feeling of the worldwide flood so central to AiG's young earth claims (figure 3.14). Inside, the layout was designed as a small, standard floor plan for a building with multiple open rooms (see figure 3.15 for a vision of the Main Hall in which a mounted moose head with sunglasses suggests a more

Figure 3.13a-f. Possible Creation Museum Names and Logos (AiG Design Archives)

Figure 3.14. Alternative Façade for the Creation Museum (AiG Design Archives)

Figure 3.15. Alternative Layout for the Main Hall in the Creation Museum (AiG Design Archives)

whimsical design). Discussions about how to construct a natural history museum were sparse and often non-existent, as the director of museum design reveals: "Well, when I first came to the Creation Museum, they had no idea what they were going to do . . . it was just a very generic plan . . . a main floor, and several mezzanine floors in it. So it was kind of like coming into a facility that was more designed as an art museum."[64] There was not a lot of internal guidance from AiG as to what its museum should look like or how it would convey its kinship with a natural history museum—rather than an art museum or a nature discovery center.[65] It is in these design phase discussions that organizations learn how to develop ideological counter-arguments and couple evidence with their alternative perspective via a built form.

Shifting to exhibits, AiG's team performed extensive research and brainstorming for each room, wall, and plaque. But some choices would have imparted a dramatically different quality to the museum experience, such as the type of human figures used. As AiG noted in its *Behind the Scenes* book, "Originally we were going to use clay sculptures, but we decided we wanted the more life-like approach that could be achieved with silicone casts."[66] These human figures are crucial for the expensive, high-quality impression and align with a contemporary mainstream museum aesthetic favoring life-like creations. These kinds of decisions about balancing quality and cost are neither rare nor surprising.

What is more interesting is that AiG hired an external consultant to work through the museum content to make sure that it was both accurate and compelling, and not just from an aesthetic perspective. Kurt Wise is a well-known creationist with a PhD in paleontology from Harvard University.[67] The head of exhibit content development outlines the prominent role Wise played in developing the museum content before it opened:

> He touched every exhibit that we have and was in a way trying to make sure it was reasonable and legitimate. The purpose was not to attack evolution . . . It's a desire just to tell a meaningful, reasonable, legitimate version of where we came from and why we're here . . . building an impressive presentation, building a creation model . . . not just attacking another position.[68]

Regarded as a leading expert in the YEC movement, the presence of Wise as a consultant highlighted how the exhibit content was tightened, controversial statements diluted, and empirical support held to a higher standard. During other conversations, the head of exhibit content showed me the background detail that went into each exhibit. These materials suggested that the approach, tenor, and content of the museum's exhibits would have been different if more of the ministry and outreach staff members had the final say; it would have been more bombastic and sharper in tone. In this case, the presence of staff research creation scientists and the ability to contract prestigious figures from broader creation science research networks ensured that the feel of the museum was aligned with the content style and form of delivery of a natural history museum.

Just Another Creationist Museum?

A comparison to another museum from the YEC movement is informative to contextualize the look and feel of the Creation Museum. The Museum of Creation and Earth History, which ICR formally operated from 1977 to 2008 in the San Diego, California area, serves as a backdrop for the Creation Museum since all of the AiG founders worked with ICR prior to their decision to branch off. As the senior director of museum operations stated about the connection, "No, they [ICR] had a small museum. Ken was really a part of that. That really whetted his appetite to do something even more in line with our particular ministry. The popular side of things and [we] used the scientific information that ICR provided hand-in-glove with what we were doing."[69] While there is an affinity with ICR's former museum, there is also a clear distancing from it as well. This is evident in numerous comments about the Creation Museum's design, its approach, and its targeted audience. The director of museum design unequivocally draws this contrast:

> Small, smaller than our space, and so you couldn't move in the same way that you could in ours . . . And the quality of the videos, the quality of the exhibits, the quality of films, etcetera, I mean we really had an opportunity to do much more than they did. But, some of the things they did well [yet] it was as a stepping stone for us . . . their teaching is different, in that they're basically after university professors and people in industry. Uh, I shouldn't say industry; I mean scientists. That, that's who they're going after more, and ours is a much broader base. It's going for the general public.[70]

Several differences between the two museums are illustrated here. First, ICR's museum was less fluid for visitors' movements, in large part due to the small scale of the site (less than 10,000 square feet). Second, the ICR museum was perceived as lower quality in terms of both the exhibits and the media used. Third, ICR targeted a substantially different audience. ICR's focus was on technical presentations aimed at the university-level specialist audience, while AiG's "teaching" is intended for a mass audience. The size of the ICR museum and detail of its exhibits reflect the movement at its earlier stage, when there were fewer resources and a smaller base of supporters.

This last argument regarding the shift in audience from technical elites to popular crowds is supported by AiG's founder. In his remarks on exhibit style and the presentation of ICR's message, Ham makes it clear how his vision differed from ICR:

> [ICR] had a lot of signs and they had a lot of writing on the wall . . . You don't need to do all technical details about a museum . . . we are all ordinary people, but even PhD scientists, I mean they may know an awful lot about a tiny little bit, but even they don't have the big picture . . . that's really what the museum does here . . . If you focus too much on the details, people sort of drift.[71]

Ham faults the poor design of displays and traces this failure to an overly intellectual approach that presented too many technical details, alienating prospective adherents and students. Ham states that the central goal of AiG's Creation Museum is to reach the ordinary person and engage them with the big picture. Here is where AiG differs dramatically from ICR: AiG does not see the museum experience as a one-time visit but rather as an opportunity to develop an accessible dialogue with visitors that will continue after they have physically left the building. That is, visitors will develop their own understanding of the material through the big picture, and then decide whether to support the SMO by purchasing related items and investing more energy into the topics that interest them. Rather than forcing visitors to wrestle with demanding details and to grasp how it all fits together, AiG offers a more effectively packaged message in a larger, more appealing building and exhibit layout through engaging displays, interactive exhibits, and the "walk through time" approach of the seven Cs. The accompanying sensory choices AiG made to drive this point home are vital for accomplishing the right aesthetic to bolster its message's plausibility.

* * *

What matters about the materiality of sites? The success of a movement's institution, like AiG's Creation Museum, is often seen as shaped by conventional social movement factors (e.g., resources, political opportunities, movement culture). Movement-created sites are not just a result of these typical social movement factors; actors make choices that in turn affect their ability to acquire resources, garner plausibility for their claims and translate them into political favor, and determine how the movement culture operates moving forward. In this chapter, I show how the qualities of physical sites directly influence the relationship between a site and the public perception of the movement. I argue that the physicality of sites themselves, how they engage our senses, influence whether the broader public sees the movement's claims as plausible as well. Sites can operate as independent forces shaping these outcomes; the built environment is not just a container for activity.

As a scholar in the materiality tradition would argue, buildings shape social activity. They require humans to interact and cooperate with non-human technological objects such as the museum's electrical system that powers the interactive displays. Buildings physically present what their creators decided would "work" while concealing the social and political interests that informed the desired sensory experience. Finally, as we saw, buildings increased the sunk costs put into one site. The creators cannot easily change the layout or readily innovate how visitors experience AiG's claims.

In the end, a unique combination of personnel circumstances, structural design decisions, and organizational resources shaped the Creation Museum's current form. Most of the changes prioritized the structural layout of the building and the visual impact; different staff members jockeyed for it to be more like an art museum, a nature discovery center, or a natural history museum. All of this points to how movements make choices not only about their ideological worldview and how best to convey it to recruits, but also how their claims engage visitors' senses. The audience is encouraged to infer material connections across science museums and does a lot of the work for AiG. Yet how movement actors package the experience matters. We will see in the following chapter how this unfolds in greater detail, when the arguments about "Lucy" are presented as a direct challenge to the museums AiG emulates.

4

"Lucy" Up Close

Visitors to any natural history museum walk through a set of arguments informed by scientific evidence, displayed according to researched artistic judgment, and guided by audience feedback. Visual rhetoric is powerful, but museums do not simply persuade visitors that they have posed the right questions, selected the correct objects for display, and provided accurate exhibit text. When effective, museums instead engage us—the audience—with bigger questions about where we, as humans, fit into the broader world, thus "inspiring awe."[1] When museums push us to consider our role in the world, they also reinforce the perception that mainstream science as an institution has the authority to guide us in exploring how we should protect the environment, interpret our shared past (animal and human), and plan for the future. Unpacking how this vision is accomplished also lays out a blueprint for how it could be challenged.

A key question that animates this chapter is how the Creation Museum's exhibits work to target scientific authority and to tackle these bigger questions about society. To examine how AiG presents a plausible counterclaim to visitors, I focus on its depiction of "Lucy," the famous Australopithecus afarensis that mainstream science uses to represent one of our common ancestors in human origins exhibits. Examining an exhibit designed to contest mainstream representations affords an understanding of how a group attempts to make ideas and objects credible. Yet the objects and styles AiG deploys reflect aesthetic appropriation and demonstrate how plausibility is necessarily political. And, science is not immune. These collections and how they are displayed come with their own set of normative assumptions and big picture orientation. Natural history museums seek to move audiences toward accepting evolutionary mechanisms that connect our contemporary species to shared common ancestors. This is precisely what AiG targets: who gets to hold sway over how we, as humans, fit into the world around us in the past, present, and future.

In the previous chapter, I showed how AiG developed the Creation Museum to persuade visitors of its plausibility as a museum by engaging visitors' senses, as so many museums do. In this chapter, I work closely through the Lucy exhibit to explain how plausibility in museum exhibits can operate. By comparing the Creation Museum's exhibit to multiple mainstream human origins exhibits, I identify what fissures in the museum world AiG may be able to exacerbate to reinforce its authority, providing insight into what an untraditional challenger must do to persuade visitors of an alternative perspective.

Lucy at the Creation Museum

To celebrate its fifth anniversary, AiG unveiled the Lucy exhibit on Memorial Day weekend in 2012. It is a modest exhibit, approximately 200 square feet. Still, it is prominently featured within the first two exhibit rooms: the Dinosaur Dig Site and the Starting Points Room. Visitors first see the conventional, well-known fossil evidence of Lucy in the mock dig site environment that marks the start of the museum walk-through. If one is facing the exhibit where two paleontologists work to excavate a fossil, immediately to the left on the rock-like walls are encased displays framed by two phrases: "The evidence is in the *Present*" and "But what happened in the *Past*?"[2] The text underneath the "Present" question provides standard information about the fossil cast. On the plaque, the Latin binominal name (genus-species) Australopithecus afarensis appears with the common nickname, Lucy, which the fossil discovery team named after the Beatles' song *Lucy in the Sky with Diamonds*.[3] The location where the team found Lucy is identified as "[a] specimen from the Hadar Formation (Pliocene Series), Hadar, Ethiopia." Interestingly, AiG presents the common museum exhibit language used to date the fossil, relying on the standard geologic timescale in which Pliocene is an epoch that occurred approximately three to four million years ago. They contextualize that this specimen was found during a series of fossil discoveries in the early 1970s.

The "Present" day discussion is a typical presentation of the information one would find in most museums, yet the follow-up section is where AiG presents its alternative. Under the question about the "Past," a series of bullet points pose skeptical follow-up questions: "When did the creature live? What did the creature look like? (For example, how much hair did it have?) How did the creature behave? (For example, could it walk like modern humans?) How was the creature related to other creatures? (For example, is it an ancestor of modern humans?)."[4] From the beginning, AiG primes visitors to reflect on how plausible it seems that Lucy could be a common ancestor for humans.

The Lucy case and accompanying exhibit text are the focal point in a series of similarly structured objects. For example, an artificial sapphire stone is encased in glass, and AiG indicates the stone was grown in a lab, which is connected to questions about how and when natural sapphires formed (perhaps not over millions of years). A cast of an archaeopteryx fossil, regarded by many paleontologists as a transitional fossil linking dinosaurs to contemporary birds, highlights how scientists can make new connections (but they are not always accurate). A piece of meteorite rock is accompanied by questions about where, when, and how meteorites form in outer space (implying that dating methods such as radiometric dating could suggest a young solar system).[5] And, the reconstructed tracks of the trilobite, a ubiquitous extinct marine arthropod organism found across the world, are displayed next to questions about the speed of fossilization since a quick burial is important for a worldwide flood theory, "How were the tracks preserved? (For example, were they strolling about or scurrying for their lives?)."

Each of these featured items set up key questions that AiG returns to repeatedly throughout the Creation Museum. The organization wants visitors to have questions at the forefront of their minds about the extent to which scientists have accurately dated items and interpreted fossils, including objects from outer space. This approach anticipates the large question painted boldly on the wall—"Same Facts, but Different Views . . . Why?"—which serves as an inquisitive push for visitors to explore further. For a group that adamantly argues the Earth is less than 10,000 years old, addressing these questions and stoking a sense of skepticism among visitors as they begin their walkthrough is necessary.

Throughout my fieldwork at the Creation Museum, Lucy was a central feature. The exhibit features Lucy in the center of the room encased in glass, accompanied by exhibit plaques fastened to the glass case and surrounding walls (figure 4.1). Most visitors spent time reading the associated placards, talked about it with their friends and family, and read aloud

Figure 4.1. Lucy's Glass Case, Creation Museum

to each other what they found interesting, demonstrating active engagement.[6] Often young children pointed at the ape-like creature in wonder and traced the outline of the blue hologram overlay with their finger along the glass. A longtime member of AiG and a key resident creation scientist on staff, Dr. David Menton, was the leading force behind the exhibit.[7]

While it matters for AiG that visitors understand how a young earth is possible and unpack how fossils are dated, the issue of human evolution is paramount. Lucy showcases how AiG can offer a plausible enough alternative that is repositioned as evidence of young earth and biblical literalism. But, most important, Lucy encourages us to care about what is at stake if we get the interpretation wrong. Mainstream natural history museums share this concern, too.

History of Human Origins Exhibits

Museums choose a variety of approaches and emphases in exhibiting evolution. The challenge for museums is to present this rather abstract

scientific material in a way that is both appealing and meaningful to the general public, while not compromising the science. After all, everyone involved is a stakeholder—part of the human family tree.
—Monique Scott and Ellen Giusti, museum consultants[8]

Given our shared human family tree, the public's interest in human origins is not new, as the museum consultants Scott and Giusti underscore. Since the 1920s, when the first human origins exhibit opened in New York at the American Museum of Natural History, and soon after at Chicago's Field Museum in 1933, how to communicate humans and primates' common ancestry required innovative techniques.[9] In the 1930s, murals and dioramas transported audiences to the savannah, and stuffed creatures stoked visitors' curiosity about our shared past with other animals (and humans). These displays made a realistic, credible argument and channeled the power of science to reveal it. This move was a sharp departure from the Victorian-era displays brimming with representative taxidermic specimens. Labels moved from simply identifying taxonomy to informing visitors about the research on display, why it was important in the past, and how it influenced future human development.

In the 1970s, tree iconography dominated how the lineage of common ancestors was depicted across human origins exhibits, and contemporary exhibits continue to feature it.[10] These phylogenetic trees show evolutionary relationships among biological species, underscoring how organisms change over time.[11] In 2012, the National Science Foundation funded a study, *Understanding the Tree of Life*, conducted by a multidisciplinary research team, " [to] provide some important insights into visitors' understanding of trees, including the ability of young children to reason with tree diagrams."[12] Education researchers have found that too often individuals think evolutionary change is simply a linear, gradual shift through which animals that adapted best survived. Instead, evolution occurs through species dying off, and adaptation is as much about timing and luck as it is about the environmental context. One solution to reflect this more nuanced, contemporary view is a "bushy tree." As archaeologist Stephanie Moser suggests, "where individuals could choose to follow a number of directions that lead to the evolution of different hominid behaviours."[13]

Part of the interest in increasing the efficacy and accuracy of these trees is that the imagery can be adopted. Museum educator and evolutionary biologist Teresa MacDonald and E. O. Wiley lamented in an *Evolution Education Outreach* journal article, "even the Creation Museum in Kentucky contrasts evolutionary trees with a series of trees depicting separately created kinds, including a solitary and independent line for humans."[14] Indeed, it is central to AiG's focus. In a book pitched to creationists' families, AiG developed a guide book full of tips and discussion points for how to navigate a secular, mainstream natural history museum exhibit on human origins:

> How to read a "family tree." Most museums feature charts that illustrate the alleged evolutionary lineage of the animal in question—birds, dinosaurs, reptiles, humans, etc. These "family trees" are supposed to show how the group of organisms has developed (evolved) over time from a common ancestor. The lines leading to the various branches on the tree represent the interpretation. The actual fossil evidence is usually pictured at the end of the branches. When viewing a family tree, it is helpful to disregard the lines (dotted or otherwise) leading to animals. If the museum has any honesty at all, the actual fossil evidence will be shown in bars or different colored lines compared to the imaginary branches.[15]

The guide book speaks to the prevalence of tree iconography in human origin exhibits and AiG's awareness of its effectiveness. AiG is careful to contextualize mainstream approaches and cast into doubt how fossil evidence is interpreted via one single tree, but not the fossil evidence itself.

Most Interested in Ourselves

Why target Lucy specifically? In 1979, *Time* magazine declared Lucy a "front-page celebrity."[16] Across the world, despite the fact that the average visitor to a science museum varies in what they find interesting about natural history (beyond dinosaurs), if there is an exhibit on human origins, it will likely focus on our common ancestors, with Lucy front and center. Lucy fosters a lot of discussion among museum-goers because, after all, we are human and typically we find ourselves to be the most interesting beings. Questions like "Where did we come from?"

can be crucial because they raise high existential stakes about who we are and how we were created. What were our ancestors like and if they were not always humans as we know them today, then what did they look like? How do we know that we are related to them? These are the kinds of questions that orient educational museum guides pitched for school-age children on field trips, but it is also what many adults want to know, too.

Lucy is a useful example because she draws out visitors' interest in evolution. For instance, as scientists and educators argue, "An evaluation study of two temporary exhibitions on the early hominid Lucy at the California Academy of Sciences found that more than three-quarters (78%) of visitors rated their interest in human evolution as a four or five on a five point scale."[17] The role of museum visits for increasing the public's understanding of evolutionary science is key as recent work finds that even one visit to the museum can influence children's views about evolution.[18] This matters for science museum educators because a prominent concern is that many visitors do not have an adequate grasp of evolution and how it works, despite its foundational prominence in the biological sciences.[19] Chimp and human exhibits evoke more discussion related to evolution when compared to other museum exhibits. As scholars and museum professionals found in their 2016 research study, "Although families spent approximately the same amount of time at each exhibit, adults were more likely to generate evolution-talk codes at the chimp/human exhibit . . . In summary, the longer families stayed at the exhibits, the more likely they were to use evolution-related concepts in their conversations."[20] While human evolution draws more audience engagement, it occurs within the context of uneven acceptance of evolutionary mechanisms among the public. Other research suggests that even when visitors do accept scientific explanations that rely on evolutionary mechanisms to explain mammalian and bird species, and other kinds of non-human species changes, many visitors continue to rely on creationist-style explanations for humans.[21]

The Creation Museum is well aware of what is at stake and Lucy's central role in that. As AiG notes, "Perhaps more than any other fossil, Lucy is presented as 'exhibit A' for evolutionists in their attempt to show that humans evolved from an ape-like ancestor."[22] Given this context, it is not surprising that the Creation Museum decided similarly to feature a common ancestor, the well-known Lucy, to advance its creationist worldview.

The Comparative Museum Landscape

I compare the Creation Museum's Lucy exhibit to natural history museums across the United States that feature Lucy in their human origins exhibits: the Cleveland Museum of Natural History in Ohio, the Field Museum in Chicago, and the Smithsonian National Museum of Natural History in Washington, DC.

"Human Origins Gallery" at the Cleveland Museum of Natural History

The Cleveland Museum of Natural History is just outside of Cleveland's city center. The Cleveland Museum's roots stretch back to the 1830s with the "Arkites," a nickname attributed to the natural scientists so enthralled with its animal specimens that it evoked Noah's Ark.[23] In 1920, the current site of the museum took shape. The museum houses exhibition, research, and educational space along with a nature conservatory and wildlife center. The museum campus is 230,000 square feet total, with exhibits on display in about 30,000 square feet of it. The publicly accessible areas are arranged into nine galleries topically focused on exploring the natural world, ranging from dinosaurs to outer space.

Positioned in between the Sears Hall of Human Ecology and the Kirtland Hall of Prehistoric Life, the Human Origins Gallery opened on September 20, 2013. The Cleveland Museum has deep ties to Lucy. Donald Johanson, a member of the research team that discovered Lucy in the 1970s, was the curator of physical anthropology at the museum during that time and remained affiliated until 1997. The museum highlights this famous connection throughout the new exhibit alongside the well-known Physical Anthropology Department that continues to conduct research on human origins, led by Dr. Yohannes Selassie. It also features commissioned work by the internationally well-known paleoartist John Gurche, whose work is featured throughout the Smithsonian's exhibit as well.

The exhibit is approximately 300 square feet and features cutting-edge research in human origins. Interactive features focused on human evo-

Figure 4.2. Human Origins Gallery, Cleveland Museum of Natural History

lution in the future introduce the exhibit. It presents different versions of Lucy, including a skeletal structure and a fleshed-out reconstruction. A large oval path, anchored by a central glass case in the middle of the room, encourages visitors to begin on the left side of the thematic timeline marked by different common ancestors' representative key traits: "The Thinkers, The Travelers, The Toolmakers, The Walkers, and The Climbers that Walked." The entire room is open and visible from any given vantage point, leading visitors' movements (figure 4.2).

The Cleveland Museum of Natural History is approximately a six-hour drive from the Creation Museum, and it is the largest natural history museum in the Ohio-Kentucky-Indiana region. AiG took notice of the new exhibit, "Her [Lucy] svelte new figure, recently unveiled at the Cleveland Museum of Natural History, has a trim waistline and arched feet. The purpose of the new reconstruction is to avoid giving the impression that humanity's afarensis ancestors retained chimp-like adaptations for arboreal life."[24] I return to the issue of reconstruction and artistic choices later in the chapter.

"Evolving Planet" at the Field Museum of Natural History

One of the leading natural history museums in the world, the Field Museum of Natural History originally formed in 1894 on the heels of the World's Columbian Exposition in Chicago. The Field Museum moved to its current neoclassical building in 1921 to anchor what would become the museum campus on the shores of Lake Michigan. The Field Museum is an internationally renowned and expansive institution with more than 480,000 square feet devoted to exhibitions and more than 150 affiliated research scientists working on-site.[25] Sue, the largest and most well-preserved Tyrannosaurus Rex in the museum world, was featured in the open-air lobby as visitors walk into the Field Museum. Relocated in 2018, Sue now sits adjacent to Lucy in the Evolving Planet exhibit.

Open to the public on March 10, 2006, the Kenneth and Anne Griffin Halls of Evolving Planet

> takes visitors on an awe-inspiring journey through 4 billion years of life on Earth, from single-celled organisms to towering dinosaurs and our extended human family. Unique fossils, animated videos, hands-on interactive displays, and recreated sea- and landscapes help tell the compelling story of evolution—the single process that connects everything that's ever lived on Earth.[26]

With its 4-billion-year-old walk through time, Evolving Planet represents a more conventional, chronological museological approach and is the oldest exhibition in the comparative analysis. Lucy is nestled two-thirds of the way into the exhibit's winding chronological path, introduced by the sign that reads, "Enter an age when mammals thrived—and discover your own origins." The exhibit guides visitors so they first see Lucy encased in glass at the forefront (figure 4.3). Directly behind the case is a center console focused on humans' common ancestry. Other exhibit content fills the half circle on the surrounding walls, providing more in-depth snapshots of different members in humanity's larger common ancestry lineage. Most visitors move from left to right around the half circle.[27]

The Field Museum is known for its active advocacy efforts to improve the public's understanding of human evolution. In the *Chicago Tribune*'s

Figure 4.3. Lucy in the Evolving Planet, Field Museum

coverage of the exhibit opening, it claimed, "The 27,000-square-foot exhibit, one of the museum's biggest, is designed to state the case for science and evolution in the national debate." The Field Museum does not
explicitly engage with any potential religious perceptions of the scientific
evidence on display. Yet the Evolving Planet's senior project manager,
Todd Tubutis, is clear about the Field Museum's aim to address gaps
in the public's understanding of evolutionary processes, "We really like
the animated video we use here, 'Evolution Essentials' . . . That is very
important in the current public debate about evolution versus creationism."[28] Given the timing of the Evolving Planet exhibit opening, just
one year before the Creation Museum opened its doors, the Field Museum looms large for AiG. Recall from chapter 1 that AiG invited Field
Museum scientist Dr. Raup to tour the museum before it opened. And,
in AiG's review of the Field Museum's Lucy exhibit, it questions what
broader takeaways visitors leave with and offers the Creation Museum
as the antidote, "Museums like the Field have a life-undermining message: that people are just the result of random processes over billions

of years. Where is a sense of purpose and meaning in a story like that? Thankfully, there will be a museum opening near Cincinnati, Ohio, next spring that will have a positive story to share: the Bible is the true history of the Creator's designed universe, and He has not created human beings without meaning or purpose."[29] AiG raises this question about the bigger picture and where humans fit into it to drum up interest in its own response to collective questions about our origins.

"The Hall of Human Origins" at the Smithsonian National Museum of Natural History

With more than seven million visitors per year, the Smithsonian National Museum of Natural History is the most widely attended natural history museum in the world. Located in Washington, DC, the National Museum of Natural History opened to the public in 1910. It is one of the world's largest scientific research institutions as well. As the Smithsonian reports, "The main building on the National Mall contains 1.5 million square feet of space overall and 325,000 square feet of exhibition and public space; altogether the Museum is the size of 18 football fields, and houses over 1,000 employees."[30] The sheer scale of the National Museum of Natural History is abundantly clear once visitors enter into a four-story rotunda where a life-size elephant is on display. After moving north through the Ocean Hall, visitors turn the corner to encounter a time tunnel to travel back millions of years in the David H. Koch Hall of Human Origins (figure 4.4).[31] Introduced to the public in March 2010, the Hall of Human Origins asks big questions, "Who are we? Who were our ancestors? When did they live? . . . [the exhibit] explores these universal questions, showing how the characteristics that make us human evolved against a backdrop of dramatic climate change. The story begins 6 million years ago on the African continent where the earliest humans took the first steps toward walking upright."[32] Thematically organized, the exhibit allows visitors to explore what it means to be human, including what distinguishes us as human and how we know where we came from, in the largest exhibit on human origins in the world (more than 15,000 square feet).

The exhibit is set up as a path that can be traversed from two distinct, opposing entrances. Regardless of one's entrance, the exhibit's chrono-

Figure 4.4. The Hall of Human Origins, Smithsonian National Museum of Natural History

logical argument is embedded into its content rather than its physical layout. Visitors may begin on the left or right side of the exhibit since exhibit areas are clustered off the main path for both entrances; it is designed so that many visitors could zigzag back and forth before moving forward.

The National Museum of Natural History is the most explicit in its discussion of religious implications in its large exhibit on human evolution. Yet much of the discussion is interactive; a few touch-screen features are located throughout the museum to encourage visitors to provide their own answers to what it means to be human. Museum staff members from the Human Origins Program host semi-regular discussions with leaders in religious communities on the museum's Broader Social Impacts Committee. The museum provides other resources on the exhibit website and related online discussion forums, such as "Human Evolution: Religious Perspectives," for which it provides this description: "Despite strong public interest in the science, however, many people find this topic troubling when viewed from a religious perspective.

Representatives of diverse religious communities encourage a larger, more respectful understanding of both the scientific evidence and religious belief."[33] Yet Ken Ham did not find the Smithsonian's approach to be compelling or accurately portrayed, as described in a *Washington Post* article:

> when asked what he hopes visitors will take away from the exhibition, Potts [curator and director of the Human Origins Program] replied: "A sense of the sacred." That almost sounds as if he wants the hall to be a kind of a temple, where visitors can be worshipful of the fossils of their apelike ancestors! The American public has largely been duped into thinking that by not mentioning God or the Bible, something like the Smithsonian is being "neutral." But there is no neutral position; one is either for Christ or against (Luke 11:23). This museum is imposing a religion on generations of Americans: the religion of atheism. It's the same worldview that is being thrust at generations of children in the public schools.[34]

Of importance for Ham, the issue of pluralism or compromise is presumably even more concerning than simply the absence of any discussion about religious implications like the other museums. He forcefully underscores the issue of secular bias and troubles any perception of neutrality in public institutions like museums or classrooms.

* * *

Through multiple field site visits, I documented each museum exhibit with photographs of all text, visuals, and interactive features.[35] I collected maps, museum and exhibit guides, exhibit archives, and other materials, including supplemental interviews with museum staff familiar with the exhibit design and development.[36] Additionally, I gathered information from each museum's website about exhibit background. I analyzed and compared each exhibit's design and content. I transcribed all of the text presented in each exhibit and used Atlas.ti software for textual analysis, using two forms of code. First, I based codes on the General Inquirer Dictionary,[37] a computer-assisted approach for content analysis of textual data based out of Harvard College. The dictionary formalizes groups of related words, and I focused on those categorized by indications of certainty (positive claims), uncertainty or doubt (negative claims), or general knowledge (neutral claims).[38] Second, I manually coded based on central themes from a close read of each exhibit to assess the frequency and proportionate coverage of different topics.

Comparative Exhibit Analysis

As I demonstrated in the previous chapter, museum-ness is conveyed through the senses. But it is also communicated by the kinds of aesthetic choices made about how to engage visitors as they move through the exhibit. Exhibit creators may ask: "Which font styles are easier to read?" or "How is the exhibit text displayed?" or "Which color palettes should be used?" While exhibit creators deploy a variety of options across the four human origin exhibits, consistent patterns emerge.

Largely adhering to museum display conventions, all of the museums' human origin exhibits use streamlined sans serif fonts. Grey and black font on white text plaques (or the reverse) are used to ensure that enough contrast is present to make it legible for most visitors. Light, off-white drywall provides a discrete backdrop with affixed exhibit cases; the walls are complemented by grey low-pile carpet (Smithsonian, Cleveland, Field) or blond hardwood floors (Creation Museum).

Interestingly, the direction of exhibit text imbues some of the most forceful contrast. In the Creation Museum, all exhibit text is set up as a binary in which Human Reason (or Man's Word) is always on the left-hand side and God's Word is always on the right-hand side. Visuals accompany this textual binary with opposing graphics—an "evolutionary tree" underneath Man's Word and a "creationist orchard" of trees on the right. The Smithsonian uses a benefit/cost binary to introduce the important milestones in human evolution. This point is tactically driven home with a set of orange board sliders at the base of each milestone exhibit showcase; slide to the left for the benefits to humans of walking, for instance, since it helped humans survive, and to the right for the cost, which in this case is connected to back pain due to human bipedality. The Cleveland Museum uses a timeline to orient the exhibit text that moves from the left (oldest known common ancestor) to the right (contemporary humans). Meanwhile, the oldest exhibit, the Field Museum, has no discernable left/right structure for the exhibit content or the visuals beyond the common setup that text is on the left and visuals presenting evidence are on the right. Across all the museums, the exhibits use a consistent left/right convention.

In its bid for leveraging its human origins counterclaim, AiG's plausibility politics becomes clear. I find the Creation Museum makes three moves in its exhibit to challenge mainstream exhibits on human origins.

Move 1: Choose Your Target Wisely

AiG selected a familiar example to target. Lucy is what many visitors expect to see when entering a human origins exhibit. Yet in many ways, Lucy embodies a key challenge that human evolution presents for religious believers: how to reconcile the possibility of common ancestry with primates and the role of a supernatural creator. Public opinion polls suggest that for many, reconciling religious beliefs with scientific knowledge does not present a challenge except when scientific issues are mobilized by interested stakeholders (movement leaders, lobbyists, politicians) and turned into social issues. Importantly, current hot button topics, such as human evolution and global warming, are not contested among professional scientists given general widespread consensus that humans evolved from a common ancestry shared with primates over a long period or that the Earth is getting hotter due to human intervention. Recent research consistently points not to an epistemological, inherent battle between religious and scientific ways of knowing among the public, but rather a "moral competition" over cultural authority: who is perceived as an expert with the most compelling evidence.[39]

Nonetheless, the impact on the public's beliefs is stark. In 2014, just under half of adults in the United States agreed with the statement, "human beings, as we know them today, developed from earlier species of animals."[40] In that same year, Gallup Poll found a clear split when it asked respondents, "Do you think the theory of evolution is consistent or inconsistent with your religious beliefs?," with 46% claiming it was consistent and another 46% stating it was inconsistent.[41] Later in 2017, only 19% of adults polled indicated that God played no role, "Human evolved, but God had no part" compared to the 38% who agreed with the statement, "God created humans in present form." While the public support for evolutionary mechanisms as an organizing principle of the biological world is common, humans present the exception for many.

The perception of human evolution as a contested area of knowledge has roots dating back to the 1920s Scope Trial, or the "Monkey Trial," as it was commonly known.[42] Think of the commonly cited Bible passage, "So God created man in His own image."[43] If humans share common ancestors with primates, then the veracity of this passage may come into question. During the Scopes era, religious conservatives forcefully yoked together concerns about biblical literalism with broader implications for societal ills (and salvation) if human evolution was asserted to be true. Their arguments continue to have relevance as evident in the recent poll data, in which still approximately 24% of adults polled are biblical literalists.[44]

Lucy's well-known status as a common ancestor for humans is precisely the right kind of target for AiG. Her prominence and her position as a cultural lightning rod for the public's division on human evolution sets her apart. What other potential evolutionary figures or theories could AiG have targeted? One classic example includes the horse fossil series as MacFadden et al. (2012) describe:

> Since the second half of the nineteenth century when many natural history museums were founded in the U.S. . . . . paleontologists typically depicted the evolutionary pattern of fossil horses in North America as a linear sequence from smaller ancestor to progressively larger descendent . . . a classic "textbook" example of evolution . . . The problem with depicting fossil horses as orthogenetic is that, by the early twentieth century, paleontologists understood that, rather than a simple, straight-line sequence, the actual fossil record of horses was a complexly branching tree . . . instead of a linear sequence in which ancestral species evolve directly into their descendants, the evolutionary tree of horses is bushy, with many species overlapping in time, multiple originations, and frequent extinctions. Despite this knowledge, to this day, the classic story of horse evolution in museums, books, and other media is still often times depicted as orthogenetic. (29–31)

Here is an example that AiG could have used to underscore that the "textbook" depiction of the macroevolution process commonly displayed in natural history museums is often inaccurate and relies on outdated information. Yet beyond a few articles published in print and online, the

Creation Museum does not discuss this horse series.[45] An exhibit unpacking the horse series in the Creation Museum would be less effective because it is unique to natural history museums (not typically discussed elsewhere in the mainstream media) and is not as innately interesting or controversial as human origins. The controversy, so to speak, is too unique to the science community and museum professionals.

Other possible issues central to AiG's argument are only of interest to creationists (e.g., flood geology) or too unique in their prominence for biblical literalists (e.g., the Garden of Eden). Instead, AiG features these topics later in the museum, once it has established key questions about the age of the Earth and origins of humans. AiG uses the museum's other big draw, dinosaurs, to introduce Lucy. Introduced in the context of the dinosaur dig site (the first exhibit), the discussion of Lucy's fossil evidence encourages visitors to think about how long ago our own human origins lineage began. It also primes the audience to consider bigger questions about scientific dating techniques (radiocarbon dating methods in particular) and fosters skepticism about how old (or young) the Earth could be.

Move 2: Portray Your Alternative Using the Same Physical Evidence

At first glance, the Lucy exhibit in the Creation Museum feels familiar. We see the fossil evidence arranged in a partial skeleton positioned upright and affixed in a museum-style display glass case. Next to it is a life-like Lucy reconstruction with skin, muscles, and hair. Yet she is in an unfamiliar position as an ape-like figure walking on all fours. To support its objections to dominant interpretations, the Creation Museum exhibit uses cutting-edge hologram technology to overlay known fossils associated with Lucy onto this ape-like figure (figure 4.5). It visually demonstrates the plausibility of AiG's arguments and depicts how the fossil record could suggest a knuckle-walking ape rather than an intermediate bipedal hominid.

When comparing the content of the four exhibits, I found evidential text—words and phrases that reference physical material such as anatomy, bone, DNA, footprint, fossil, fragment, replica[46]—was prominent across all of them. For instance, at the Smithsonian, a plaque outlines the

Figure 4.5. Holographic Lucy, Creation Museum

differences in the types of items on display: "Objects from 48 countries are displayed in this exhibition, including both original finds and exact reproductions [cast, replica, and model] of unique and fragile specimens kept in their country of origin." At the Field Museum, availability of evidence structures the timeline of the exhibit's physical layout as it claims:

> Epochs are just smaller chunks of time in Earth's history. The rest of your walkthrough time today will be organized by epoch. Why? Because fossils from the more recent past are more common—and better preserved—than more ancient fossils. More fossils paint a more detailed picture of evolution, allowing us to study it using a more detailed time scale.

And, finally, the Cleveland Museum contextualizes fossil evidence within our own bodies: "Bone for bone, we are closely related to ancient hominins like Lucy, and modern apes like chimpanzees." How often does AiG reference this kind of evidence compared to the other exhibits? The evidence code received substantially more coverage at the Creation Museum (66% of the mentions) than the Smithsonian (50%), Cleveland (45%), and the Field (40%).[47] This is not surprising given what is at stake for AiG. It needs to convince the audience that there is another way to interpret its counterparts' evidence, and it uses that same fossil evidence as the platform to launch its counter-claim.

Fossils lie at the heart of AiG's alternative argument, because fossils are accessible to everyone. As museum education researchers suggest, "Early elementary children can understand the importance of fossils— that fossils provide evidence about the plants and animals that lived long ago."[48] For instance, AiG highlights both the fossil evidence and its incompleteness in its exhibit:

> Lucy's fossilized skeleton consists of 47 bones out of a possible 207, including parts of both upper and lower limbs, vertebrae, ribs, and pelvis (hip bones). While most of the hand and foot bones are missing, as well as most of the skull (except for the lower jaw called the mandible), these have been partially filled in by the discovery of other presumed specimens of A. afarensis.[49]

Important for AiG's framing, mainstream exhibits do acknowledge consistently the partiality of Lucy's skeletal remains. The Field Museum displays the partial skeleton with an interactive feature highlighting how they filled in the skull. Both the Cleveland Museum and the Smithsonian depict the entire skeleton, noting where they filled in the gaps within the known fossil record: "The brown bones are casts of the parts of Lucy's skeleton that were excavated. The black bones represent missing parts" (Smithsonian exhibit; see figure 4.6 for a side-by-side comparison). AiG roots its challenge in a direct comparison to the skeletal frame constructed out of the known fossilized bones associated with Lucy in all museums. This move allows AiG to portray its alternative Lucy narrative and model using enough similar presentational conventions to evoke plausibility for their interpretation of an incomplete skeleton.[50]

Building on its alternative interpretation of the partial fossil record, the depiction of Lucy on all fours in the Creation Museum stands in direct opposition to all of the other exhibits' portrayals. The three examples of Lucy in the Field, Smithsonian, and Cleveland Museum exhibits demonstrate a striking similarity: Lucy stands upright with elongated arms at her side (Figure 4.7). AiG works to support their interpretation and display by targeting the most common evidence natural history

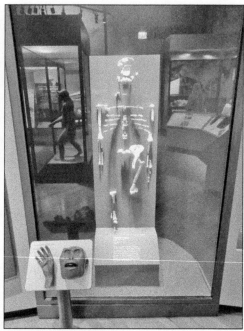

Figure 4.6a-c. Lucy Skeletal Frame, Comparative Exhibit Features (Clockwise Left to Right: Cleveland Museum of Natural History, Field Museum, Smithsonian National Museum of Natural History)

Figure 4.7. Lucy Reconstructed, Comparative Exhibit Features (Clockwise Left to Right: Cleveland Museum of Natural History, Field Museum, Smithsonian National Museum of Natural History)

museums use to depict their case for upright bipedality—anatomical structure and fossilized footprints.

An Anatomy Lesson

AiG addresses the familiar anatomical evidence feature by feature to support its case for how Lucy could be interpreted as more akin to a gorilla than anything human. It follows the mainstream exhibits' leads. The Field Museum instructs visitors in the *Evolving Planet* exhibit:

> How to tell the hominids from the apes. When scientists look at fossils, several features can tell them whether they are dealing with an ape or a hominid: (1) pelvis, (2) femur, (3) teeth, (4) skull, (5) toes, (6) foot arches . . . The hominid story is still being written. There are gaps in the fossil record, and many fossils are fragmentary. But each new discovery brings us closer to a clear picture of human evolution.

In the Smithsonian, visitors work through a series of anatomical features to determine how "Walking Upright" emerged over time. This detailed approach provides a tangible type of evidence to walk through systematically to see first-hand how scientists interpret Lucy's fossil evidence.

In table 4.1, exhibit text is displayed side by side between the Smithsonian and the Creation Museum. It underscores a striking similarity in the type of information conveyed but, of course, dramatically different conclusions are drawn. The Smithsonian's distinction between "Apelike Arms" and "Humanlike Hips" is a fundamental point echoed in all of the mainstream exhibits; it demonstrates how Lucy represents a bridge between primates and humans.[51] It is what AiG focuses on in its counter. AiG frames its anatomical discussion with a question: "Just an extinct type of ape? As with many other high-profile creatures that have no living survivors, a layer of interpretation lies between the original and the reconstruction. The less complete the fossil, the thicker the interpretation, as in Lucy's case. The existing data appear to show a stronger similarity between Lucy and the great apes rather than humans." AiG follows this up by highlighting how the fossil record is damaged, how her hips are more gorilla-like than human-like, and how her feet are curled, suggesting a tree-dweller rather than a creature who walked

TABLE 4.1. Anatomical Features, Comparative

Smithsonian National Museum of Natural History	Creation Museum
Apelike Arm	Lucy's Arms and Legs
Notice how long this arm bone is compared to the rest of the skeleton. **Its length is a clue that Lucy's species climbed trees.** Powerful chest and upper arm muscles pulled on the bone during climbing, creating the ridge—or crest—at the top.	All of Lucy's **long bones were fragmented.** Evolutionists who believe that Lucy was a link between apes and humans **close the gaps in her arm bones and lengthen the gaps in her leg bones so that they more closely resemble human proportions.** However, the bones fit together just as well with ape proportions.
Humanlike Hips	Lucy's Hip Bones (Pelvis)
Chimpanzees and other non-human apes have hip bones that are tall and narrow. Lucy's pelvis is short and broad. **It enabled the hip muscles to hold the body upright as each leg swung forward to walk.**	While Lucy's pelvis (hip) has **some distinctive features,** in the most important respects **it resembles the pelvis of a gorilla.** In particular, the front or "anterior" portions of the upper wings of the pelvis, called the iliac blades, face laterally (to the side) in humans, but not in Lucy and other apes, such as gorillas and chimps.
Flexible Feet	Lucy's Feet
Lucy's species had compact feet that supported the body's weight during upright walking. But look at the toe bones. **They are longer and more curved than those of a modern human foot,** more like those of tree-climbing apes.	Illustrations of Lucy always show her with essentially human feet, but the fossil evidence reveals that the feet of creatures like Lucy had **the long, highly curved toes of tree dwellers.** The most cited evidence that Lucy walked like a human with human-like feet is an amazing trail of very human-like footprints found in Tanzania.

upright for long distances. Typically, AiG does not question the fossils themselves but rather the interpretation, specifically what that interpretation suggests, how it could fit into the larger known body of fossil evidence, or how the evidence is displayed. It is important that AiG stays close to how mainstream exhibits portray fossils; this part of AiG's counterargument depends on the display of familiar, scientific evidence and relatively technical anatomical language. It also relies on peer-reviewed journal articles and provides citations from mainstream publications suggesting that multiple interpretations of fossil evidence continue to circulate within the scientific community.

A Walk with Lucy

The Laetoli footprints are another central feature in all three of the mainstream museums. These footprints have been widely publicized in the media for decades, and they represent a different kind of fossil evidence from bones. The Cleveland Museum of Natural History describes them under the exhibit title, "Walking without a Doubt":

> These famous footprints prove that early hominins walked upright as early as 3.6 million years ago. They belong to a member of Australopithecus afarensis—Lucy's species. The Laetoli footprints show the tracks of 3 individuals walking upright across an open grassland at a time when a nearby volcano was emitting clouds of ash. These human ancestors' tracks were almost immediately filled in with more ash, preserving them until they were discovered in 1976.

The Cleveland Museum demonstrates the importance of these footprints for bipedality and the details of how they were preserved.

Interactive features anchor both the Smithsonian and Field Museum exhibits. The Smithsonian encourages visitors to "Compare Your Stride" with a mirror set approximately six inches from the floor so visitors may view their own feet and walk four or five steps to assess their stride:

> How does your stride measure up with that of the early humans who made these footprints? Australopithecus afarensis had short legs and therefore a short stride. Later species evolved longer legs and therefore a longer stride, enabling them to walk farther and faster and to cover more territory each day (figure 4.8a).

The Field Museum uses footprints embedded in the floor to highlight how scientists know that the footprints are not human:

> Could those be an ape's footprints? No. Hominids and apes have very different feet. Apes have thumb-like big toes that diverge sharply sideways. Hominids do not. Chimpanzee foot [on the left] Modern human foot [on the right]. This fossil footprint could only have been made by a hominid.

The museum presents the footprints so that they clearly make the case for how members of Lucy's species made these footprints walking

Figure 4.8. Compare Your Stride, Smithsonian National Museum of Natural History |
Laetoli Footprints, Creation Museum

upright. In its exhibit at the Creation Museum, AiG argues that the distance between Lucy's remains and the footprints leaves room for doubt:

> To this day these footprints are the evolutionists' best "evidence" that
> Lucy walked upright with the same distinctive stride as humans. However, there is no evidence that a creature like Lucy made these footprints.
> In fact, the Laetoli footprints were found in Tanzania, about 932 miles
> (1500 km) from northern Ethiopia, where Lucy and other representatives
> of her species were found (see figure 4.8b).

Beyond challenging the connection between the footprints and Lucy
by questioning the interpretation, not the fossilized footprint itself,
AiG offers its alternative explanation for how these footprints could
fit into its shorter timeline in which humans always have been present
in the world (and the fossil record): "The Laetoli footprints . . . have a

very human-like shape and stride. In a young-earth creationist model of geology and anthropology, these footprints were probably made by post-Flood humans sometime after the biblical account of Babel and the scattering of humans over the earth." Weaving together references to the fossil record and the biblical story of Babel evokes AiG's push for an interpretation that relies on both scientific and religious references.

Move 3: Explicitly Confront Mainstream Exhibits

The political realities of what Lucy represents are not lost on AiG. Yet, interestingly, it is downplayed frequently, if addressed at all, in most natural history museums. Conflict is perceived as antithetical to revered public institutions such as science museums. Archaeologist Stephanie Moser reviews museum exhibits' more conventional, conservative approach taken in human origins displays: "It appears that developments in museum display that have led to the creation of new understandings of science and culture have escaped human origins exhibits because there has been so little criticism or reflective thought on their nature as representational and interpretive devices."[52] This stands in contrast to other exhibits within natural history and science museums that reflect more contemporary museological approaches. Often the focus is on communicating new, more emotionally evocative stories about society and its relationship to science in terms of the human race or climate change.

In human origins exhibits, however, the default approach is to rely on standard conventions or insert new approaches in an area off the beaten path due to concerns about potentially offending certain audiences, namely religious museum visitors. The perceived conflict is rooted in the implications of common ancestry—the undermining of creationist beliefs—which both religious audiences and science enthusiasts understand quite well.[53] While natural history museums make different decisions about the extent to which they engage with visitors' intertwined sets of beliefs, they worry about too much discussion of conflict.

AiG positions itself in stark contrast to conflict aversion in its Lucy exhibit. The Creation Museum grounds its claims of marginalization within the secular, largely conflict-avoidance bias of mainstream human origin exhibits. Many connected to the museum world, like Moser among others, argue that more recognition of individuals' nuanced perspectives is needed within science museum exhibits for them to be effective. Indeed, the National Science Foundation even funded a touring exhibit, "Explore Evolution," to proactively engage visitors, humanize evolutionary scientists' research process, and shore up mainstream natural history museums' authority on the topic (explicitly targeting efforts like the Creation Museum).[54] It reflects a new approach but one that is not widely adopted in the museum world as it goes against the long-running presumption that museums should simply stick to the facts and let the information speak for itself. AiG capitalizes on its challengers' status—and pivots.

With this context in mind, AiG adopts direct engagement with the audience as people with multiple ways of knowing and a strong set of preexisting beliefs. It accomplishes this by adopting a forceful tone and approach as well as by redirecting the emphasis of the human origins exhibit's content.

Tone and Range of Exhibit Content

A common breakdown of patterns across all four museums was clear in the exhibit content despite some minor differences in the individual exhibits' composition of positive, negative, and neutral claims.[55] A total of 41% of all coded text was positive, with three codes capturing exhibit text that made a positive claim through an assertion or conveyed certainty.[56] For example, the Field Museum stated, "Different early species of the genus *Homo* lived at different times and in different parts of the world," while the Creation Museum informed visitors that "You can see how the artist has a very powerful influence over what the viewer believes about the evidence." Negative tone, tracked by three measures of doubt, uncertainty, or negation, were reflected in approximately 34% of exhibit text across all of the museums.[57] For instance, an exhibit plaque at the Smithsonian asserts, "The last common ancestor of humans and chimpanzees lived between 8 and 6 million years ago. We do not yet have its remains." Finally, neutral tone, namely straightforward knowledge claims without interpretation, were the least commonly present in 25% of the coded text, such as when the Cleveland Museum noted,[58] "An international team of scientists, including Donald Johanson, a former curator at the Cleveland Museum of Natural History, discovered the partial skeleton in 1974." While the dominance of certainty (positive claims) is not surprising across the exhibits, it suggests that neutrality is less common not only in the Creation Museum but also in mainstream museums.

Statements indicating an overemphasis of "accuracy, certainty, and extremity" are the most common at the Creation Museum (19% of coded text). "A more recent study shows that Lucy and her kind were in fact long-armed knuckle walkers with wrists capable of locking to support the hands during knuckle walking. While some recent illustrations of Lucy do show ape-like hands with highly curved fingers, none show her in a knuckle-walking position as this exhibit does." While the Creation Museum overstates the most, it is not alone in this trend. A tendency to be forthright and overstate an argument was the most common across all the exhibits (approximately 38% of all coded text). And the negation keywords "that show the denial of one sort or another" were much more common at the Creation Museum than the three mainstream human origins exhibits. The highest overlap occurred with "certainty" keywords that indicated "a feeling of sureness, certainty, and firmness" and references to physical evidence.[59] This underscores the continued reliance on objects to support broader exhibit claims. For instance, the Creation Museum asserted, "Claimed to be 3.66 million years old, these footprints are identical to modern human footprints—with a well-shaped heel, strong arch, and a distinctively human left-right stride." These two patterns are in keeping with expectations that a challenger exhibit would be more forceful in its claims to bolster its position as outside of the mainstream.

Redirection of Exhibit Content—Artistic Choices

AiG establishes its explicit position against mainstream representation by challenging the most familiar, conventional aspects of human origins exhibits. All of these exhibits discuss family trees that consist of early ancestor primates and humans and use reconstructed head busts to showcase variations in our phenotypical features. And, all of these exhibits focus on walking upright as a key evolutionary milestone in human evolution.[60] The exhibits display the skeleton frame of the known fossils associated with Lucy's discovery and use it as an opportunity to underscore how this fossil discovery was a significant step toward capturing the public's interest in better understanding human origins.

These similar patterns across the mainstream exhibits serve as a blueprint for AiG's focal points in its Lucy exhibit. Assessing the exhibits' text, keywords related to common ancestors were prominent across all of the museum exhibits (26% to 38% of coverage in coded exhibit text) compared to the Creation Museum (approximately 9%).[61] Instead, the art of reconstruction—words that point toward artistic choices made in how sculptures, artifacts, and scenes are depicted—were most prominent at the Creation Museum, ranking most common (21%) after physical evidence supporting its alternative claims (66%). AiG backs up its exhibit text in its visual depiction.

The full reconstruction of Lucy as a gray gorilla-like creature on all fours is a striking visual alternative and it anchors AiG's argument in two important ways that map onto the consistent exhibit features. First, it de-emphasizes common ancestor connections often drawn to Lucy by coupling this gorilla-like rendering of Lucy with a question boldly written above it: "Is Lucy Your Ancestor?" This suggests that Lucy is just another primate, a claim that AiG dedicates a lot of space to unpack in the exhibit. Second, AiG's reconstruction of Lucy introduces skepticism regarding Lucy's bipedality by drawing out how fossil discoveries may have multiple interpretations. The rendering suggests that Lucy walked mostly on all fours and only occasionally bipedally, more akin to some primates than early humans.

In a separate portion of the exhibit, in a display case titled, "What Did Lucy Look Like?," (figure 4.9a) AiG's artists outline how secular paleo-artists (as well as paleoanthropologists and paleontologists) have made decisions that extend beyond the physical evidence in their depiction of Lucy in conventional natural history museums. To support that claim, AiG's staff display five potential life-sized heads developed from the same fossil evidence to highlight the many ways a museum could choose to depict Lucy. It deploys the anatomical features discussed elsewhere in the exhibit. Under the title "Creative Decisions," the plaque centered in the middle of the potential Lucy heads states (figure 4.9b):

Surrounding the skull are five examples of how an artist can take the same sculpture and apply different colors and hair patterns to influence

Figure 4.9a-b. "Creative Decisions," Creation Museum

a viewer's belief about the fossil. Amazingly, all of these models were cast from the same head mold used in the full body Lucy reconstruction in the front of this case.

AiG further discusses the role of bias in how artistic details are decided by using the five head busts to illustrate how choices about skin tone, hair color, and eyes have a dramatic effect. Notice the distinction between "Lucy with human-like coloration" and "Lucy as a gorilla" (figure 4.10a, 4.10b).

Lucy as an ape-man
An artist who believes that Lucy was an "ape-man" might give her more human characteristics. Notice how human-like this version looks with human eyes and hair patterns.

Lucy as a chimp
This version shows Lucy with chimp-like colors and hair patterns. See how different the eyes look?

Lucy with human-like coloration
This version may strike you as absurd, but it demonstrates that any color and finish could be applied to this sculpture. Notice how different Lucy looks with human eyes, skin tones, and hair patterns.

Lucy as an orangutan
Some people think Lucy might have resembled an orangutan. Remember, this version is made from the same sculpture as all the rest, just with different colors and patterns.

Lucy as a gorilla
This version shows that if *Lucy is nothing more than an extinct ape*, then she may have resembled a common gorilla. (Creation Museum Lucy exhibit text, emphasis added)

Figure 4.10a-b. Creative Decisions Up Close, Creation Museum

To complement its reconstructions, AiG has scattered comparative pictures from current Lucy exhibits from around the world in the glass case below these replicas. AiG suggests that all too often Lucy is rendered unnecessarily human-like (e.g., a white sclera surrounding the pupil, instead of a primate's dark brown or black eye). This display explicitly references and counters familiar Lucy exhibits in natural history museums around the world, many with eyes similar to the one AiG's critiques.

Mainstream museum exhibits focus much less on how they created their displayed reconstructions. Among the three, the Cleveland Museum of Natural History dedicates the most exhibit space to this discussion under the title "Art and Science Bring Bones to Life." The museum explains, "Our understanding of what early hominins may have looked like stems from a blend of art and science. Paleontological artists work closely with scientific experts in order to reconstruct extinct creatures based on anatomical clues from the fossilized bones." The Smithsonian exhibit briefly discusses the reconstruction process, mostly focusing on John Gurche, the famous paleoartist who contributed sculptures to the exhibit. It also offers an interactive booth, but the focus is more on common ancestry rather than the process of reconstruction.[62] The Field Museum does not address the artistic reconstruction process in relation to Lucy, but it does discuss its three-dimensional reconstruction of a 15,000-year-old Magdalenian woman using CT scan technology.

These museums' modest attention to the role of paleoartists in creating the reconstructions on display may be due to their authoritative mainstream position. Yet contemporary discussions in the museum world encourage exhibit designers to engage the audience more in the lesser-known areas of what human ancestors may have looked like and why it matters. Museum consultants Monique Scott and Ellen Giusti point to the importance of describing reconstructions effectively to engage audiences:

> [museums] are becoming aware of the reality that visitors come into human evolution exhibitions with a cache of preconceived beliefs. One of the most significant interventions museums can make, then, is to give visitors the tools to understand how popular scientific reconstructions—those images they encounter in *National Geographic* and on the Discovery channel—are made. Fossil Fragments [The Yale Peabody Museum], for example, discusses how reconstructions of Neanderthals are made,

step-by-step from "fossil fragment" to musculature to fleshed-out recon-struction, explaining the steps from the scientific to the speculative. Ide-ally, then, museum visitors become drawn into that classic Neanderthal image, and then also learn to decode and deconstruct it.[63]

Despite this encouragement, the mainstream exhibits above only moder-ately address this topic; the Cleveland Museum outlines its process, and the Smithsonian provides an interactive opportunity. Unsurprisingly, these two exhibits are newer, but neither dedicate the amount of pro-portional attention that the Creation Museum does.

AiG uses its Lucy exhibit to critically examine the practice of artis-tic reconstruction that occurs in natural history museums across the world. For AiG, artistic reconstruction relies heavily on the content an artist chooses to emphasize and what they use that content to suggest. When paleoartists transform fossils into reconstructed head busts and full bodies, AiG claims that bias may feed into different structural and phenotypical renderings of Lucy. The bias leans toward rendering her more and more human-like. Of course, this argument could be lobbed back at AiG since its artistic rendering is more gorilla-like, but as an institutional outsider to mainstream science, it simply needs to focus on drumming up plausibility in order to make its case. Hence the in-depth discussion of artistic interpretation in the Creation Museum and the focus on an alternative reading of what Lucy's structural anatomy may suggest contrasts heavily with the proportionally scant coverage these reconstructions receive in the mainstream exhibits.[64]

AiG's emphasis on artistic representation replaces what is decidedly not present in its exhibit: recent fossil discoveries that further connect human evolution via other common ancestors as well as the physiologi-cal and sociocultural processes of becoming human. Active research using improved CT scans and new fossil discoveries is not mentioned. Instead, AiG connects fossil evidence to its literal reading of the Bible. As AiG argues online in its article about the exhibit:

> It is very easy to get off track and fear the discovery of some variety of ape that could waddle around on two legs might de-rail someone's faith. How-ever, faith should be grounded in a correct understanding of Scripture and a discernment of the difference between *observations* of the fossils

and *interpretations* about them . . . But even if Lucy and her cousins had a more versatile anatomy than some other apes, tiptoeing through the jungle didn't make anything ape-like turn into a person. Nothing could.[65]

According to AiG, the Bible contains the ultimate story of how humans came into being and no other fossils or incremental steps, such as the use and development of language, matter in this narrative. A focus on the close reading of the Bible renders those other arguments obsolete or simply inaccurate from the perspective of AiG's biblical literalists.

Presenting Human Origins in Context

Historically, museums are not well positioned to deal with controversy or sociocultural shifts in understanding, and natural history museums even less so. Faced with politically fraught topics, yet decidedly not contentious given widespread agreement among scientists, the main-stream exhibits examined in this chapter reflect a collective misstep to not adapt some of the lessons from what other natural history museum exhibits do so well, including facilitating open discussions of uncertainty and a focus on meaning-making rather than solely "fun fact" transmission. This work, however, is being done elsewhere in the natural history museum world. As archaeologist Stephanie Moser notes:

> The fact that natural history exhibitions have also started to engage more openly with the political dimensions of their content offers a further incentive for adopting this practice in exhibitions on human evolution . . . by addressing environmental and conservation issues, where visitors are encouraged to contemplate the effect of their behaviour on biological diversity.[66]

But exhibit curators appear hesitant to incorporate these tools. Surely, museum professionals do not operate outside of the demands of administrative oversight, funding demands, and politicized public perceptions. Yet an emphasis on how science gets done and how it changes is vital for consistently engaging a broader, if at times skeptical, audience, particularly when it comes to human origins. As science educators suggest, "Through constructivist exhibition designs (building on visitors' existing frameworks while simultaneously challenging their preconceptions), through explanation of scientific methodology and also by demystifying the museum and science, museum visitors are given the tools to think critically about the science they encounter both in the museum and, perhaps more importantly, in the larger cultural sphere."[67] This approach is most clearly adopted in the Smithsonian, but that museum still hovers around the question of human meaning-making. It largely leaves discussions about religious traditions and other ways of making sense of our humanity off-site or relegated to temporary programming. AiG exacerbates this oversight in human origin exhibits to advance its own claims in the Creation Museum.

Beyond avoiding engagement with topics that may have religious or political implications, science communication scholars caution about the potential dangers of relying on presenting a polished outcome. Hine and Medvecky (2015) refer to this as "finished science": "There is a tendency towards stasis . . . and in order to achieve this there needs to be not only a separation of science from real-world issues that impact on its practical application, but also an elimination of scientific debate" (4). Comparatively, unfinished science contextualizes the scientific process and knocks off balance the notion of science as a universal truth. Instead, science is portrayed as a process. As science education researchers highlight, "Science isn't about proving claims true—which are what we need for finished science—it's about disproving false ones."[68] In this chapter, I show that, indeed, these three mainstream human origin exhibits display various theories and sources of scientific evidence to suggest one explanation or another, leaving only occasional room for uncertainty. This dynamic is embedded into a larger authoritative frame.[69] Yet museums do not always accurately present scientific claims or frequently discuss how these explanations shift over time, fall out of favor, or are otherwise less than complete.

When museum exhibits exclusively present finished science (or at the very least let it dominate), they open the door for visitors to not fully understand how scientific inquiry operates in practice or how to evaluate scientific claims. Visitors also do not gain a sense of the ties between scientists, policymakers, and the public. I find it is precisely in these moments when AiG exacerbates the disconnect that exists in the museum world with its public. There is a fissure between a contemporary ethos for pluralism and a historical impulse to offer a singular authoritative voice in museums—in this case, a finished science. AiG does not want to dismantle the authority of science, but rather to shift the grounds upon which it stands. The irony, then, is that mainstream museums laid in some of the groundwork for a group such as AiG to mobilize.

A long line of work within social sciences and philosophy examines the cultural and social foundations of science. This body of scholarship unearths how scientific findings do not simply emerge from the natural world but rather are actively pursued with theoretical frameworks and constructed using techniques shared among scientists. AiG implicitly draws from this line of work to gain traction among the public and make its three moves: challenge a meaningful target, ground the challenge using material objects, and make claims explicitly and transparently against mainstream framing.[70]

The public maintains high levels of trust in science while being skeptical of scientists' perceived unfettered reach into moral and ethical questions. Overwhelmingly, the public does not want scientists determining the meaning of life. What does this have to do with human origins? As we have seen across the exhibits, questions about who we are, where we come from as a species, and subsequently how we should engage in the world, are at the top of visitors' minds as they gaze into Lucy's eyes. Recall the 46% of American adults who state that the theory of evolution is inconsistent with their religious beliefs.

A key difference between AiG and scholars who study the institution of science and wrestle with the premise of unequivocal objectivity is that these scholars do so from within the academy, using the same kind of systematic research and secular principles to bolster their critique. Conversely, as a challenger, AiG's presentation of science in its museum is far from exhaustive. AiG claims that science as an institution is not failing, but rather, scientists and science educators as a professional community are to blame for mainstream science's problems. Undoubtedly, this rankles many science enthusiasts. Yet for AiG, objectivity is guided by religious texts, and witnessing is not simply a matter of peers verifying findings. To explore alternative explanations, the Creation Museum demonstrates that long-held beliefs are feasible and aligned with both biblical religious convictions and scientific proclivities. In many ways, the Lucy exhibit at the Creation Museum adopts enough conventions to evoke the plausibility politics at play while inserting its forceful view to a crowd that reaches well beyond its supporters.

Without explicitly directing more attention toward critical audience engagement and attending to different ways of knowing and creating meaning around human origins, mainstream museums may have left the public's acceptance of human evolution vulnerable to challenges from multiple fronts. In the next chapter, we will see the extent to which AiG reaches a broader audience.

5

What Audiences Think of the Creation Museum

Who pays attention to the Creation Museum? Do people take it seriously as making a viable argument or simply fear its ability and its professionalism? Preceding chapters largely draw from data collected on-site to examine internally why the Creation Museum emerged and how it operates. Yet what does it do for the movement? Who else besides the media is noticing or visiting the Creation Museum? To understand the extent to which this broader engagement occurs, I examine the kind of media attention that the Creation Museum receives.

Like any other metrics for assessing audience reception (e.g., the number of attendees, new members, or hits on a website), newsworthiness indicates how different members of the public perceive the Creation Museum. I use a multilevel media analysis (conventional news media and personal blog posts) to trace perspectives of various audiences outside of the movement. It provides an external vantage point necessary for determining the extent to which AiG's efforts have an impact. One of AiG's primary goals is to reach a layperson audience more effectively. In this chapter, I explore whether AIG achieved that goal, unpacking the extent to which those outside of the YEC movement have noticed its efforts.

Social Movements Vying for Media Attention

Social movement scholars consistently point to any media coverage as evidence that a social movement matters because coverage signals its cultural influence and credibility.[1] Beyond designating a movement's (or organization's) standing as "newsworthy," scholars find the media plays an informational role in publicizing movement activity and messages. For example, social movement scholars Andrews and Biggs (2006) found that coverage of 1960s sit-ins in the American South was a means of informing potential allies to be aware of what was occurring and to

be inspired by the scope of the movement's sit-ins. While media attention matters for social movements writ large, specific coverage patterns
can be linked to identifiable social movement organization characteristics such as the state of its bureaucratic organization.[2] Why? A well-run
organization can dedicate more energy and resources to framing movement events for the media, to calling attention via press releases, and to
mobilizing members with the media in mind. For instance, an organization may encourage large crowds to gather at movement events/protests
to attract interest.[3]

Still, any social problem, as translated by social movements, can only
expect to receive finite media attention. Peaks and valleys often characterize this attention, increasing during legislative sessions and decreas-
ing after policy decisions, and other events gain hold of the media cycle.[4]
Specifically, in these cycles, many scholars find movements' events receive more media attention when they occur close to a news media
outlet's location, when they are large and disruptive, or when they are
routine and take place annually.[5]

In the end, scholars have long acknowledged that while an array of factors influences media attention, a sizeable amount of coverage is driven
by the journalistic process itself, such as where events/items of interest
occur and whom they affect.[6] Conflict always attracts attention, whether
in entertainment, politics, religion, or cultural events. But, in part, conflict is created by messages that capture intense emotions. Historically,
movements used music, clothing, street theater, parades, and other cultural objects, as cultural sociologist Wendy Griswold highlights, "to stir
people up, to move people. This requires making not simply a cognitive
appeal but an emotional one. Movement activists will often use [these
forms] . . . to reach the hearts of potential converts to their cause."[7] This
explains why some movements may gain more attention than others, but
it also requires a further understanding of just what becomes culturally
resonant.[8] And, the question of resonance or how well culture works
hinges on how well it solves problems for AiG.[9]

Clamoring for "cultural change" does not provide much insight into
what a movement specifically desires. Instead, a scholarship that focuses
on the cultural consequences of social movements has gained traction.[10]
This body of work draws from studies of the production of culture and
its subsequent reception, otherwise referred to as "audience studies." The

assessment of audience impact frequently relies on popularity and visibility measures.[11] Williams (2004) argues that effective media coverage depends on a movement's ability to establish two components for a viable "cultural opportunity structure" or a cultural context for collective action: *intelligibility* (is it understood by group members) and *legitimacy* (its broader moral, ideational authority is in public). He goes on to assert that "social movement expressions do not stay the sole symbolic property of the groups who first used it. They become open for rival interpretation and potential transcendence in meaning" (102–104). Cultural producers cannot always anticipate or manipulate how a given audience or multiple audiences will receive their efforts.[12] Media coverage takes on a life of its own.

Andrews and Caren (2010) point out that the media can affect public views of a social movement's professionalism. Success in the creation of this appearance can in turn increase media attention and ensure a broader audience.[13] Ghaziani and Baldassari (2011) contend that the extent of coverage "itself signals the movement's cultural effects" (185). From this vantage point, it becomes clearer how an SMO building an "alternative" museum may be useful for attracting media attention and introduce AiG's broader attempt to produce cultural change.[14]

One way to measure the reach of a movement is to count the number of recruited members; another way is to measure media discussions of these alternative institutions.[15] By linking physical buildings to movement protest events, design consultant Ann Thorpe (2014) argues, "although a building, for example, cannot be 'an event' given its durability, certain points in the building's design, construction or use (e.g., the opening of a new building) can be event-like" (282). This physicality may become particularly important for social movements seeking to achieve cultural change. Schudson (1989) observes, "It seems obvious that culture works better if it is brought into the physical presence of a potential audience, and that it has more lasting impact if it is incorporated into a culturally sanctioned form of public memory " (163). In the end, the news is defined by what mass media outlets drag to the top: what gets more attention is not necessarily what is most important, impactful, or even accurate. But, like any other metric for reception, newsworthiness is tethered to social problems embraced by movements jockeying for coverage to reach the largest audience. The extent to which the Creation Museum accomplishes this for AiG is a key question.

In the case of the Creation Museum, the issue of plausibility becomes paramount. Given AiG's claims about the age of the Earth and the potential coexistence of dinosaurs and humans, its perspective is directly at odds with the beliefs and authority of the mainstream scientific community. Yet, as science and technology scholar Steven Epstein (2008) signals, "Science and technology do not merely change how we live our lives; they also lend power to those who speak in their name, and they offer new tools for establishing what counts as credible or true" (177). Whether the Creation Museum gains any traction in the media depends in part on how outsiders view its controversial stance on creation science and to what extent the museum is indeed recognizable as a museum.

Success for AiG would mean media attention. Coverage might suggest either that the museum is a laudable strategy or is perceived as a big mistake, but it helps to insert AiG into the public sphere and broader cultural conversation. Media coverage suggests that the museum may indeed pose significant questions about the interface between religion and science in public life and serve as a site to reframe the politics of plausibility. Or, at the very least, it is perceived as noteworthy enough to attract interest for its desired audiences. Ultimately, success in this case would imply sustained media attention and creation of a more permanent platform from which AiG can reach the masses.

Media Coverage: Magazine and Newspaper Articles from 1994 to 2018

The first part of the analysis is based on data from a range of magazines and newspapers.[16] I focus on the content of the media attention on creationism, not on its coverage of related protest events, as is conventional in scholarly literature.[17] I gathered data on what the media covered, when the coverage occurred, and which media outlets covered the story. By tracking references to AiG and its Creation Museum within the broader media coverage of creationism, I trace the public reception of AiG's efforts.

I also assess how the level of attention varies across different intended audiences. To capture differential coverage, articles used in the content analysis come from both mainstream and specialty media outlets.

Mainstream media outlets focus on reaching the broadest audience possible. Comparatively, specialty media outlets look to capture readers who share common interests and values. Christian media outlets, specifically targeting evangelical pastors and rank-and-file believers, frame issues biblically. Science media outlets' readers, typically scientists and science enthusiasts, are interested in attaining the latest scientific updates and gaining a better understanding of the natural world. Historically, creationism and evolution have divided these two communities. The analysis of media coverage is designed to show where AiG and its museum fits into this long-running opposition of claims.

I selected seven media sources according to a non-random purposive sampling approach designed to capture a range of perspectives and various circulation sizes.[18] I draw from three sources for mainstream media coverage and two sources for each type of specialty outlet. The total number of relevant articles is 1,719; the largest number of articles comes from mainstream media outlets (approximately 60%), science media outlets (approximately 30%), and the fewest from Christian evangelical media sources (approximately 11%) (table 5.1).[19]

TABLE 5.1. Magazine and Newspaper Articles from 1994 to 2018

Media Outlet	N (of articles)	Percent
Christian Evangelical Media Outlets	182	10.59
World	124	
*Christianity Today**	58	
Science Media Outlets	503	29.26
Reports of the National Center for Science Education	378	
Science Magazine (published by AAAS)	125	
Mainstream Media Outlets	1034	60.15
New York Times	745	
Chicago Tribune	162	
USA Today	127	
Total	1719	100

Christianity Today articles collection began in 1996 when the website was created.

Mainstream Media Outlets

The newspapers selected to represent the mainstream national media attention include the *New York Times* (New York Times Company, New York), the *Chicago Tribune* (Tribune Publishing, Illinois), and *USA Today* (Gannett Company, Virginia). Besides differences in location and ownership, the first two large-market newspapers are widely circulated: The *New York Times* is consistently one of the largest newspapers in terms of circulation and the *Chicago Tribune* is often among the top ten in the United States.[20] Meanwhile, *USA Today* is a unique source given its explicitly centrist, national focus and widespread distribution.[21]

Christian Evangelical Media Outlets

In 1956, Billy Graham founded *Christianity Today* in Carol Stream, Illinois, as a religious non-profit media ministry. The non-profit has grown into one of the largest evangelical multimedia companies worldwide. The publication has managed to keep up not only with religious and cultural shifts, but also with the latest technological innovations:

> with 6 print publications, several digital-only publications, and practical web and mobile resources that together reach over 2.5 million people every month, *Christianity Today* changes the people who change the world. Men and women—in the US and abroad—who are serious about their faith. Leaders and influencers—young and old—who are serious about wanting their lives to be used by God as a counterculture for the common good.[22] This Christian media source remains a longstanding and dominant voice of the evangelical community.[23]

The second Christian-oriented source I used to capture the evangelical media sphere is *World*, a magazine published by World News Group (WNG). Founded in 1951, WNG or, as it is otherwise known, *God's World Publication*, is a non-profit organization in Asheville, North Carolina. Similar to *Christianity Today*, WNG delivers a widely read magazine, website, radio program, and a host of podcasts. Regarded as a bit more controversial within the evangelical community for its outspoken coverage of internal movement dynamics, the publication's "About

Us" page plainly states, "*World* tries to be salt, not sugar." It goes on to specify what it envisions the magazine to represent:

> We stand for factual accuracy and biblical objectivity, trying to see the world as best we can the way the Bible depicts it. Journalistic humility for us means trying to give God's perspective. We distinguish between issues on which the Bible is clear and those on which it isn't. We also distinguish between journalism and propaganda: We're not willing to lie because someone thinks it will help God's cause.[24]

Together *Christianity Today* and *World* represent the two largest evangelical publications with both national and international audiences. Given their prominence, they provide a sense of how those within the evangelical community view both AiG and its YEC museum.

Science Media Outlets

Founded in Oakland, California, the National Center for Science Education (NCSE) emerged in 1983 during the height of court battles over creationism in the public schools. Serving as a clearinghouse for best practices in science education, NCSE is a leading non-profit advocacy organization directly engaging creationist challenges on all levels (local, state, and federal).[25] Its mission is "[t]o promote and to advance the teaching of science in the public schools, and to educate and inform the public about issues concerning science education through the dissemination of informative materials to schools, libraries, and interested individuals."[26] Under the determined leadership of Eugenie Scott, who became an increasingly well-known figure due to her role in prominent court cases, NCSE publishes a regular newsletter, *Report of the National Center for Science Education (RNSCE)*, six times a year.

The second science-oriented source is the popular magazine, *Science*, published by the American Association for the Advancement of Science (AAAS) based in Washington, DC. AAAS is a non-profit professional society with roots that go back to 1848. As a "leading voice for the interests of scientists worldwide," AAAS has maintained an active web presence since 1995.[27] It produces a variety of scholarly-oriented publications along with more accessible information in *Science*, which includes research summaries, commentary, and even information on science products.

Because of the scope and consistency of these publications, along with their interest in issues pertaining to evolution and creationism, both *RNCSE* and *Science* provide a comparable counter to the explicitly evangelical ministry-oriented publications of *Christianity Today* and *World*. All of the specialty media sources are non-profits, a point of contrast from the mainstream media sources, all of which are for-profit corporations.[28]

I considered all articles if: (1) any references were made to "creationism" or "creationist" or "creation museum," and (2) the publication date fell between January 1, 1994 and December 31, 2018.[29] The twenty-five-year period was determined by AiG's founding in 1994 and continued to 2018, more than a decade after the Creation Museum's opening in 2007. I sought to trace how media attention fared before and well after the opening event. I included all types of articles—news, opinion, letters to the editor—as I consider them all media attention. I saved and coded every article that explicitly mentioned the creationist movement in some capacity, regardless of its length, location in the newspaper, or detail in describing the event(s).[30]

While every sentence had the possibility of being coded, not all of them were, since any instance of a code was only counted once per article. I adopted this strategy for two reasons. First, I wanted to be able to determine how many unique articles captured a particular code at least once. Second, I sought to create a more conservative count estimate.[31] As the goal of the analysis is to compare patterns of media attention as a proxy for cultural reception, I did not want a handful of articles to drive the underlying patterns or exaggerate the count. Put another way, the analytic focus is on how many different days a publication decided to devote media attention to creationism, not how often an author used the same terminology within one article.

Given the emphasis on multiple sources across various types of media outlets, much of the focus in this analysis is on the frequencies and patterns of coverage. I do not analyze the qualities of the article's content, the placement of the article in the source, or whether the media attention was positive or negative. (I will focus on this in the blog posts later.) Instead, I follow the lead of social movement literature, which asserts that the level of media coverage alone for an event, SMO, or movement outcome can measure public influence.[32]

Media Coverage Trends and Patterns

Media attention to creationism varied over time. From 1994 to 2018, the median number published per year was fifty-one articles (1,719 articles total). The highest number of creationism articles was published in 2005 (345 articles) and the lowest number, in 1994–1995. Clearly, in 2005, Intelligent Design and the Dover trial in Pennsylvania attracted the lion's share of media attention, given that the parents' successful lawsuit against the school district's attempt to adopt Intelligent Design curriculum received extensive national coverage. The most dramatic drop in overall media coverage was from 2005 to 2006 (345 to 145 articles). Yet reviewing the median number of articles published per year between 2004 and 2006 (145), I found that the coverage is not limited to 2005. The pattern over time suggests that the Creation Museum's opening in 2007 brought the movement greater attention as well, since a median of 107 articles were published per year from 2007 to 2009. Coverage remained relatively steady from 2010 to 2018, but much more moderate with forty-five articles on average.

What kinds of topics were the focus of this coverage? How are articles on creationism framed? I constructed five context codes to trace various frames across time: education (science and Christian), legal, political, and sociocultural (see table 5.2 for search terms and descriptions).[33] While I coded each context separately, often one article referenced multiple contexts, and thus I coded all applicable contexts appropriately (1,569 codes in total).

Overall, education (36%) was the most common context for media attention on creationism. This outcome is unsurprising. The long-running combative history of local school boards hashing it out over curriculum choices in biology classrooms is a steadfast feature in media coverage. Yet, when legal and political contexts are separated from explicitly educational conversations, the sociocultural context emerges as second in frequency of media coverage (32%). This suggests that education and sociocultural contexts propel media attention, not just the recent history of court cases (legal context, approximately

TABLE 5.2. Contextual Codes

Search Terms	Brief Description
courts | legislation | plaintiff | defendant | Dover | Scopes | trial	Legal: References to legal system with some sort of reference to the creationist movement
Example: "As recent court cases in Kansas, Georgia, and Pennsylvania demonstrate, we are still, more than 80 years after the so-called Scopes monkey trial, suing one another over whether evolution ought to be taught in the schools, and for those who are opposed, it's not just an idle matter." (January 2009, *New York Times*)	
politic | elected | campaign | Congress | GOP | Republican | Democrat | electorate	Political: Politics discussion with reference to creationist movement, e.g., not just mention of Congress
Example: "In Republican and Democratic primaries conducted last week, pro-evolution candidates won party nominations for three of the five board seats that are up for reelection in November. Three of the board's other five seats are held by moderates. The results mean that, regardless of the individual winners in the November election, the board's composition will flip from its existing 6–4 conservative tilt to at least a 6–4 majority controlled by moderates." (August 2006, *Science*)	
culture | cultural | culture wars | culture clash | cultural divide | public understanding | public opinion | play | movie | theater | television | tv	Sociocultural: Cultural references to creationist movement or the public understanding of science within the context of creationism (non-technical)
Example: "Practicing healthy dialogue prepares us for when we feel fired at or worse—we find ourselves behind the verbal trigger. Such preparation also has missional benefits, as we find ourselves dissenting from the cultural norms or defending our faith. We must practice." (March 2016, *Christianity Today*)	
school board | classroom | teacher | science education | curriculum | bio homeschool | human evolution	Education: Needs to discuss some element of science education explicitly and not just a group with "Education" in the title, such as NCSE or an author's biography who is a teacher
christian schools | christian college | christian university | Liberty University| Christian Heritage College | Wheaton College | academ	Education: Regardless of whether it is positive or negative coverage, the article must be explicitly connected to Christianity and education

24% of coverage) as is presumed in much scholarship on creationism. Political context is relatively small, with only about 8% coverage.

The Creation Museum

Overall, 5.2% of the media coverage on creationism mentions the Creation Museum, while 14.2% mentions either the Creation Museum or AiG. The Museum received some attention during its earliest design phase from 1996 to 2000, and that attention slowly increased in 2004. Coverage of the Creation Museum reached its first peak in 2007 when it opened. However, other significant peaks in coverage include when Bill Nye and Ken Ham debated at the Creation Museum in 2014 and when AiG opened the Ark Encounter in 2016. The pattern suggests that beyond the development of the Creation Museum itself, other AiG movement activity fostered media attention for the movement overall. Much of the coverage consistently mentions controversy surrounding the event, often citing protestors like *Christianity Today*'s coverage of the Ark Encounter: "Visitors called the park 'breathtaking' with 'a lot of attention to details.' A group of atheists also turned out to protest."[34]

What kinds of outlets give the most attention? The Creation Museum was mentioned most frequently within mainstream outlets—39.8% compared to 36% in science outlets and 25% in Christian outlets. Yet out of the articles specifically covering the idea of creationism, the Creation Museum constituted 18% of all science media articles and 23% of all Christian media outlets' articles. Compare this to only 9% of all mainstream outlets. Interestingly, then, while articles referencing the Creation Museum were more frequently covered in mainstream media outlets, the specialty media outlets devoted more nuanced attention to the museum within its coverage of creationism, albeit in fewer articles when compared to daily news outlets. I revisit this pattern in further detail later in the blog coverage analysis.

From 1994 to 2018, media outlets referenced secular museums more consistently than any other type of Christian sociocultural site (the Creation Museum and other Christian attractions/museums). Approximately 17% of all specialty media outlets reference sociocultural sites. This suggests that while sociocultural sites received consistently moderate attention, secular sites seized greater attention than Christian sites. This was despite Christian sociocultural sites' best efforts to equate their own site's level of quality to secular sites. As *World* reports:

> The Creation Museum doesn't draw nearly the numbers of visitors as the nation's top science museums, which boast larger facilities and government funding. The Smithsonian's National Museum of Natural History in Washington attracted 5.8 million visitors in 2006; the Children's Museum in Indianapolis brought in 1.2 million that same year, according to a list compiled by *Forbes* magazine. "But for its size and budget, the museum has been an overwhelming success," founder Ken Ham said. "We made a decision quite a few years ago, that we wanted to do it first-class . . .

as good as you would see at museums or Disney World or Universal Studios," Ham said. "It's become an attraction in its own right, regardless of the message that we have here."[35]

As Ham demonstrates in the preceding passage, many Christian organizations compare their sites to secular sites to acknowledge their smaller scale and outsider status yet to assert their professionalism despite limited resources. Ham's and AiG's efforts to align the Creation Museum with other internationally well-known secular sites are attempts to acquire credibility through established markers of professionalism (e.g., the operating budget, attendance figures, and relative size of the museum). AiG's approach relies on global understandings of what it means to be a professional attraction, like the Smithsonian National Museum of Natural History's scientific credibility or Disney's status as a well-known tourist destination.

These widespread understandings can remain intact alongside the SMOs; the YEC movement regards the Creation Museum as its own version of an attraction, which is reflected in the words the media chooses to describe it. Alternatively, AiG could have used a new word or simply played down any mention of secular sites. Instead, AiG as well as other YEC movements cultivate this global/local tension as they seek to establish a professional attraction. And, it appears AiG is reasonably successful in doing so within the media. Social movement scholars likely expect the media coverage of sociocultural sites in the context of news stories about creationism broadly. But creationism scholars may be surprised by this factor because the coverage is not solely concentrated on what is happening in the classroom or courtroom, for instance.

Media attention to the Creation Museum as a "ground zero" for the culture wars between secularists and YEC coincides with a familiar finding in social movement literature. Increased coverage often follows bombastic mobilization efforts.[36] I argue the Creation Museum attracted attention because of its ability to draw together temporarily disruptive events within its overall non-disruptive efforts. It is, after all, a museum in the Cincinnati area, which hosts routine visitors every day and annual events on-site. This pattern is evident in similarly routine yet controversial events such as the Nye vs. Ham debate and the protestors at the Ark Encounter opening. All of these factors—disruptive and non-disruptive events, conflict, frequent events, and sustained on-site sociocultural activity—explain the rise in media attention and presumably also in public interest.

AiG and the Creationist Movement

How is AiG situated in the creationist movement, including the YEC branch and the broader former creationist branch that coincides with Intelligent Design? Throughout the late 1980s and 1990s, Intelligent Design leaders created more connections with mainstream, secular universities and officially maintain a religiously neutral position; meanwhile the roots of the movement are Christian and often overlapped with Young Earth Creationism. But the movement strategies varied. Intelligent design maintained a "tent strategy" where all religiously minded science enthusiasts were welcome regardless of affiliations or beliefs for movement insiders.[37] A "wedge strategy" was used to engage the broader public where Intelligent Design proponents would substitute religious language with more secular, non-sectarian references to a supernatural force.

The first step is to discern which internal movement strategies and tactics were covered by external media and influenced public opinion. The second step is to establish how media attention may or may not reflect internal movement trajectories—such as shifts in organizational prominence or dynamics between YEC and Intelligent Design.

Media coverage of the Creation Museum and AiG was most frequently framed in the sociocultural context (55.8%). A key peak in coverage for this framing occurred in 2007, when the Creation Museum opened. Ham's comments make it clear how AiG sought out this type of contextual framing, as *Christianity Today* reports:

> AIG president and CEO Ken Ham said he has wanted such a museum for more than two decades. "Twenty-five years ago, we didn't have all the arguments fine-tuned," Ham told CT. "This is part of the maturing of the biblical creationist movement . . . Christians have problems answering the questions of skeptics because churches and Christian colleges don't teach apologetics," Ham said. "The museum is a rallying point to call the church and culture back to the Word of God by confirming the Bible's accuracy!"[38]

As one might expect by now, the educational context (27.3%) was the second most prominent context in which the media referenced the Creation Museum or AiG. Both legal and political contexts were considerably less frequent. This confirms expectations that both AiG and the Creation Museum were received by the media as primarily sociocultural sites. Also, it points to a complex tension between the SMO's strategic goal to increase the public's awareness of it through media attention. The media frequently downplays AiG's tactic of institution-building as an act of protest because it lacks ties to institutional politics (courts and classrooms) and is neither violent nor disruptive (i.e., building a museum).[39] Instead, AiG engages in political activity but through other means. The goal is to shore up plausibility for its cultural efforts. It is not necessary for media coverage to frame it as a protest or social movement activity because the goal is simply to get noticed, consistently.

Moving to the broader movement, how do patterns of media attention compare between YEC and Intelligent Design? Specialty media outlets mentioned YEC slightly more often than Intelligent Design, with Christian media at 62% coverage and science media at 52% coverage (figure 5.1). On the other hand, Intelligent Design overwhelmingly dominates mainstream media coverage with more than 70% of the media coverage. These patterns reveal a stark bifurcation in specialized media outlets focused largely on YEC and mainstream media focused on Intelligent Design. While the Creation Museum receives modest coverage overall in the creationism media coverage, Intelligent Design's efforts in the classroom still garner a lot of attention. Interestingly, those presumably more familiar with creationism, like Christian or science specialty audiences, perceive YEC efforts as more newsworthy. This is not necessarily unexpected, but how coverage focused on Intelligent Design and YEC may operate in tandem is a prospect I return to later, in the conclusion of this book. Regardless, when examined at the movement level, Intelligent Design attracted the most coverage from mainstream sources, even though it was short-lived.

Online Efforts

Of course, not all movement tactics or media coverage were confined to specific physical sites. When comparing these physical institutions

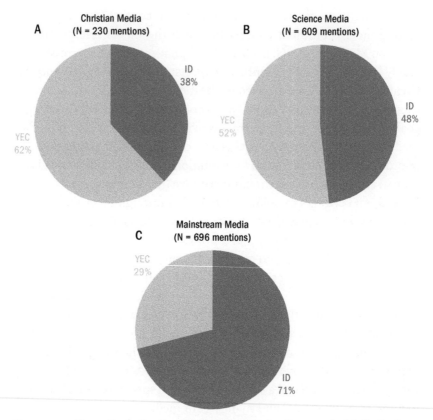

Figure 5.1a-c. Young Earth Creationism/Intelligent Design Coverage by Media Outlets

to online efforts there were sporadic patterns of attention. Online creationist-related efforts emerged in 1997, which demonstrates that both movement efforts and media coverage were relatively on pace with larger trends in the development of the internet.[40] From 1997 to 2018, media coverage of online efforts increased steadily, but peaked in 2009 and 2014. For instance, a 2009 *USA Today* article, written by the leaders of the BioLogos organization, showcased its online efforts:

> We have launched a website to spread this good news (www.biologos. org) and—we hope—to answer the many questions those of faith might have. BioLogos is a term coined by Francis Collins in his best seller *The Language of God: A Scientist Presents Evidence for Belief*. Collins, the

Christian scientist who led the Human Genome Project, joined "bios," or life, with "logos," or word, from the first verse in the book of John in the New Testament. The project aims to counter the voices coming from places such as the website Answers in Genesis, which touts creation scientists, and the Discovery Institute, a think tank in Seattle, that calls on Christians to essentially choose between science and faith.[41]

Citing one website as a means to counter other online presence of competing organizations, BioLogos made a clear attempt to strive for a different kind of broader public reach. Yet media coverage of these kinds of efforts, either specialty or mainstream media coverage, never comes close to surpassing the amount of attention devoted to physical sociocultural sites.

This pattern of media attention is in accordance with scholarly expectations. Social movement researchers and news media alike skew toward covering events when movement members are co-present and mobilizing for a protest, or when a large SMO is associated with a visible event.[42] Earl and Kimport (2011), on the other hand, anticipated that in the future, the focus would be more on tracking collaboration and less on physical co-presence (182). While contemporary research is mixed and coverage often varies depending on the type of movement (think of hacktivism), in this case, the SMOs have maintained an ongoing presence in media coverage.[43] AiG was a relatively early adopter of an active website. Its use of the web is organized around non-protest forms of action, such as the promotion of the SMOs and their physical sites, and around the dissemination of educational information and resources. Petitions and other forms of protest are rare. Yet their website generates a sizeable amount of traction–a recent report tracked more than 1.4 million visitors during a six-month period in 2018.[44]

AiG used a multipronged approach effort to introduce the museum and the organization itself to the largest audience possible. As the director of communications remarked during our interview about how the museum as a physical site compares to the website:

There's a wisdom, of course, in doing a lot of things online. Someone in Nigeria may never come to the creation museum or ever hear Ken Ham speak, but what I think is one of our strengths is the physical presence . . .

coming to the creation museum, they have a physical encounter with somebody that they may get excited about sponsoring the next project . . . When it comes to things like raising revenue and raising interest, there's nothing better than either you connect to a speaker, an event, or come to the physical plant. It's hard to build a relationship online. You're not connecting with a person typically. While we have a very strong online presence, and you've seen that, there's no substitute for having a physical connection rather than an electronic one.[45]

AiG's website and social media presence has two goals: first, to engage individuals potentially interested in its mission, or at least sympathetic to its efforts to advance its view of Christianity in the public sphere; and second, to reinforce the commitment of those who are already well versed in AiG's efforts and want to attend, follow up, or otherwise support the organization and its sponsored activity. Despite large metrics for its website, AiG regarded the museum as an anchor for its efforts—a place where interested members of the public could come see the "attraction" for themselves.

Audience Engagement: Blogging about the Creation Museum

How often is the Creation Museum discussed by regular visitors? How does the audience reception vary across bloggers who range in their support? Shifting to visitors and those directly interested in the Creation Museum, I examine personal blog posts to understand the characteristics of this individual-level engagement. Recent literature ranging in topical focus—from nursing professionalization to climate change denial—highlights the breadth of blogging activity online, or the blogosphere. Blogging is a form of social media that began shortly after the internet took hold and continues to this day in various forms, making it well positioned for social science analysis.[46] Drawing from 151 blog posts published from 2005 to 2018, I trace patterns in what is identified by the bloggers as interesting, inflammatory, or otherwise noteworthy to their readers. I show how a blogger's stance toward AiG and its museum's mission coincides with the extent to which they find the Creation Museum to be effective, sometimes in counterintuitive ways.

Why blog posts? The advantage of blog posts is that individuals select what to share with their readers, both text and images, unprompted or biased by any kind of survey. Those who strongly support or oppose may be as likely to create a blog post—similar to open-ended questions in survey results. Yet examining blog posts potentially increases the ability to capture a broader public's varied responses, many of whom may have indifferent or neutral reactions, for example, and choose to simply describe the site. I did not want to capture only sheer coverage amount or frequency. Audience attendance is a better metric for that, which is largely between 200,000 to 300,000 people per year despite media attention to some variation.[47] Instead, the ability to work with a feasible sample size for manual coding, assisted by Atlas.ti software, allows me to account for contextually thorny issues like satire, which is particularly relevant in this context as I'll show.[48]

To produce a dataset of blog post coverage, I piloted a series of Google searches of blog posts that are open to the public.[49] I identified which keywords produced the most valid results, not just about creationism, but specifically about AiG's Creation Museum.[50] I searched through sixteen popular blog hosting sites.[51] Since the Ark Encounter opened in 2016, posts that primarily focused on that attraction but also mentioned AiG or the Creation Museum were included as well (15 blog posts). WordPress was overwhelmingly the most common site for individuals to host their blog (approximately 57.6%), followed by LiveJournal (13.9%), among others.[52]

From 2007 to 2018, 151 blog posts from 101 personal blogs discussed the Creation Museum.[53] The coverage is relatively steady throughout the twelve-year period. The largest number of posts occurred from 2007 to 2009 (15 posts per year on average) and 2013 to 2015 (22 posts per year on average). On average, bloggers with a site posted once about the Creation Museum (81.2%), 7.9% of bloggers posted twice, and roughly 10.9% of bloggers post more than twice. In terms of how bloggers who posted about the Creation Museum self-identify, the most common were those who posted about a wide range of topics (47.2%); 36.8% were religiously oriented bloggers, and 16% were science-oriented. Comparatively, since most bloggers only posted about the Creation Museum once, the topic of blog posts were split evenly across each area, with approximately 33% coverage in general, religious, or science.

Overwhelmingly, 77.5% of blog posts have at least one image. On average, bloggers shared seven photos per post. What do bloggers post most? They focus on the Creation Museum exhibits, with approximately 54% of the photos dedicated to them. Comparatively, 18.2% of blog posts include snapshots of individuals and their families while they were on-site. The predominance of images in blog posts highlights that it is equally important to assess both images and texts for contextual evidence.

Ranging Levels of Support

What kinds of stances do bloggers who post about the Creation Museum take? Overall, I found thirty-nine posts to be generally supportive (25.8%), ninety-six posts unsupportive (64%), and sixteen posts neutral (10.6%). Eighty percent of the supporters self-identify as Christian, many of whom are mothers with school-age children, and a few are explicitly invested in critiquing evolution. For example, here is one blogger's description: "I am a children's novelist . . . But before I am an author, I am a Christ-follower." This post is typical of supporters:

> If you've ever felt like you're the only person left in the world who doesn't buy into evolution, go to the Creation Museum. If you've struggled with balancing your faith with what the scientific community passes off as "fact," go to the Creation Museum. If you're looking for solid science that does not contradict God's Word, get yourself to the Creation Museum in Kentucky. It's run by Answers in Genesis, and every hypothesis, every theory, every answer is carefully weighed against the authority of scripture. If it doesn't align, it's discarded. My family and I made a stop at the museum on our vacation last week. It's a beautiful facility—bright, colorful, and kid-friendly. And their message is a super antidote to the crap constantly dished out in our schools. It's nice for Christian parents to have some solid backing by real scientists.[54]

As the blogger notes, the Creation Museum helps them feel less isolated in their minority worldview and acknowledges the challenges people face when balancing faith and science, and in turn finds the creation scientists compelling. This kind of reflection occurs in the context of a family vacation in what they perceive as a well-done facility that feels modern and family-oriented. Finally, this visitor circles back to the feeling of not fitting into mainstream society, giving the museum's message equal footing to secular institutions such as the public school classroom and declaring the museum the winner. The blogger found the Creation Museum plausible, and not simply because it feels expensive or slick.

Those labeled as neutral are largely generalist bloggers focused on travel, cultural attraction reviews, and a few who identify more with old earth creationism. They did not appear to indicate one opinion over another, and they did not provide a balanced review of pros and cons. As one blogger, who describes himself as focused on writing about "oddities," reports, "I'm not sure about who is right and who is wrong here, but the irony behind a picture of an empty space in the museum with this sign did make me smile: 'This Space is Still Evolving.' You have to admit, that's pretty funny. Check the video at the bottom, for a tour of the Creation Museum and more insights on this place."[55] Notice that no particular stance is taken by the blogger, who identifies something charming, funny, or otherwise interesting, and largely focuses on providing readers a descriptive tour of the Creation Museum or the Ark Encounter.

Overwhelmingly, however, most bloggers indicate a general lack of support for the Creation Museum and AiG. Using the title "Welcome to the Anti-Natural History Museum. Please Check Science at the Door," one blogger captures the central themes across many similar bloggers' posts: a refusal to acknowledge the site as a museum and persistent questions about the scientific credibility of the information presented (and about creation science in general).[56] Most identify as general bloggers or specifically science enthusiasts and educators. Others identify as atheists or non-believers. What is telling is that individuals who do not support the museum overwhelmingly are the ones who post the most about it. On one hand, it is not surprising given that outliers were expected to be the most prolific; people with strong convictions against the AiG and the Creation Museum will want to discuss it. On the other hand, it also suggests that these bloggers find it noteworthy, if not concerning. If the museum were simply wacky and poorly done, then bloggers' coverage would likely wane much faster and be more infrequent over time. To address this nuanced dynamic in which a blogger may vehemently disagree with the Creation Museum but still find particular aspects impressive or striking, I examined within each blog post the different sentiments about the museum's effectiveness. While the level of support was assigned once overall to each blog post, effectiveness could be assigned as frequently as statements fit the description, even if one statement contrasted with other statements in the same post.

Effectiveness

Surprisingly, more bloggers made comments about the effectiveness of these sites (177 statements) for the Creation Museum, or the Ark Encounter after 2016, compared to the sites being perceived as ineffective (105 statements). Many bloggers referred to the Lucy exhibit as being particularly effective. Approximately 10% of the blog posts mention the Lucy exhibit and often document it with images. As one atheist blogger recounts:

> One display I found really interesting was their model of Lucy, the three-million-year-old fossil. Holograms of the fossil finds were projected onto the three-dimensional model which I found to be fascinating and a great way to present an incomplete fossil find. Of course, the point of the holograms was to demonstrate how the very incompleteness of Lucy left her open to interpretation. The argument was that those who reconstruct the Lucy specimen bring their scientific bias to the interpretation and, therefore, choose to see her as more human whereas someone with a Biblical bias would choose to reconstruct her as more apelike. I thought that was actually an interesting interrogation of how biases influence concepts and thought there was a chance that would set the tenor of the discussion in the museum, a dialogue between different stances.[57]

This level of detailed engagement stood in contrast to many of the exhibits' write-ups posted from this attendee, but it was also characteristic of many blog posts about Lucy. The use of the hologram technology did stand out to many attendees, but so did the argument that researchers' interpretation of the fossil evidence could reasonably vary and may be informed by other presuppositions. It was perceived as compelling and plausible.

Other exhibits tend to split the audience along more predictable lines. Science enthusiasts took issue with the Garden of Eden or Noah's Ark.

Religiously oriented bloggers focused on how combative some of the AiG's apologetics tools were and their potential effectiveness for engaging a less committed audience. For instance, one of the religious bloggers concerned about AiG's style of apologetics made this comment:

> The intention of the Creation Museum is to defend the truthfulness of the Bible and to point people to Christ. I suspect that many of these paleontologists [referencing a group visiting from a nearby conference] were more likely to walk out of the museum with their minds hardened against Christianity . . . Will it be because of their atheistic, anti-Christian world views (not all paleontologists are atheists, nor are they all hostile to Christianity), or because the museum presents something that just isn't true (not required by the Bible, not scientifically accurate) as apologetics?[58]

Given this frustration with AiG's apologetics approach, more bloggers argued consistently that the Creation Museum was effective more for others (55.9%) than for themselves (44.1%). Referring to Christians who do not believe in a literal interpretation of the Book of Genesis as "compromisers" or insisting that the Earth is less than 10,000 years old due to flood geology theories concerned some bloggers about AiG's approach toward defending their faith. These were visitors who may otherwise view AiG as having some arguments worth sharing with others.

Interestingly, about 30% of those who found the museum to be effective in some aspect (for themselves or others) were the same bloggers who were unsupportive. This lends credence to initial trends that more blog posts were negative than positive in support of the Creation Museum. Yet many of them were concerned about the efficacy of the site. As the blogger who titled her post "Anti-Natural History Museum" shared:

> a woman standing next to me points out an animatronic dinosaur looming over our heads to her daughter, who's sitting in a stroller . . . I ask her what she thinks of the museum. "It's so state-of-the-art," she tells me . . . That doesn't mean she won't visit traditional natural history museums . . . "We're actually members of the Cincinnati museum," she tells me. I ask her what she makes, then, of the scientific facts put forth there. "Oh, we just don't agree with it. We just look at the things, but don't agree with the dating."[59]

Since this blog post excerpt focuses on conveying a discussion the blogger had while visiting the Creation Museum, it is interesting to note the level of detail and nuance they identify. In the broader blog post, this atheist attempts to forgo the standard mocking in favor of highlighting an example of a fellow visitor who was impressed by the Creation Museum. Yet the implications of the person's comments concerned them because the blogger could see how effective the Creation Museum was when the person compared the Creation Museum to nearby mainstream natural history museums. It unearths a strategy AiG actively promotes as well: selective and critical engagement with mainstream natural history museums rather than avoidance. When some dissenting bloggers sensed that other visitors could engage actively across mainstream and creationist sites, they deemed this ability as unfortunate and alarming from their vantage point, shaken by the idea that others could find the museum so plausible.

Continuing this theme of plausibility, a sentiment of professionalism emerged among many of the blog posts. A generalist blogger conveyed a presumably frequent assumption among the broader public:

> I expected a sort of homemade museum—something really cute, modest, wacky, and with a kind of charm. Nope, this place is BIG, with extensive grounds too. It's slick, like a theme park. The exhibits themselves are, in terms of quality, as good as any museum in the country and are [sic] use a lot of pseudo-science. This pseudo-science includes lots of graphs, charts, and maps that are completely inaccurate, but appear to give the exhibit legitimacy.[60]

Defying their own stereotype, the size, quality, and format of the museum all feel familiar to the blogger despite the creationist context. An admitted old earth creationist blogger went even further in comparing the Creation Museum's professionalism and mainstream museums: "As I anticipated, the exhibits at the museum are all of the highest quality. Whether the displays were animatronic dinosaurs, dioramas of the garden [sic] of Eden, fossils, mounted insects, or reconstructions of hominids, they were at the same level of quality one would expect to find in the Smithsonian Institution."[61]

The line between professionalism—signaled by sentiments conveying quality—and unprofessionalism—signaled by arguments about exhibits being cheap, tricks, or gimmicky—is arguably blurred for many bloggers. Yet how they interpret it ultimately reflects their position. For instance, the cost of building the museum (more than $27 million), or the Ark Encounter (which received city tourism bonds) or the price tag for admission were often mentioned across blog posts. Perceptions were largely bound to individuals' overall support of or distaste for the site; supporters found the construction costs served as a testament to its professionalism, and detractors balked at the cost of admission. Overall, only four blog posts mentioned examples framing different components as either professional or unprofessional within the same post. Otherwise those in support found it to be professional and effective; non-supporters did not. But one-third of the non-supporters were not sure how to rectify the professionalism they perceived at AiG's Creation Museum. Another twist took a satirical turn.

Satire

Predictably, given the general lack of stated support among a sizeable group of bloggers, more than a third of them (38.4%) include a satirical statement or image. Approximately 16.5% of the blog posts include satirical photos ranging from people saddled on the triceratops (a side exhibit that has since been removed), individuals interacting with the human model figures in exhibits, or an animated image referencing the Flintstones. Indeed, 30% of the satirical photos focus on dinosaurs. For example, PZ Meyers, a well-known blogger who is a biology professor and ardent critic of the Creation Museum, is pictured riding the infamous triceratops with a saddle on it. As described by another blogger, "The best part of today by far, though, was when PZ himself got atop the famous saddle-wearing triceratops . . . I've made my own version of a 'motivational poster' with the picture, in honour of the day."[62] Interestingly, even non-satirical photos often depict museum-goers' active engagement with dinosaurs, for example, of people posing with their heads in the mouth of a looming dinosaur. Notably, many Christian families posted the professional portraits they had taken in the museum lobby, which include a T-Rex approaching them ominously, courtesy of a green screen backdrop.

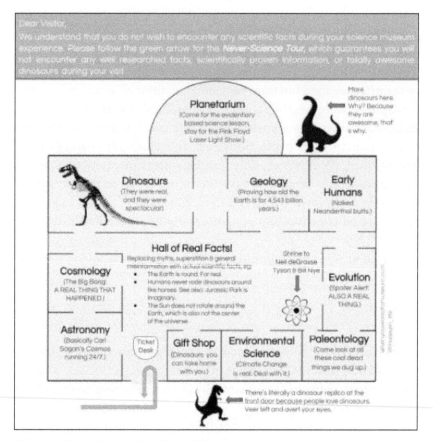

Figure 5.2. Never-Science Tour, Blogger Generated

Finally, after chatting online and reviewing the Creation Museum's website, a museum professional went so far as to create a detailed natural history museum map they call "Never-Science Tours." In figure 5.2, the text above the floor plan states: "Dear Visitor, We understand that you do not wish to encounter any scientific facts during your science museum experience. Please follow the green arrow for the Never-Science Tour, which guarantees you will not encounter any well-researched facts, scientfically proven information, or totally awesome dinosaurs during your visit."[63] Their motivation for creating this tour came from a Facebook thread where another museum professional conveyed dismay about having to curate tours they give in a mainstream science museum presuambly for religious groups that want to avoid what are perceived as charged exhibits on human origins and evolution, among other topics.[64] Notice in figure 5.2 the centrality of dinosaurs and the presumed general common topical structure of any science museum. It becomes clear that the audience, regardless of their perspective, is familiar with what a science museum should look like and what topics should be addressed. Accordingly, AiG weaves its perspective into that set of assumptions and, regardless of how the audience receives that point of view, the organization appears to be well on its way to achieving "museum-ness" among the public, even to some bloggers' chagrin.

Measuring Media Attention Success

This chapter focuses on the broader reception of the Creation Museum and what media attention might signify in terms of success for AiG and the YEC movement. The Creation Museum receives attention across different types of outlets and bloggers, but overall, its share of media coverage on creationism is moderate; it neither dominates the conversation nor withers into obscurity.

Media attention on creationism increased overall from 1994 to 2018. This was a period when most scholars discussed the movement as generally limited to state-level courtroom battles, with the exception of Pennsylvania's Dover Trial in 2005. But coverage of the Creation Museum differs from the coverage of the court case, as the former is not limited to the period of active debate. It is a building, open every day, hosting numerous people and events. Conflict occurs on-site (e.g., counter-demonstrators, negative media attention) and additional movement efforts are grounded in the place itself. Nevertheless, the museum is an unfamiliar and somewhat unexpected tactic for the YEC movement. Media attention suggests that AiG and its Creation Museum have already succeeded. The museum was mentioned in 5.2% of articles on creationism across all media outlets (including ID efforts); together with references to AiG, coverage is approximately 14.2%. AiG has edged its way into a public sphere that was initially, if not continually, indifferent to its goals. To break out and appear as a "new development" is challenging. For the AiG to receive media attention not only when the Creation Museum opened in 2007, but also throughout its operation and the subsequent opening of related sites almost a decade later, is a solid indicator of some success.

Cultural change is not an easy, tractable outcome to pin down. According to social movement scholar William Gamson's (1998) well-known discussion of movement outcomes, success is signaled when an SMO is regarded as speaking on behalf of the movement. AiG unarguably forged ahead in the YEC movement. These patterns suggest two insights. First, a physical site has a staying power social movement literature currently underestimates and that cultural sociologists do not typically connect to collective organizing capacities. Second, the Creation Museum and sites like it matter for the movement's persistence, as it continues to attract media coverage and advance the movement's efforts.

Other patterns of media attention suggest AiG's presence on the internet is also important, but in an unexpected way. Online efforts do receive media attention, but never surpass Christian sociocultural sites. AiG uses its website to gain leverage to subvert some of the previous control that conventional media outlets wielded in disseminating and framing information.

By way of blog posts, coverage is largely unsupportive but not entirely critical. Many find the museum effective, even if not for themselves. With ability to experience AiG's arguments and see how well it displays them, many bloggers appear to be persuaded to take AiG seriously, even if that feeds into more support for AiG's opponents, including evolution science education, mainstream museum professionals, or secularist groups. Otherwise, many Christians who attended with high hopes appear to feel that AiG more than delivered. AiG strengthens and continues to build its base, as evident in some visitors' comments about their experience attending both the Creation Museum and the Ark Encounter. Overall, these media attention trends suggest that AiG has succeeded; so many other SMOs' tactics never receive coverage, let alone sustain across the years.

Conclusion

The Future of Plausibility Politics

Why did creationists build a museum? The short answer is because the Creation Museum would be unexpected. Who would anticipate that an extreme, creationist group would build something that professional—or that it would endure for so long? Throughout *Creating the Creation Museum*, I argue AiG's success is about a distinction between *accuracy* and *plausibility*. Rather than making claims to the accuracy of knowledge, AiG's focus is to provide enough evidence to make its narrative *plausible* to a broader public. I analyze the Creation Museum as a site of social movement activity, a place to contest the secular mainstream, to persuade people of AiG's point of view, and to provide believers new narratives to defend their beliefs. The Creation Museum possesses many typical museum features—and just as a natural history museum reinforces the credibility of evolutionary theories, the Creation Museum legitimates creation science.

In our walk through the museum in chapter 1, I show that AiG built a museum to proclaim a point of view that may resonate with a much broader audience than critics and scholars frequently acknowledge. Throughout the historical review of the creationist movement in chapter 2, I examine how social movement leaders developed in the Creation Museum an opportunity to convey a clear target (secular culture) and a physical anchor for asserting AiG's grievances. Internal factionalism led to AiG's focus on building its own site, which demonstrates how cultural sites are not neutral and how internal resistance and protests may occur. AiG developed the museum to dominate the creationist organizational field and to try something else because other strategies failed.

By displaying an alternative argument for others to see, touch, feel, and hear, I show in chapters 3 and 4 how sites like the Creation Museum present an experiential opportunity, a sense of the broader movement for attendees. It also allows rank-and-file members to support the movement—whether it is through monetary donations or in-kind services to help maintain the site. I examine how a social movement physically anchors its efforts to engage in plausibility politics. AiG created its own plausible site to showcase its professionalism; they know how to present creationism in a way that is forceful, but more compelling than previous efforts. AiG directly challenges the secular mainstream status quo and does so by using the material signifiers of scientific authority: museums and their objects.

Finally, analyzing media outlets and bloggers' discussion, I explore in chapter 5 what the general public—a mix of intellectual sympathizers, antagonists, and curious folks who fall somewhere in between—think about the Creation Museum. A site creates a tangible entity on which all parties can focus their support or their protests. More generally, it provides an opportunity for audiences to explore other possibilities with minimal effort or commitment, thus gaining a clearer sense of the movement as a whole. The professional quality of the museum is frequently mentioned in antagonistic media coverage as an example of why strong opposition is needed. Bloggers are largely unsupportive but not entirely critical. Many are concerned about the potential effectiveness of the museum for others who hold any feelings of embattlement with the secular mainstream. It is important to note that, with its museum, AiG bypasses external metrics of success or failure like that of a school board decision or courtroom ruling. AiG maintains its own attendance records and can influence the narrative of its successes or struggles.

Researchers often view the success of a social movement's site as a byproduct shaped by more typical movement factors such as the availability of resources, a receptive political environment available to be marshaled for support, and the movement's internal culture. In *Creating the Creation Museum*, however, I found that movement-created sites are not just a result of these typical factors. I examined how the qualities of a physical site influence a movement's success directly. To assess the plausibility embedded in movement-built sites, we must better understand the social relationships connected to them. I show how a site's physicality can affect whether targeted audiences see a movement's claims as credible. Movement actors make intentional choices about their own sites that subsequently shape their ability to acquire more resources and influence their claims' effectiveness for garnering political favor and the ways their movement culture evolves. It is difficult to determine whether these alternative sites mobilize new supporters or simply reflect the outcome of existing adherents' efforts. Do they cause movements to extend their reach or are these sites a consequence, a result of core members' efforts? I find both are possible at different points in the movement trajectory. By contextualizing the Creation Museum in the broader creationist movement, in chapter 2, I unpack how the Creation Museum was first an outcome of long-term movement efforts. Later, in chapters 3 through 5, I demonstrate the impact of its operation during the following decade and how it shaped the persistence of the movement, expanded its reach among the public, and spurred additional sites such as the Ark Encounter.

The need to better understand what, how, and why social movements build sites does not subside in light of the internet and the rise of digital tactics. Rather, the need to understand becomes more urgent given the patterns of media coverage, to take one example of a movement's reach. Recent scholarly attention focuses on the use and power of social media for mobilizing movement adherents and for sustaining new members. Yet, media and popular attention often still focus on the physical setting of movement activities—think of Zuccotti Park for the Occupy Wall Street Movement, Tahrir Square for the Arab Spring, or the streets of Ferguson, Missouri for the Black Lives Matter movement. Creationists wield this to their advantage. The Creation Museum is a building, open every day, hosting large numbers of people and events. If conflict arises, it typically occurs on-site in the form of counter-demonstrators or negative media attention. Additional movement efforts use the place itself as a platform from which to engage and sometimes antagonize, like the debate between Bill Nye and Ken Ham. These kinds of public-facing sites extend face-to-face interactions in a lower risk environment. It is not just about protests in the streets or sit-ins but planned attendance at events, which foster internal value for supporters, cementing a sense of shared identity and connection to the movement. In other words, the built environment normalizes social movement tactics since it proceeds in a way that is "business as usual" and not only during charged events such as protests. It is built for the long haul.

The Creation Museum is not representative or typical, but when studying social movements, this is an asset. It reveals more about how

AiG's alternative worldview resonates with members of the public who seek to resurrect a conservative status quo across multiple institutions. *Culturally*, these adherents want heteropatriarchy to remain unquestioned. *Politically*, they want to revitalize concerted evangelical lobbying tactics dating back to the Moral Majority of the 1970s. *Scientifically*, they want observable data and for the Bible and other sources of authoritative knowledge to be deemed relevant and consulted when data are incomplete or unknown. Finally, *religiously*, these believers want the country to see itself as a Christian nation. These institutional ideals are bound together to form one cohesive narrative on display, despite their anachronistic origins. Ultimately, the Creation Museum and later the Ark Encounter anchor the movement for outsiders so that when other sites emerge, such as the Museum of the Bible (MOTB) in Washington, DC, they are positioned to yoke themselves to these broader-reaching, less extreme sites, securing their continued relevance and affirming steady persistence.

The Future of Plausibility Politics

In 2007, the Creation Museum opened its doors in the midst of the country reeling from the Great Recession. Less than a year later, President Barack Obama became the first African American elected to the Oval Office. Sweeping progressive social change felt imminent to many. President Obama was decidedly pluralistic in his calls for reform—both in terms of repositioning the United States in the global landscape and re-envisioning domestic social policies. He was a steadfast champion of science and technology and was the first president to sign a bill protecting the religious freedom of non-believers.[1] Yet more than just a decade later, not much feels the same. Over time, Republicans reclaimed the majority in Congress. As of 2014, fewer Republicans believe in evolution than they did just a few years ago in 2009.[2] And, as the 2016 election approached, many evangelical leaders professing "Never Trump" began to concede. An overwhelming 80% of white evangelicals voted for Donald Trump, ushering in his presidency.[3] Afterward, some evangelical leaders declared that it was all in God's plan to anoint him as the leader.[4] Trump questions the need and expense of scientific data collection, appointed a secretary of education who is sympathetic to alternative scientific worldviews, and assigned leaders to the Department of Justice who consider Christians among the most in need of religious freedom protections. Yet Trump's presidency is not all that happened in the nation's capital to create a more welcoming environment for the plausibility of creationism.

Most people in the United States generally agree that the Bible is an important historical document, even if they do not elevate it as a sacred text for themselves personally. At first pass, then, sites like MOTB appear relatively neutral. Yet there is another history at play here, which is unevenly discussed among the broader public. It is a history of concerns over secularization and the broader implications of a pluralistic society that is less Christian-centric. These are concerns that both MOTB and the Creation Museum share.

Located just off the National Mall in Washington, DC, the MOTB opened in 2017. Walking into its sprawling 430,000-square-foot space spread across eight floors, history looms large. The cascading set of glass stairs leads visitors to the first floor, where a sign reads, "Perhaps no other book in history has had a greater impact than the Bible." While biblical quotes and testaments to the beauty of God are found easily throughout the museum, the role of history and historical artifacts grounds the experience for visitors. Exhibits explore the Bible's influence on the founding members of the United States and present various historical interpretations of the Christian scriptures. For instance, the museum juxtaposes the vantage point of slaves and slaveholders to underscore how the Bible may be read distinctly and often in opposition with itself. Throughout MOTB, the Bible is treated as both a sacred icon and a historical object whose academic study is associated conventionally with seminaries and divinity schools rather than secular, public institutions. For its more than two million visitors, one central takeaway from the Museum of the Bible becomes clear: visitors should approach the Bible as a historical artifact that requires serious and sustained attention by everyone.[5]

MOTB is illustrative of a larger question about how various members of the public relate to the academy. Given long-standing distrust or negative associations with the academy's perceived secularity, social science research continually suggests that many religious and political conservatives do not hold secular institutions—including science—in as high a regard as the rest of the public.[6] However, they still believe in science as an approach or a set of tools with which to better understand the world around us.

Historical efforts to distance Christian ideals and norms—specifically its Protestant roots—from central social and political institutions in the United States are at the root of the perceived cultural crisis presented in the Creation Museum. Social phenomena such as same-sex marriage, racism, and abortion are regarded as social problems constitutive of this larger cultural crisis, spurred by humanity's rejection of the authority of biblical text. Building off the historical sense of urgency, fundamentalists initially cultivated around this concern in the late nineteenth century, conservative evangelicals and their network of colleges and organizations embraced a moral righteousness. Throughout the twentieth century, many would insist on closer readings of the Bible as a guide for sociopolitical actions and scholarship.[7] Creationists drawing from the cultural crisis ideology focus on a broader moral indignation across educational systems, the media, and politics rather than a narrow emphasis on the religious roots of a singular perceived social problem. Creationists lament the erosion of a Christian United States, specifically a Christianity that does not emphasize biblical literalism.[8] Where does MOTB fit into this history?

The chairman of the Museum of the Bible's board and primary funder, Steve Green, is the CEO of arts and crafts store Hobby Lobby, and his family founded the national chain. They are MOTB's primary funding force, contributing more than $500 million to it and its vast collection of historical biblical artifacts. The family's religiously conservative philanthropy and political stance is well known due to the 2014 Supreme Court case *Burwell v. Hobby Lobby*, in which the store successfully fought to deny medical coverage to their employees following the contraceptive mandate in the Affordable Care Act. The founders' background positions them as receptive to creationism.

Yet, what ties, if any, exist between the Creation Museum and MOTB? Some scholars argue that we should draw minimal meaningful connections between MOTB and the Creation Museum. The sites are vastly distinct and reflect a deep split within the evangelical community. Christa Ballard Tooley and Matthew Milliner, two faculty from the evangelical Wheaton College, argue in a *Washington Post* article titled "The Ark vs. the Covenant" that the Creation Museum reflects an outdated fundamentalist "Ark" model in which only believers will be saved from God's judgment. Instead, the Museum of the Bible reflects "the covenant between God and all creation that followed the flood [which] entailed both accountability and critical embrace."[9] For scholars like Tooley and Milliner, who are embedded within the historic evangelical network of colleges and universities, the stark contrast between the two museums could not be more pronounced: "The embattled ark mentality of the Creation Museum and the engaging covenant approach of the Museum of the Bible finally help us see the historic difference between fundamentalists and evangelicals."[10] Drawing a distinction between fundamentalists' embattlement and evangelical engagement is of long-standing importance for many within Christian communities.

More explicit supporters feel the critical attention directed toward the Museum of the Bible is just another example of biased media coverage. As the website editor of the *Creation Evolution Headlines* laments, "Inviting people to 'consider' what the Bible says is not the same as pushing religion on them, since people can freely choose to visit the museum or not. But the fact that the Green family is Christian and wished to have people 'consider' the Bible was enough to send secular reporters into attack mode."[11] Skepticism about MOTB's mission is viewed as a by-product of partisan journalism.

Still, some other academics question the nonsectarian framing of the museum. They suggest that places such as MOTB serve as rallying sites for strengthening a broader swath of evangelicals to sympathize, if not outright identify, with calls for a more sustained engagement with the Bible. In their in-depth research on Hobby Lobby and the Green family, professors in theology and divinity schools Candida Moss and Joel Baden lay bare how the contemporary version of the Museum of the Bible's mission shifted over time—a trend that the Green family downplays. From 2010, they cite the IRS nonprofit paperwork submitted on behalf of the museum's foundation, in which the focus centered on elevating the word of God and "to inspire confidence in the absolute authority and reliability of the Bible."[12] By 2012, this language disappeared, and statements about engagement and education appeared. When questioned, the Green family denied that this broader shift was significant or reflective of any substantial changes. Yet their interviews with scholars previously associated with MOTB and detailed investigation leave Moss and Baden to conclude otherwise. They write:

> The difficulty is that the museum portrays itself to the public as something else: It presents itself as a nonsectarian independent organization, intimates that it contains the best academic research available, and claims to issue an open invitation to everyone. These may be sincere and well-intentioned claims, but they are impossible to support.[13]

A few journalists go even further. Katherine Stewart forcefully declared in a *New York Times* op-ed:

> The museum is a safe space for Christian nationalists, and that is the key to understanding its political mission. The aim isn't anything so crude as the immediate conversion of tourists to a particular variety of evangelical Christianity. Its subtler task is to embed a certain set of assumptions in the landscape of the capital.[14]

Stewart highlights the strong ties between the museum and Secretary of Education Betsy DeVos, whose family's foundation provided generous support for MOTB.[15] When asked by reporters about the political significance of opening the museum in Washington, DC, the museum's staff indicated that a consultant merely suggested that this location offered access to a steady flow of visitors.[16]

While MOTB maintains that it "is an innovative, global, educational institution whose purpose is to invite all people to engage with the Bible," its own framing as an apolitical, pluralistic museum is hard to justify.[17] Its positioning is well suited for some national leaders. For the first time in more than a century, a weekly Bible study group is hosted in the US Cabinet, which Vice President Mike Pence and Secretary DeVos, among others, attend.[18] The Bible study is led by Ralph Drollinger, a pastor who frequently holds events at MOTB. Drollinger founded Capitol Ministries—a non-profit organization that convenes meetings in many state legislatures across the United States. The organization's long-term political and religious aspirations are not ambiguous given its mission: "Making Disciples of Jesus Christ in the Political Arena Throughout [*sic*] the World."[19] Drollinger's political, religious, and sociocultural views align with AiG's positions. For example, both entities believe that the United States should eliminate LGBT rights such as marriage equality and that women should not hold leadership positions in the church. As scholarship and writers like Stewart have noted, the political influence and religiously conservative roots of MOTB are remarkable. The museum is part of the elite and politically influential arm of the broader evangelical community positioned to remain influential for years to come.

Revisiting the ties between the Creation Museum and the Museum of the Bible, evidence from the Creation Museum suggests multiple long-lasting network ties, collaborations, and overall support. In 2012, the Creation Museum hosted a traveling exhibit from the Museum of the Bible "Verbum Domini," which showcased rare biblical texts. The former chief operating officer at Museum of the Bible, Cary Summers, was a long-term consultant for the Creation Museum. And, on his blog introducing MOTB, Ken Ham features a picture of him and his wife attending the museum's opening gala. He goes on to outline the complementary relationship between the Creation Museum and the Ark Encounter, "The Ark and Creation Museum's focus is on apologetics, particularly in regard to Genesis, which is the foundation of our Christian doctrine, and on the gospel of Jesus Christ. *The Museum of the Bible's emphasis is to get a conversation going about God's Word, have people be interested in the Bible, and see people reading it.*"[20] Ham's framing of the relationship between the Creation Museum and MOTB makes it plain how AiG sees itself as the more focused Christian ministry follow-up to MOTB's broader appeal to educate a range of visitors about the historical significance of the Bible. In so doing, he maintains the evangelizing mission of the creationist movement while leaving intact the public appearance that MOTB is a more neutral institution.

This move lends credibility to AiG, given the prominence, scale, and influence of MOTB's operation in Washington, DC, yet it does not put AiG in a position to compromise its own long-term movement goals. Interestingly, however, MOTB has not cited AiG or the Creation Museum anywhere on its website or in its materials since it opened in 2017. The absence of any mentioned connections is striking given the multi-layered relationship between the two institutions, including exhibit collaboration, explicit ongoing public support from Ken Ham, and shared broader goals as outlined in MOTB's previous mission statements.[21] The question becomes, why is MOTB downplaying its ongoing ties to the Creation Museum?

If the lack of parity in acknowledging ties to creationists or the removal of religiously explicit language in earlier mission statements feels familiar, it is likely because the Museum of the Bible's approach looks a lot like the tactics of the Intelligent Design movement. Increasing in popularity throughout the 1990s, Intelligent Design's *Of Pandas and People* textbook became the subject of the well-publicized 2005 *Dover v. Kitzmiller* case in Pennsylvania. The court overruled the school board's desire to assign the textbook when expert witness Barbara Forrest demonstrated in her testimony (which the judge appeared to find particularly noteworthy) that Intelligent Design was simply another variation of the religious creationist movement, albeit more palatable for a broader audience.[22] For example, in the 1989 textbook, creationist terminology and references to creationism were simply replaced with words like "intelligent design" and "agency" among other seemingly non-sectarian language.[23] Meanwhile, Intelligent Design explicitly and consistently denies any connections to creationism or biblical literalism, and continues to do so into the present.[24]

As I discussed in chapter 5, Intelligent Design's multipronged approach by which the inclusive "tent strategy" engages everyone with general religious leanings who is interested in how the origins of the universe began with a supernatural creator. Comparatively, the "wedge strategy" aimed to foster discussion about religiosity, not to challenge science. Instead, Intelligent Designers challenge "materialism" which they define as "*scientific materialism*—the simplistic philosophy or world-view that claims that all of reality can be reduced to, or derived from, matter and energy alone. We believe that [fighting against] this is a defense of sound science."[25] The target becomes the perceived necessity of science to be secular, not advancing a singular view of the Bible or necessarily the Bible at all, which public opinion surveys suggest draws in more people to be sympathetic or even receptive to Intelligent Design's positioning. In 2019, the Pew Research Center studied how the public thinks about God, generally, in relation to human evolution by evaluating participant responses in public opinion polls. It asked one group of participants a single question about their views that would indicate how they felt about both human evolution and the role of God. Pew compared these responses to participants' answers to two survey questions in which the evolution and God components were separated and questions about human evolution came first. Pew found more members of the public were apt to indicate they believed God guided the process but also that humans did evolve, which would fall within the Intelligent Design perspective.[26] Overall, people often want to assert their belief in God before they fill out questions about evolution—a way to identify both their religious beliefs and scientific knowledge.

Creationists continue to go to natural history museums and other cultural attractions. But increasingly they seek out Christian alternatives. Why does this matter? The history of the creationist movement underscores that it plays the long game. In turn, this is not a blip or a fluke. Even the most extreme site of them all, the Creation Museum, continues to fare reasonably well. Attendance records are steady, expansions and new exhibits continue, and media coverage rolls along. Institutions like MOTB capitalize on what the Creation Museum represents and then mainstream it.

Perhaps the group with the most immediate concerns are science educators focused on the public's understanding and support of science. Approximately 10% of school-age children in the United States attend private school (predominantly religiously affiliated) and 3% are home-schooled.[27] The overwhelming majority of students are still in the public school system, so it is vital to carefully evaluate more effective ways to engage students, particularly for those seeking to combat antievolution. *Creating the Creation Museum* highlights just how important it is to engage families and discuss science in the broader context of their social lives. As Lucy illustrated, we are most interested in ourselves. And, we are a society full of believers. The sooner that is acknowledged and engaged in the science classroom around practical moral and ethical questions that emerge in scientific research, the better.[28]

Some may think science education is not as high a priority. It is a niche concern among science educators and parents of school-age children. Yet broader implications extend well beyond science education as groups like AiG identify the "cultural crisis" as its primary target. Lessons from decades of activism against Intelligent Design are a fruitful starting point. Unearthing connections between the Creation Museum and the MOTB reveals that both sites have their own political implications, just like any other museum. They are not neutral, educational institutions. Indeed, MOTB is religiously and politically conservative and has established connections to groups like AiG and sites like the Creation Museum. While the Creation Museum leans into polarization, it can do so, in part, because of MOTB's pluralistic public efforts. AiG becomes the extremist, young earth creationist counter to the mainstream, intelligent design approach of MOTB. MOTB can implicitly position itself as the reasonable alternative to the extremist Creation Museum for the broader Christian community, who may appreciate AiG's apologetics but fear that it comes across too forcefully for many potential adherents. AiG benefits from the perception of its steadfast commitment to biblical authority for the more orthodox members of the evangelical community, and MOTB poses broader questions about the role of secularity from the nation's capital.

The evidence from *Creating the Creation Museum* suggests that the moral conflict over secularity is long-standing, and movements increasingly mobilize alternative cultural sites to challenge the secular underpinning of key social institutions such as science. Until we better understand how various groups can frame plausibility politics using the built environment—not just ideological rhetoric online or protests in the street—we will continue to be surprised by the relevance of groups such as AiG and sites like the Creation Museum in the future.

ACKNOWLEDGMENTS

As with any major endeavor in life, this book only came about because of the encouragement and unwavering support from my colleagues, family, and friends. Truly, I am indebted to you all. I would like to acknowledge some of the key individuals, opportunities, and sources of financial support that made transitioning this project into a book possible.

My deepest gratitude to my dissertation committee at Indiana University: Tom Gieryn, Brian Steensland, Fabio Rojas, and Bernice Pescosolido. Tom, your discernment and indefatigable support gave me the footing to take the necessary leaps to see this project through. Brian, your persistent nudge to analytically challenge myself and continued support to help me make sense of the leaps, including the publishing process, were always invaluable. Fabio, your keen methodological insight, candor, and spot-on suggestions, such as the idea to concentrate on plausibility politics, kept me focused on how to present the most persuasive argument. Bernice, your rigorous encouragement to always think about the big picture helped me keep in mind how my ideas would land for a broader audience. And, to Bloomington, Indiana, your proximity to the Creation Museum (less than a three-hour drive) inspired an auspicious beginning to grad school in 2008, when I joined my colleagues on a field trip to check out the new local attraction.

I am grateful to the team of scholars who supported this project by providing feedback on chapter drafts and grant applications, inviting me into your classroom to discuss it, or chatting about the project in narrow hallways and long email threads: Aaron Ponce, John H. Evans, Elaine Howard Ecklund, Terence McDonnell, Steven Epstein, Ronald Numbers, Carla Yanni, Bill Leslie, Aimi Hamraie, Jenna Tonn, James Skee, Libby Sharrow, Kody Steffy, Shiri Noy, Ann McCranie, Oren Pizmony-Levy, Gemma Mangione, David Yamane, Rory McVeigh, Michael S. Evans, Christopher Scheitle, Edward J. Larson, Bernard Lightman, Gary

Alan Fine, Brigittine French, Henry Reitz, Leah Claire Allen, Karla Erickson, Lesley Wright, David Cook-Martin, Charlotte Christensen, Ross Haenfler, Audrey Devine-Eller, Sharon Quinsaat, Kesho Scott, Patrick Inglis, Ruth Braunstein, Jeff Guhin, Lisa Bergwall Herzog, Christena Nippert-Eng, and many others.

I benefited from constructive feedback on earlier presentations or writings leading to this manuscript. I am particularly lucky to have participated in many small community gatherings of sharp and engaged colleagues: the Spaces of Inquiry group along with many others from "DPDF camp" funded by the Social Science Research Council, University of Notre Dame's Young Scholars in Social Movements Conference and the Department of Sociology's Culture Workshop, the Ethnography Workshop at Northwestern University, Public Perceptions of Science and Religion Conference at the University of California–San Diego, and the Installed Knowledge: The Material Culture Network Meets Museum Practitioners at the Science History Institute.

Grinnell College was a wonderfully productive and intellectually supportive environment in which to complete the manuscript; overwhelmingly this was driven by many curious and kind colleagues, staff, and students who asked good questions and nudged me to make the project accessible to a larger audience. Thanks to my fabulous student research assistants, SoYeong Jeong and Quynh Nguyen, for your thoughtful and meticulous work.

Chad Anderson, I appreciate your editorial attention to detail, consummate professionalism, continued interest in the work (and spot-on television show suggestions). Thanks to you, I could move drafts out the door with that extra boost of confidence.

Thank you to New York University Press. I value the focus on the larger audience for this book that my editor, Ilene Kalish, kept at the forefront, the steady guidance that Assistant Editor Sonia Tsuruoka always offered, and the entire editorial office for their careful work.

I received support for this research from several institutions. Thank you for vital research funds: National Science Foundation (NSF 1126535), Social Science Research Council, Friends of the University of Wisconsin–Madison Library, Indiana University's Department of Sociology, and Grinnell College's Faculty Development Fund. Thank you for helpful email communications with staff at the Field Museum and the

Cleveland Museum of Natural History; I'm particularly grateful to Richard Potts and Briana Pobiner at the Smithsonian National Museum of Natural History for taking time to speak with me during my visit. And, sincere gratitude to the members of the Answers in Genesis organization for granting me access and for their sustained generosity with their time. Any opinions, findings, and conclusions or recommendations expressed in this material are mine and do not necessarily reflect these institutions.

To my parents, Tom and Regina Oberlin. For the newspaper clippings, understanding of the long process on all fronts, and above all continued belief (and at times insistence) that your daughter do her best: You embody not only what it means to be loving, supportive parents, but also lifelong learners. To my grandparents: Jeanne and Wayne Oberlin, Dolorita and Edwin Baecher. You made it possible for your granddaughter to take risks and go after whatever I wanted to pursue. To my broader family, for your encouragement and respect for my work, even when it interfered with so many family gatherings and trips for far too long. To so many dear friends who constitute my chosen family. Your support was not based on external markers of success, but instead always on whether I stayed true to the course I set out for myself. It helped carry me through many uncertain moments.

And, to my family. Paloma, our beloved greyhound, you taught me about the benefits of having good snacks and taking breaks for walks throughout the writing process. To my partner in life and love, Kenn. Words are inadequate to express what your intellect, patience, and pursuit of getting a laugh out of me at any cost have meant throughout this decade-long process. You selflessly allowed me to dedicate the time I needed to do my best work without complaint (and, later, often synthesized my own arguments better than I could). For everything, thank you.

APPENDIX

TABLE A.1. Timeline of Creationist-Oriented Events Receiving National
Media Attention, 1994–2016

Year	Event Description
1994	Answers in Genesis (AiG) founded in Petersburg, Kentucky by proponents of Young Earth Creationism (YEC).
1994	National Academy of Science publishes federal standards for K-12 science education, an emphasis on evolution. Many states push back.
1995	AiG begins planning Creation Museum under Ken Ham's leadership.
1995	John D. Morris assumes leadership of Institute for Creation Research (ICR), from movement YEC legendary leader Henry M. Morris.
1996	The Center for Science and Culture is formed by the Discovery Institute, proponents of Intelligent Design (ID), in Seattle, Washington.
1999	Kansas Board of Education passed curriculum standards, which made teaching evolution non-mandatory.
2000–2008	George W. Bush serves as the US president. In 2005, he made remarks suggesting that intelligent design should be discussed in relation to evolution, "so people can understand what the debate is about."
2000	Field Museum Opens "Sue the Tyrannosaurus Rex" exhibit.
2001	The Discovery Institute helped Senator Santorum craft a failed amendment advocating ID be included in the No Child Left Behind Act. Despite its removal from the Act, it gained national media attention.
2005	*Kitzmiller v. Dover Area School District*: Parents successfully challenged the teaching of Intelligent Design in science classrooms by linking it to creationism and the court upheld it as violating the First Amendment.
2005	Kansas Board of Education passed curriculum standards that mandated "equal time" in the classroom for evolution and ID—amendment rejected in 2007.
2006	"Evolving Planet" Exhibit Opens at the Field Museum.
2006	American Museum of Natural History's Dinosaur Wing is renamed David H. Koch, after he donated $20 million.
2007	Creation Museum opens in Petersburg, Kentucky. More than 400,000 patrons attend the museum in the first year.
2007	PBS premieres "Judgment Day: Intelligent Design on Trial," a documentary on the *Kitzmiller v. Dover* trial. Gains widespread national media attention and won a Peabody Award in 2008.
2008	Political candidates' beliefs regarding evolution and the role of intelligent design in K-12 classroom instruction becomes a prominent talking point in the US presidential election.

2008	ICR sells Museum of Creation and Earth History in California and relocates headquarters to Dallas, Texas. Meanwhile, plans to administer Master of Science degrees through their online graduate school are ruled against by the Texas Higher Education Coordinating Board.
2008	*Religious*, a film hosted by comedian Bill Maher, is released. It features the Creation Museum in its critical and often satirical exploration of religion in public life.
2009	Texas Board of Education voted to include ID arguments alongside evolution in textbooks adopted by the state—one of the largest markets for textbooks in the country. This decision gained national media attention as well as inspired a documentary *The Revisionaries* (2012).
2010	Smithsonian Institution's National Museum of Natural History opens David H. Koch Hall of Human Origins after he donated $15 million.
2010	After a failed lawsuit to reverse the accreditation refusal from the Texas Higher Education Coordinating Board, ICR discontinued the online Masters of Science graduate program. They now focus on apologetics.
2010	AiG announces plans to build the Ark Encounter, a theme park revolving around a full-size replica of Noah's Ark from the Bible.
2012	Again, in the US presidential election, candidates' beliefs regarding evolution and the role of intelligent design in K-12 classroom instruction becomes a prominent talking point, particularly among Republicans.
2014	Bill Nye debates Ken Ham at the Creation Museum; it is aired on YouTube and receives more than seven million views online.
2016	Ark Encounter opens, AiG's for-profit sister attraction to the Creation Museum. Media coverage focuses on the tax incentives and bonds given to the venue by Williamstown, Kentucky, where it is located.

NOTES

INTRODUCTION

1 "Evolution Versus Creationism Debate," C-SPAN, February 20, 2018, www.c-span.org.

2 This count was retrieved on September 26, 2019. "Bill Nye Debates Ken Ham," Answers in Genesis, February 4, 2014, www.youtube.com.

3 This short timeline is the key factor that distinguishes the Young Earth stance from Old Earth Creationism, and Intelligent Design, which varies in explanations for how old the Earth is, but adherents often align with mainstream geologic accounts for the Earth to be billions of years old. For more on the Intelligent Design movement see, Forrest and Gross 2004.

4 The Creation Museum in Kentucky cost more than $30 million to build and it was fully funded upon opening its doors to 4,000 people and more than 100 members of the press on May 28, 2007. It has maintained an average of 300,000 attendees per year from 2008 onward (Ham 2007; McKeever, Vaterlaus, and King 2008: 45–47; AiG internal documentation). For comparison, the median attendance for science and technology centers/museums was 216,250 in 2012 (Association of Science-Technology Center 2013).

5 To contextualize the entrance fee at the Creation Museum, in 2009 the median cost per visitor across museums was $31.40 (American Alliance of Museums 2009).

6 Redfern 2007; Rothstein 2007.

7 Slack 2007; Slevin 2007.

8 Opinion, Editorial. *Los Angeles Times*, 2007.

9 Asma 2007; Leahy 2007; Phelps 2008.

10 See Duncan and Geist (2004) for a longitudinal analysis and Swift (2017) for an update to these figures. These are the two most prominent national surveys with questions striving to capture public beliefs regarding the role of God and evolutionary biology in human origins or the age of the Earth. While there is continued discussion regarding how well these survey items capture "creationist beliefs," since not all creationists are biblical literalists, the antagonism of conservative Protestants, like biblical literalists, to secular science remains prominent (Evans 2013; Roos 2014).

11 National Center for Science and Engineering Statistics 2016.

12 Desilver 2017.

13 While field and laboratory work would later come to serve as central sites of scientific knowledge production in the twentieth century for fields like geology,

evolutionary biology, and anthropology, the role of natural history museums as research institutions that participate in experimentation and publication continues to this day. Nevertheless, the centrality of science centers and museums for the public's engagement with the institutions of science is unparalleled, see Bennett 1995, 1998; Conn 1998, 2010; MacDonald 1998.

14 Numbers 2006; Larson 2006; Scopes Trial exhibit in the Creation Museum during 2012.

15 Worthen 2014.

16 Numbers 2006.

17 This quote is from the monthly organizational newsletter, *Acts & Facts*, published in 1974, volume 3, issue 6 by Institute for Creation Research, a young earth creationist group.

18 Casanova 1994: 5, 147.

19 *Science* 1980: 1214, published by the American Association for the Advancement of Science.

20 Pew Research Center 2015.

21 Goodstein 2005.

22 Eve and Harrold (1990), in their review of the movement, identify the four most prominent areas in which creationists concentrate their efforts: federal courts, state-level legislatures, state educational bodies, and grassroots-level organizing around local schools.

23 Nelkin 1977; Binder 2002, 2007.

24 Larson 2003; Forrest and Gross 2004; Lienesch 2007.

25 See Kaden (2019) for a contemporary review of the creationist landscape and who considers creationist and anti-creationist organizations as engaged in conflict with one another as the organizations are with the public. While there are clear divisions and offshoot branches of the creationist movement, for the sake of brevity, I will use young earth creationist movement interchangeably with creationist movement unless specified otherwise.

26 Only one other book is published on the museum. In *Righting America at the Creation Museum* (2016), the Trollingers draw primarily from museum visits to produce a close reading of the exhibits on display and the book is directed at scholars interested in creationism, evangelicalism, and the use of religious rhetoric in museums.

27 In the *Ark Encounter* (2018), James Bielo examines the theme park created by AiG and run by the for-profit corporation Ark Encounter, LLC. Bielo focuses on entertainment attractions that seek to evangelize and the emphasis is on the creative team's work throughout the process of design and production.

28 The exact definition of a social movement varies among scholars, but most agree that the phenomenon consists of a collective group of people who assert strategic goals via non-institutionalized discourse or practice (Zald and McCarthy 1980; McAdam, McCarthy, and Zald 1996; Armstrong and Bernstein 2008). Goals may address or articulate a shared grievance, challenge extant socioeconomic conditions, or demand recognition and consideration.

29 For historical overviews of the literature on state repression, see Davenport 2007 and Earl 2011.

30 Armstrong and Bernstein 2008: 78–79; Polletta 2008: 81–82.

31 Tarrow 1998: 7, 25.

32 The cultural orientation seeks to avoid a previous tendency to focus only on the state as a viable movement target but retains an interest in political changes sought and achieved by a movement. Cultural institutions are salient targets for movement initiatives. The goal is to understand how the state and other targets are often inextricably connected in the pursuit of political change (Taylor et al. 2009). The elaboration of movement outcomes and their contexts, in turn, led to the idea of "cultural outcomes." Empirically, the range of outcomes is vast. They include: social psychological impacts on the broader public, a readjusted world-view among movement members, and, specifically, a cultural product such as media coverage, or an alternative site, or changed scientific practices (Earl 2000, 2004).

33 Frickel and Moore 2006; Moore 2008; Breyman et al. 2016.

34 An exception would be health and medical movements studied within science and technology studies where alternative medicine and direct challenges to medical authority are well documented, see Epstein 1996, 2007; Morello-Frosch et al. 2006.

35 Bennett 1995; Conn 1998.

36 Toumey 1994.

37 See classic social movement work on the "iron law of oligarchy" (Michels 1962[1911]) for how mass demonstrations invariably become run by a small group of elites; Piven and Cloward (1977) for work on mass disruptive collective action dissipating. For contemporary work on movement institutionalization, see Meyer and Laschever 2016.

38 The word "institution" is a familiar but often analytically ambiguous concept used by scholars interested in how practices and ideas become formalized into rules. As Friedland and Alford (1991) argue, institutions are: "supra-organizational patterns of activity through which humans conduct their material life in time and space, and symbolic systems through which they categorize that activity and infuse it with meaning" (232).

39 It is a practice that often arises from a social movement's negotiation of how to match its goals with effective tactics that align with the institutional target it seeks to challenge. The type of institution constructed is often rooted in the movement context—ranging from "indigenous" community institutions (e.g., churches), transmovement connections (e.g., halfway houses), or prefigurative sites created by ongoing movements to showcase their autonomy (e.g., feminist bookshops) (Polletta 1999).

40 As Clemens's (1993) work on the twentieth-century women's movement for voting rights and political representation notes, institutions are not invested with self-reproducing meaning. Rather, they are constructed based on rules made by

those with more resources and power. She emphasized that what matters most for the disenfranchised is the ability to adopt a new organizational form (such as women's voluntary associations associated with domestic work), "to transform their public identity in ways that largely sidestepped the culturally embedded equation of the political with masculinity" (776). See also Clemens 2005; Konieczny and Rogers 2016.

41 Clemens and Cook 1999.

42 Bordt 1997.

43 Described in extensive detail by Morris (1984) and, later, Pattillo-McCoy (1998).

44 Taylor and Whittier 1995; Bordt 1997; Staggenborg 2001; Taylor and Van Dyke 2004.

45 Davis and Robinson 2012: 20–24.

46 See Marsden (1980) for a historical review of fundamentalism as a movement and Numbers (2006) for a specific historical examination of the creationist faction.

47 Verta Taylor's (1989) landmark study of the women's movement documented how these "abeyance structures," organizations and structures developed to sustain the women's movement, helped the movement endure through a period of decline from 1945 to the early 1960s. Throughout the expansive discussion of abeyance, Taylor continually reverts to discussions of the Alva Belmont House and its ability to sustain the movement in abeyance. But what did it do? It served as: the national headquarters, a hub of lobbying efforts in Washington, DC, a publishing house for movement materials, and a prominent site for movement members to bring their personal recruits (often their friends) to visit. However, this vital site for the movement is discussed largely in symbolic terms in the analysis—the details noted above were not drawn together or assessed in relation to the House or the movement itself. What is it about the House that made so many members "feel at home"? How did so many functions of the movement come to be located there? To what extent the Alva Belmont House facilitated, the ability of the movement to endure is bound up in these abeyance structures and it warrants a closer look.

48 Morris 1984.

49 For instance, Polletta (1999) points to how free spaces afford a better understanding of mobilization and identifies actors' network ties as what holds these spaces together with minimal attention to the physical context. These relationships enable actors to identify opportunities, recruit members, inspire leaders, and develop a strategy for action, see also Rao and Dutta 2012.

50 Inserting materiality back into social movement discussions may strike social movement scholars as regressive—resources and materials were often the central factor examined in social movement literature throughout the 1970s and 1980s. In the 1990s, calls to take culture seriously in the social movement literature hovered around the need to unpack the importance of symbolism and expressive qualities rather than the instrumental components so focused on in resource mobilization frameworks. However, I focus on how cultural authority is fostered through ma-

teriality and the built environment, examining how material and symbolic forces relate to other structural factors, political and otherwise.

51 See Berezin (1994) and Zubrzycki (2011, 2013, 2017) for formative work on the role of aesthetics in the State's attempts to politically persuade its constituents. For scholarship on how collective commemoration and memorial sites inform competing discussions about what social change is envisioned in the future based on how it was portrayed to be accomplished in the past, see Armstrong and Crage (2006); Wagner-Pacifi and Schwartz (1991); Wagner-Pacifi (1996).

52 While institution-building is most prominent, even for the Occupy Wall Street movement or Arab Spring, commandeering a park or taking over a public square requires significant coordination in order to demarcate the hub for collective action from which to protect against and resist outsider efforts to decamp.

53 See Polletta and Kretschmer (2013) for a review.

54 Somers (2008: 257); I lean on contemporary scholarship that is emblematic of the "practice turn." The emphasis on what people do with their beliefs, resources, or values—and when—came to the forefront for both cultural sociology and social movement scholarship in the 1990s (Griswold 2004; Sewell 2005; Isaac 2009). This body of scholarship dovetails with sociology of science's long-standing emphasis on scientific knowledge production as it pertains to the maintenance of scientific credibility as well as expertise and the sociology of religion's focus on examining religious believers' actions (Epstein 2008; Edgell 2012).

55 See Earl et al. (2010) and Earl and Kimport (2011) for an overview of the relationship between social movement organizations and online activity. Vasi and Suh (2016) examine this dynamic in the Occupy Movement.

56 Schradie (2019) offers a critical examination of the digital activism gap where technology fails to level the social movement playing field—well-resourced groups are able to leverage digital tools like social media more effectively than groups with fewer resources or members. Digital activism is not always democratizing or driven from the ground up.

57 Merriam Webster Dictionary, www.merriam-webster.com.

58 AP-NORC 2015.

59 Mitchell et al. 2014.

60 Seib 2016.

61 Smith and Martínez 2016.

62 Letzter 2016.

63 The stakes are particularly variable for science, as Gauchat (2011) even found that where scientific activity is perceived to occur (university laboratories) affected the likelihood of the public maintaining favorable general attitudes toward science.

64 Weber 1978: 212.

65 Funk, Gottfried, and Mitchell 2017.

66 Contemporary museums are not just relics of years past. As Conn (2010) argues, "We live in a museum age. At the turn of the twenty-first century more people are going to more museums than at any time in the past . . . measured at the gate, in

philanthropic giving, and in the cultural influence they command" (1). However, cultural and demographic shifts as well as technological advances underscore that a museum's reception is historically contingent and contextual.

67 MacDonald 1998: 14; O'Neill 2004.

68 See Conn (2006) for a review of how controversy has been handled in science museums throughout the twentieth and twenty-first centuries.

69 Despite this persistent attention to museums as social institutions within organizational fields or as hubs of cultural classification, museums have been understudied by social movement scholars as sites for social and cultural change, particularly regarding how groups establish their own museum rather than challenging a single exhibit (Zolberg 1996, 1998; Blau 1991; DiMaggio 1991; Pachucki 2012). See for exceptions MacDonald 1998; Knell, MacLeod, and Watson 2007; Jansen 2008; Autry 2013.

70 Hetherington 2002; Knell et al. 2007; Cooper 2008; Autry 2013.

71 Indeed, these types of conflicts recently came to a head, as Sharon Macdonald (2006) summarizes, "Museums found themselves at the center of wider 'culture wars' over whether it was or was not possible or permissible to see some cultural products and forms of knowledge as in any sense more valuable or valid than others. Museums became, in short, sites at which some of the most contested and thorny cultural and epistemological questions of the late twentieth century were fought out" (4).

72 Now, more than ever, historically marginalized groups are able to influence the content and focus of exhibitions in order to inform what a museum space provides the public (Knell et al. 2007). It is a direct push beyond the historical role of the government and ruling classes "to civilize the masses" (Foucault 1972; Bennett 1995). The new direction for this work is presumed to be negotiated between established museums engaging with their respective "community," which as Tlili, Gewirtz, and Cribb (2007) highlight, is often a stand-in phrase for discussing oppressed groups.

73 Sharon MacDonald (1996) underscores, "museums remain powerful and subtle authors and authorities whose cultural accounts are not easily dislodged . . . a museum is a process as well as a structure, it is a creative agency as well as 'contested terrain'" (4). This suggests that neither museums' leadership nor exhibit content is challenged or changed quickly as exhibitions are closely tied to vested members' interests and classificatory values. See also Alexander 1996; Pachucki 2012.

74 Specifically, structural opportunities that would commonly be used by scholars and advocates alike to indicate historical discrimination based on a minoritized status typically include data to track differential employment opportunities, wealth accumulation, incarceration rates, and educational attainment.

75 While science has never been objective, apolitical, or irreligious, the goal of secular inquiry has marked the contemporary institution of science since the late 1800s as a result of active pursuit among scholars intent on disentangling science from its religious roots. In the case of Europe and the United States, this largely

meant Protestantism. As a higher number of non-Protestants such as Catholics and Jews joined the academy, efforts to assimilate became stronger since a shared religious tradition no longer served as a singular foundation for the academy. Today the perception that religion and science are inherently in conflict is a minority position among faculty and not widely held, see Smith 2003; Ecklund 2010; Ecklund and Long 2011; Ecklund, Park, and Sorrell 2011; Beit-Hallahmi 2015.

76 For instance, Ecklund and Scheitle's (2007) analysis of available General Social Survey data suggested 52% of scientists reported no religious affiliation in contrast to the 14% of the entire population. Yet Gross and Simmons (2009) have argued that even though atheism and agnosticism are more readily indicated among faculty compared to the general population, "religious skepticism represents a minority position, even among professors teaching at elite research universities" (103). Similarly, in examinations of how specifically religion and science are perceived in relation to one another, Stirrat and Cornwell (2013) discovered that while members of Great Britain's Royal Fellows (who are nominated based on substantial, influential scientific work) indicated less belief in a personal god or the supernatural compared to the general public, there was also no consensus among Royal Fellows about the relationship between the two spheres of authority either.

77 See Golinksi (2005) for a comprehensive historical review of constructivism as it relates to science and technology.

78 While the billions of years' timescale is not in question among mainstream scientists, see Falk (2016) for an overview of current debates among physicists about how to understand and explain the origins of the universe. The question of transitional fossils is regarded typically as specious within mainstream science, see Shermer 2005.

79 Smith 2003.

80 Asma 2007; Leahy 2007; Slack 2007; Slevin 2007; Phelps 2008.

81 Green 2017.

82 Goodstein 2018.

83 Mukerji 1994: 159.

1. A WALK THROUGH THE CREATION MUSEUM

1 Throughout the chapter, field notes and interview citations indicate the date of the observation or conversation being referenced.

2 In a 2014 Pew Religious Landscape Study, about half of Kentucky identified as evangelical compared to 31% and 29% in Indiana and Ohio, respectively (Pew Research Center 2015).

3 Answers 1994 1(2): 2. *Answers* was a publication produced by Answers in Genesis for its supporters from 1994 to 2006. It was an internal movement newsletter featuring organizational updates and editorials from AiG leaders. After 2006, a series of more targeted internal publications were developed, such as *Answers* magazine, organizational blog posts, and the *Answers: Research Journal*.

4 Answers in Genesis materials are often published through Master Books, a Christian publisher with the slogan "Where Faith Grows!" Hailing from an established tradition of evangelical presses publishing materials for various ministries and groups, Master Books was started in the 1970s by creationists to produce their own movement materials. Later in the 1990s, New Leaf Publishing group, another evangelical publishing house based in Arkansas, purchased Master Books, and since then they have published the majority of AiG's materials.

5 Butler 2010; Caudill 2010; Barton, 2012; Kelly and Hoerl 2012; Moran 2012; Lynch 2013; Rosenhouse 2012; Kaden 2019.

6 See Trollinger and Trollinger (2016) for their close reading of the Creation Museum exhibits.

7 Field Notes, December 14, 2012.

8 Text quoted from Stop #101: Portico, Audio Tour. Audio tours are available through a website adapted for smartphones. Signs mark thirty-six stops on the Enhanced Tour throughout the museum (Answers in Genesis 2014). Each stop provides additional detail behind the exhibit, and this material is accessible as a written transcript or narrated by Ken Ham in his Australian accent. All the transcripts are also available in Spanish.

9 FotoFx is a company based in Tennessee and works with many museums and public attractions. For the Creation Museum, it provides customized digital backdrops.

10 Text quoted from Stop #122 Mastodon and Stop #123 Turtles and Animatronic, Audio Tour.

11 McKeever, Vaterlaus, and King 2008: 53.

12 Interview conducted, July 28, 2012.

13 Answers in Genesis 2008a: 31.

14 For example, in the early 1900s, the Piltdown man was purported to be the link between man and apes but later was discredited as fraudulent because the fossils were not old enough and were manipulated to fit together in order to deceive the public (Natural History Museum Archives, London, n.d.).

15 Numbers and Wiley 2015.

16 Numbers and Wiley 2015.

17 Answers in Genesis n.d.; The reference to 1841 is regarding when Sir Richard Owen, renowned Victorian-era scientist and museum director, first used the term "dinosaur." However, technically it was in 1842 (Yanni 2005: 134).

18 Answers in Genesis 2008b: 81.

19 Carey 2010.

20 Answers in Genesis 2010.

21 When a dinosaur was displayed in the United States for the first time at Philadelphia's Academy of Natural Sciences in the late 1800s, "officials there worried that the building would collapse under the crush of all the visitors. Little has changed since. . . . Dinosaurs—and all manner of extinct creatures—have always been and remain a central attraction for natural history museums" (Conn 2010: 152).

22 Field Notes, March 10, 2017; McKeever et al. 2008: 57.

23 See the website: https://creationmuseum.org/planetarium.

24 Phelps 2008.

25 McKeever et al. 2008: 58.

26 Answers in Genesis 2007.

27 "Mineral crystals, which have been growing in the 6,000 years since the creation, show not only beauty but also consistent patterns and diverse shapes," Treasures of the Earth, exhibit placard text, December 14, 2012.

28 Interview conducted May 23, 2012. See also the National Academy of Sciences' biographical memoir on David Raup, where Raup mentions his visit to the Creation Museum (Foote and Miller 2017).

29 Text quoted from Stop #170 Dig Site, Audio Tour.

30 Answers in Genesis 2008a: 10.

31 See Worthen (2014) for a thorough detailed historical analysis of evangelicalism's factionalism in the United States throughout the nineteenth and twentieth centuries.

32 Text quoted from #190 Biblical Relevance, Audio Tour.

33 Text quoted from Stop #124 Main Hall Case Exhibits, Audio Tour. Trollinger and Trollinger (2016) provide a lucid discussion of how the Creation Museum's "7 Cs" is closely tied to the much earlier "7 Ds" of dispensationalism, a long-standing historical interpretation of the Bible for nineteenth-century fundamentalists. They claim that the museum aims to engage visitors with similar religious traditions and draw upon their general familiarity with this type of framing device for biblical understanding (44–48).

34 Hodge 2010.

35 Genesis 2:19–20, New King James Version.

36 Baraminologists are creation scientists who study this kind of classificatory system and were central to the Ark Encounter's exhibits, where an emphasis on the animals aboard Noah's Ark becomes pivotal in their life-sized re-creation (Gishlick 2006).

37 McKeever et al. 2008: 86.

38 Answers in Genesis 2008a: 26.

39 In November 2017, the Museum of the Bible opened just off the Washington, DC National Mall. One of the largest funders for the operation is the Green family, who own the national corporation Hobby Lobby.

40 Petting Zoo, Audio Tour, July 2012.

41 Interview conducted May 23, 2012.

42 As the founder of the YEC movement Henry M. Morris wrote, "Pressures towards conformity and uniformity imposed by secular accreditation bodies, though often denied, are very real, and the impact becomes increasingly obvious with the passing of time" (Morris 2010[1988]).

43 American Alliance of Museums n.d.

44 Answers in Genesis 2009; Evangelical Council for Financial Accountability 2017.

45 Answers in Genesis Collections Management Policy 2012: 1.
46 Interview conducted March 22, 2012.
47 Field Notes, September 30, 2011; July 27, 2012.
48 Field Note, September 19, 2012.
49 Interview conducted September 20, 2011.
50 McKeever et al. 2008: 97.
51 Interview conducted May 23, 2012.
52 Interview conducted September 30, 2011.
53 Interview conducted July 27, 2012.
54 McKeever et al. 2008: 25.
55 Field Notes, July 28, 2012.
56 Internal correspondence with AiG in 2012.
57 Interview conducted December 14, 2012.
58 Interview conducted May 23, 2012.
59 This publication is a fee-based subscription and it is actively advertised at the Creation Museum bookstore and online: www.answersingenesis.org.
60 Ham 2014.
61 Interview conducted July 23, 2013.
62 Interview conducted September 20, 2011.

2. THE CREATIONIST MOVEMENT IN THE UNITED STATES

1 The concept of "tactical repertoire" focuses on distinct constellations of tactics and strategies developed over time and used by different protest groups when making their claims (Tilly 1978; Tarrow 1998). As Clemens (1993) extends the concept to identify how disruption occurs, a tactical repertoire is "[t]he set of organizational models that are culturally or experientially available [to an SMO] . . . when deployed in novel ways by unfamiliar groups, even the most familiar organizational models can have unsettling consequences for political institutions" (758). The success of an SMO depends in part on its ability to translate what is considered appropriate or institutionally normative into the goals and tactics of the movement. By considering organizational repertoires, social movement scholars have discovered multiple models of organization, revising classic Weberian theories of inevitable bureaucratization and Michels' iron law of oligarchy (Weber 2001[1905]; Michels 1962[1911]). Attention has shifted to the strategies and tactics selected by SMOs.
2 See Taylor and Van Dyke 2004.
3 See Armstrong (2005: 189) for a definition of SMO. The emphasis on the significance of social movement organization has increased in the last twenty years due to an increasing synergy between social movement scholars and organizational theorists (Davis et al. 2005). But the interaction between SMOS and their environment is an old issue. More recent work suggests a movement's use of an organizational form is an attempt to shore up its position among the SMO population and to effect change in the broader sociopolitical environment (Loonsbury and Ventresca 2002; Scully and Segal 2002).

4 See Zald and McCarthy (1980) for foundational work on the social movement industry.

5 See Taylor and Van Dyke 2004; Frickel and Gross 2005.

6 Freeman 1983; Blee and Creasap 2010.

7 See Blee 2002; Rydgren 2007; Caiani, Della Porta, and Wagemann 2012.

8 See McDonnell, Bail, and Tavory (2017) for a discussion on how to analyze resonance rather than get trapped in a common research cycle, i.e., objects matter or work because they are resonant, but what's driving its resonance is tied into the fact that it "works." Why do some ideas, places, or arguments resonate more than others? To answer this, they claim researchers must focus on audiences' interaction with the object to tease out the extent to which the intended meaning is produced in process. Inspired by this analytical approach, I focus on how AiG as an SMO within a field of other SMOs tries to compel others that what they offer addresses an existing question they may have, or in the case of creationism, how individuals could rectify their faith within a secular, scientific society.

9 Soule and King (2008) find that as the number of SMOs in an SMI increases, specialization within each organization typically increases in a way that makes it harder for each of them to survive. More established SMOs typically maintain general goals and tactics in order to avoid this kind of factionalism (1575). Succinctly put, established SMOs are less likely to specialize and generalists are more likely to persist, but this is at the risk of being potentially upstaged by an SMO willing to take a risk and specialize. Interestingly, however, Zald and McCarthy (1980) suggest that conflict and/or competition between two new SMOs, with no common history, is more likely than between spin-off organizations within the same movement.

10 I gathered archival materials from three collections. First, *Creationism Believers Movements* (Brown University, John Hay Library Collection), which contained items from twenty-one different creationist organizations including internal documents such as letters (correspondence), newsletters, press releases, and other movement-specific promotional materials. Second, *Science and Religion Collection* (University of Wisconsin, Special Collections Library), which was donated by the premier historian of creation science, Ronald L. Numbers, and features more than 700 items pertaining to creationism and evolution, including documents produced by a range of OEC and YEC movements. Finally, each SMO's own archival collections is available online. I only used the organizational newsletters for this analysis—all four SMOs directed their newsletters at members and potential recruits. The SMO leaders had a hand in the content either by writing it themselves or featuring activities and goals they favored. There is a clear precedent for using organizational newsletters—it reflects a movement's own account of protest events (Taylor et al. 2009). Whether or not they were co-present in terms of petitions, letter-writing, campaigns, boycotts (Earl and Kimport 2011; Lienesch 2007; Lindekilde 2008), and the general need to signal that events took place as well as identifying actors involved in legal battles and public debates (Taylor and

Van Dyke 2004: 267). I read the data considering salient issues suggested by the literature. Analytic factors were generated using a retroductive scheme; I alternated between a priori and inductive codes to offset concerns of reliability and validity (Ghaziani and Baldassarri 2011). I used several features in Atlas.ti, such as auto-coding and co-occurrence to ensure coverage as well as reliability; I also read every newsletter by hand in order to verify validity and to discover emergent search terms via open coding.

I also relied on the extensive secondary literature on creationism, particularly Toumey (1994), Numbers (2006), and Lienesch (2007).

11 Drawing on Irwin A. Moon's "Sermons for Science" and from the formidable Moody Bible Institute, many conservative evangelicals encountered college-level students who were concerned and "eager for reassurance that modern scientific knowledge does not rule out faith," during the 1940s. References to newsletters will follow this format, when information is available, as it varies over time and across SMOs (Source Year: Volume(Number), page #). JASA 1951, page 4.

12 JASA 1951, page 3.

13 ASA 1963: Vol. 5(2), page 7.

14 The association was run like any other professional society, with elected council members and a president; the membership increased to almost 2,000 members by 1971. (ASA 1972: Vol. 14(1)). Yet during this same period, ASA received minimal attention from the media and lacked support from the scientific establishment (Lienesch 2007: 202).

15 Numbers 2006: 116. The contemporary development of creationist ideology dates back to rejecting John Tyndall's 1874 assertion that "naturalism" was the only legitimate means to pursue a scientific agenda (often referred to as "scientism") (Gieryn, Bevins, and Zehr 1985; Livingstone 2003; Attridge et al. 2009). Instead, the YEC movement increasingly drew upon both a literal interpretation of the Bible (dating back to James Ussher's seventeenth-century biblical chronological work on the Young Age of the Earth) and Baconian inductive scientific methods to develop their creation model of a young earth (inspired by Price's scientific creationism).

16 Numbers 2006: 189.

17 While the text did not receive the expected book review in the journal of ASA that year, ASA directly referenced Morris and Whitcomb in the society's informal newsletter in 1961 (ASA 1961: Vol. 3(1), page 4).

18 Throughout 1961 they assembled what Tinkle referred to as the "team of ten" and arranged to meet in a separate caucus, to be held concurrently during the annual ASA convention held in June 1963 at Asbury College in Kentucky (CRSQ 1964: Vol. 1(1), page 1).

19 Numbers 2006: 254.

20 CRSQ 1964: Vol. 1, page 2.

21 CRSQ 1964: Vol. 1, page 1.

22 CRSQ 1973: Vol. 10, page 46.

23 BSCS 2001: page 10.
24 BSCS 2001: page 7.
25 CRSQ 1965: Vol. 2(1), page 5.
26 Moore and Slusher 1970.
27 Moore and Slusher 1970: 266–267.
28 CRSQ 1969: Vol. 6(1), page 3.
29 This focus is evident in a 1966 ASA newsletter: "Dr. Robert Fischer rolled off some very disturbing statistics showing the dominance of research and development by the Federal government. Christians, said Fischer, are doubly obligated to analyze the strings attached to Federal grants" (ASA 1966: Vol. 8(4)).
30 "Baconian" refers to scientist Francis Bacon, who introduced a focus on empiricism in the scientific revolution during the sixteenth century (Klein 2012).
31 With origins in the mid-twentieth century, secular humanism was constructed largely by creationist opponents rather than advocated for by self-identified humanist groups during federal court cases concerning the First Amendment (Toumey 1994: 78–81; Lienesch 2007).
32 See Gerring 1997.
33 Oliver and Johnston (2000) assert that, at its core, "Ideology is rooted in politics and the study of politics, and points to coherent systems of ideas which provide theories of society coupled with value commitments and normative implications for promoting or resisting social change" (37). Values in this context refer to ethical or moral judgments; norms refer to sometimes idealized behaviors that enact a desired change, whether nostalgic, contemporary, or future-oriented. These idealizations are interest-oriented but also based on personal experiences. Platt and Williams (2002) suggest that ideologies are localized, "On the bases of such varied local knowledge and circumstances, different groups calculate and derive distinct ideologies and courses of action" (337).
34 Durkheim 1995[1912]); Geertz 1973; Wilson 1973.
35 Platt and Williams 2002.
36 Gerring 1997; Jost, Federico, and Napier 2009; Sociologists regard ideologies not only as individual mind-sets but also as collectively shared worldviews. This differs from psychologists who tend to focus on the situational and dispositional needs shaping an individual's mindset and from political scientists who emphasize the role of ideology in individuals' and groups' political behaviors and attitudes.
37 Pattillo-McCoy 1998: 769.
38 See Kniss and Burns 2004. Almost non-existent in the literature is analysis of ideological formations and splits within science-based social and intellectual movements (Frickel and Gross 2005). Nevertheless, some social movement scholars have recently highlighted the multidimensional and dissonant nature of ideological worldviews since group members interpret things differently due to differences in their social locations and backgrounds (Platt and Williams 2002: 338). Movement factionalism may at times result from the negotiation of ideological

differences in debates among movement members, even within science-oriented social movements.

39 Ganz 2000, 2004. Charisma is a well-known quality that develops from identifiable relationships between leaders and followers. Its sociological roots date back to Weber's classic conceptualization of how unique supernatural abilities were imputed by followers to a leader—abilities that legitimated the leader's authority within the group (Weber 2001[1905]). As Ganz (2004) states, "as sociologists of religion and others have documented, many groups have charismatic leaders but few devise strategy effective [*sic*] enough to achieve institutional stability, much less to become successful social movement organizations (180). Morris (1984) underscores this point, suggesting that in Weber's focus on the salience of charisma in leadership, Weber did not account for how or why a given charismatic leader would emerge nor offer guidance as to how these attributes translate (or not) in to an effective use of resources and opportunities. Using the case of Dr. Martin Luther King Jr. for the Civil Rights Movement, Morris argued, "the movement did not create charismatic leaders out of a vacuum; charisma as a social form already existed within an enduring institution of the black community" (ibid.: 279).

40 Ganz 2004: 188, 197.

41 Historian of creationism Ronald Numbers (2006) suggests, "it signified a major tactical shift among strict six-day creationists. Instead of denying evolution its scientific credentials, as biblical creationists had done for a century, the scientific creationists granted creation and evolution equal scientific standing. Instead of trying to bar evolution from the classroom, as their predecessors had done in the 1920s, they fought to bring creation into the schoolhouse" (269–270).

42 A&F 1972: Vol. 1(1), page 3.

43 A&F 1972: Vol. 1(5).

44 A&F 1972: Vol. 1(1).

45 A&F 1981: Vol. 10(10); Morris explains the rationale behind the dizzying number of debates: "Few developments in the creationist movement have stirred as much interest as have the creation-evolution debates that have been held on various campuses the past two years. Some may question the value of such engagements (I do, myself), but there is no doubt that these serve to get the creationist message heard by more non-Christians and non-creationists than almost any other method. Other things being equal, one can be sure a debate will draw a larger audience than a regular lecture. Maybe it's like the crowds in ancient Rome anticipating a bloody confrontation between the Christians and the lions! (A&F 1974: Vol. 3(3), page 2).

46 Numbers 2006: 259, 313.

47 A&F 1975: Vol. 4(6), page ii.

48 "The hatchet job accomplished on the fundamentalists by the news media and the educational establishment following the Scopes trial in 1925 is a type of what could happen, in the unlikely event that favorable legislation or court decisions could be obtained by this route." A&F 1973: Vol. 2(1), page 7.

49 A&F 1974: Vol. 3(6), page 5.

50 ICR was focused on public opinion polls to showcase the broader support among the public for creationism. Here they outline why it matters politically, "the emergence of the public opinion poll as a strong policy-making tool . . . politicians seem to base their campaigns and programs almost entirely on a wide assortment of popularity polls conducted, supposedly, by scientific statistical techniques of opinion sampling. So far as we know, neither the Gallup poll nor the Harris poll nor any other 'official' sampling agency has conducted a survey of public opinion on the issue of creation or evolution. Nevertheless, evidence is accumulating that such a poll would show that a large majority of American citizens would say—if they had the chance—that they favor including creation as an alternative scientific model of origins in the nation's public schools and colleges, rather than the present practice of teaching only evolution" (A&F 1976: Vol. 5(12), page 3).

51 A&F 1982: Vol. 11(10), page 6.

52 CRSQ 1987: Vol. 24, page 109.

53 For instance, CRS printed one member's letter to the editor about perceived unfavorable coverage, "The letter was written as an answer to a report published in *Science* [182]: 696 with false allegations about the C.R.S. Barnes' letter that clarified the fact that C.R.S. is not a lobbying organization, nor is it officially engaging in any dispute with any other organization" (CRSQ 1974: Vol. 11, page 127). The aforementioned lack of engagement with the surrounding external context was underscored in the re-statement of CRSs' goals in 1982, "the essential and primary purpose of the CRS was and remains the publication of its journal as a quarterly. This would contain articles of a scientific nature impinging on an alternate view of origins, namely creation" (CRSQ 1982: Vol. 19, page 149).

54 A&F 1983: Vol. 12(3), page 4.

55 A&F 1989: Vol. 18(10), page 3.

56 In 1986, ICR moved its own campus to Santee, several miles from CHC in El Cajon, but still within a thirty-minute drive from San Diego. ICR continued to produce educational materials, participate in debates, and even increased the number of its on-site seminars. By spreading the word throughout the 1980s and early 1990s, attendance at ICR's museum reached more than 25,000 attendees in 1992 (A&F 1992: Vol. 21(11), page 1). Still, during this period, ICR remained primarily focused on its educational efforts through the graduate school, seminars, and research trips.

57 A&F 1995: Vol. 24(11), page c.

58 Answers 2006: July, page 1.

59 While Alton Everest was a leader of the broader ASA who did not have more than a Bachelor of Arts degree, ASA was not affiliated with the YEC movement.

60 Answers 1994: Vol. 1, page 3.

61 Answers 1995: Vol. 2.

62 A&F 1999: Vol. 28(11), page 3.

63 AiG wanted to be innovative in how they secured laypersons for the movement and coupled their appeals for funds to construct physical buildings with new technology such as creating a website early on (circa 1995) and increasing the professionalism of their video programming. AiG also moved ahead with other advancements in technology, offering lectures on CD-ROM before ICR, even though AiG had a much smaller pool of resources. AiG converted this smaller pool of financial resources into a strength, "There were over 1,600 CSM [AiG] supporters who gave two or more gifts over the year that amounted to under $50.00. Yet, these donations totaled [*sic*] $26,310" (Answers 1994: Vol. 1, page 3).

64 Answers 1995: Vol. 2, page 3.

65 The direction is gleaned by in-depth analysis and reading the entire passage rather than just auto-coding; Answers 1999, August.

66 Williams 2004.

67 A&F 2007: Vol. 36(6), page 1.

68 A&F 1977: Vol. 6(3), page 2.

69 A&F 1988: Vol. 17(9), page 5.

70 Overall, ICR mentioned the museum in 65 instances throughout Episode 2, approximately 40% of the total 157 instances across both episodes. Compare this to 92 times, approximately 60%, in Episode 3. The increase in Episode 3 was also during a shorter time span, as Episode 3 covers fourteen years compared to twenty-one years for Episode 2. Why the uptick in discussion of the museum rather than the continued silence from Episode 2 into Episode 3? The timing and coverage pattern suggests that the discussion of the museum began to spike when Ken Ham joined ICR in 1986. Ham began contributing a regularly featured series of lay-oriented articles in comparison to previous "Impact" newsletters, which often discussed a technical matter directly related to creation science. Instead, Ham's series "Back to Genesis" referenced the seminar series he created with the same title when he joined ICR. In these seminars, he was explicit about the organization's goal, espoused in the header of the series: "Foundation for Family and Nation" (A&F 1989: Vol. 18(1)).

71 A&F 1994: Vol. 23(1), page 4.

72 A&F 2007: Vol. 36(1), page 2. Later in 2008, an outside buyer, Tom Cantor, stepped up to take over the museum. He is the owner of Scantibodies Laboratory in the San Diego region and has subsequently changed quite a bit of the museum. He was never affiliated with ICR or the movement.

73 A&F 1992: Vol. 21.

74 A&F 1993: Vol. 22(11), page 1.

75 A&F 1994: Vol. 23(9), page 1.

76 A&F 1996: Vol. 25(5), page c.

77 Wilson 1973; Snow and Benford 1988; Benford and Snow 2000.

78 Answers 2005: May.

79 As Ham proclaims, "Though no one knows exactly what other logical outcomes of an evolutionized, humanized worldview are around the corner, we can already

discern glimpses through such things as school shootings, euthanasia lobbies, and the like. One powerful way to help confront the humanistic worldview that demeans life and hides its real purpose is the building of AiG's Creation Museum near Cincinnati, where the true history of the world will be presented. Won't it be exciting to see busloads of students exiting our museum having learned true history, from the Bible, including the fact that sin is the real cause of death, pain, and suffering?" (Answers 2001: Vol. 8, page 4).

80 A&F 1979: Vol. 8(12), page i.

81 Supplemental analyses are available from the author upon request.

82 Answers 1995: Vol. 2, page 5; Answers 1995: Vol. 2, page 3.

83 A&F 1991: Vol. 20(2), page a.

84 A&F 1994: Vol. 23(2), page 8.

85 A&F 2002: Vol. 31(1), page 1.

86 A&F 1995: Vol. 24(11), page 1.

87 Binder 2002; Lienesch 2007; Moran 2012.

3. ENACTING A MUSEUM

1 Interview conducted September 18, 2012. Throughout the chapter, interview citations indicate the date of the interview being referenced.

2 See Sewell (2005) for a historical treatment of the practice turn. See Polletta (2008) and Isaac (2009) for the importance of tracing cultural practices in social movement activity. This body of scholarship dovetails with a current focus in the sociology of religion on unpacking religious believers' actions. For a review, Edgell (2012). And see Epstein (2008) for a review of this tradition as it pertains to science and technology studies.

3 See Latour 1983; Ophir and Shapin 1991; Knorr-Cetina 1992, 1997, 1999; Shapin 1994; Kohler 2002; Henke and Gieryn 2008.

4 The case of the Museum of Jurassic Technology (MJT) in Culver City, California is illustrative of how attention to materiality may persuade or, in this case, confuse visitors (Biagioli 1995; Weschler 1995; Gieryn 2001; Roth 2002; Jansen 2008). Robert Jansen (2008) examined how individuals and groups came to understand the MJT, a museum whose reception ranges from being seen as an oddball art project/prank to a provocative exercise. As Jansen explains, "Most museums ask visitors to take their spatial 'materiality' . . . for granted. The MJT, on the other hand, complicates these spatial elements" (130). He highlights how the MJT obfuscates visitors' expectations through the museum-form, where the labyrinth structure leaves visitors frequently disconnected and lost from their group, and the museum-content is complete with a wide array of bewildering, at times incoherent, exhibits.

5 For historical context of natural history museums' development, see Bennett 1995, 1998; Conn 1998, 2010; Golinski 2005; Forgan 1994, 2005; Yanni 2005, 2014.

6 For more on the Hezbollah Resistance Museum, see Krieger (2007). Autry (2013) highlights that the Black Museum movement in the 1970s developed in response

to the neglect or negative portrayal of African Americans across museums in the United States. They offered not only alternative museums but also an alternative to the American Alliance of Museums, one of the largest professional museum organizations in the world, the Association of African American Museums. This network of black museums continues to maintain its own professional organization (71).

7 See Forgan (2005) for the importance of multisensory analysis of museum visitors' experiences; Griswold, Mangione, and McDonnell (2013) for a discussion of proximity and spatial arrangement in museums; Mangione (2016) for insight into situated museum conventions and choices about multisensory engagement; Klett (2014) for how sound shapes our experience in ways that often go unrecognized by visitors and undertheorized by sociologists; and Rose-Greenland (2016) for the role of color in a museum exhibit's negotiation of accuracy and authenticity. See Brennemann and Miller (2016) for a comprehensive call to focus more on the significance of religious buildings in order to better understand how its materiality impacts believers; and Hirschkind (2006) for an example of how the politics of sound operated through the widespread distribution of cassettes with recorded popular Muslim sermons on them (khutaba') in Cairo, Egypt.

8 Questions about how people create or wield culture have long animated the interdisciplinary field of materiality, see Mukerji (1994), Knorr-Cetina (1997), DeNora (2000), Keane (2003), Dominquez-Rubio (2014), McDonnell (2016), and Greenland (2019).

9 As architectural historian Carla Yanni (2005[1999]) points out about nineteenth-century natural history museums, "Most of these buildings were the architectural products of multifarious committees, and as a result the buildings communicate ambiguously or ineffectually" (3).

10 de Vaujany and Vaast (2013) unpack how, on the heels of the 1968 student protests, a Parisian university was crafted out of a former North Atlantic Treaty Organization (NATO) building, a hub for Cold War activity. They underscore the ongoing maintenance and "mutual construction of organizational space and legitimacy" and thereby destabilize notions of coherency associated with the built environment (713).

11 For this chapter, I collected data from July 2011 to March 2017, throughout more than thirty multiple-day visits (e.g., two to three days each) to the museum, which resulted in more than one hundred hours of observation and approximately one thousand photographs of museum exhibits, floor plans, and the museum grounds. I also conducted twenty-three interviews with twenty participants, eighteen of whom worked at AiG.

12 Field Notes, March 11, 2017.

13 My emphasis on AiG's purposeful decisions is informed by the interdisciplinary work bound up in the aforementioned interdisciplinary "practice turn." To trace how audiences are encouraged to "infer" meaning, I draw on McDonnell's (2010, 2016) work on "enunciation" inspired by de Certeau (1984) whereby audiences

relate and stretch in varying directions the creators' intended meaning of a given cultural object or, in this case, exhibits in a museum's built environment. See Stoltz and Taylor (2017) for an analysis of "purposeful enunciation" where physical forms of money (cash, coins) are used by "instigators" to protest and to foster an alternative interpretation of money that is captured by the media. Interestingly, their concept of "purposeful enunciation" elides what I keep analytically distinct in this chapter. First, I capture what AiG, as instigators, purposefully do to impart their worldview in their site, in comparison to what a generalized audience enunciates in their walk-through of the Creation Museum. I explore the specific audience inferences in greater depth in subsequent chapters as captured by the news media and as discussed in social media.

14 See Rose-Greenland (2016) for a detailed account of how museum visitors' perception that ancient Greek and Roman marble sculptures should be white and austere trumped curators' desire for a more historically accurate use of color on the statues. Rose-Greenland unpacks how the general public's desire for authenticity is rooted in what they had become accustomed to rather than an evolving conception of what these statues should look like based on new research.

15 Asma 2007.

16 Interview conducted September 18, 2012.

17 Field Notes, August 24, 2010.

18 Interview conducted July 28, 2012.

19 See Gieryn (2008) for a discussion of contemporary laboratory buildings whose hallmark is large glass, transparent walls and open floor plans. And, many evangelical megachurch structures now embody visual connections to contemporary commercial building trends, too. They are often complete with landscaped campuses, earth-tone color schemes inside, large, open multipurpose spaces, floor-to-ceiling glass windows, and extensive use of technology. By drawing on the look and feel of commercial real estate, megachurches have become a fixed part of the American cultural landscape since they are not a "special destination" but instead yet another public building that happens to be infused with religious meaning (Kilde 2006: 236–238). Since the late 1970s and early 1980s, these structures have been on the rise and reflect a long-standing evangelical commitment to reach as many people as possible and to congregate in large, shared spaces as a symbol of commitment (Kilde 2002; Loveland and Wheeler 2003). It underscores how the evangelical movement's approach, its layperson, broad-base support, is reiterated in choices of the built environment.

20 Rothstein 2007. And, cultural critic Stephen Asma (2011) makes the observation, "It also seems ironic that secular museums historically borrowed the visual rhetoric and architecture of sacred temples to lend gravitas and credibility to their claims, and now the Creation Museum is borrowing the visual rhetoric of secular museums to make their religious claims more credible" (146).

21 Interview conducted September 18, 2012. AiG comments on this aspect tongue-in-cheek in its *Behind the Scenes* book, "Looks like rock, feels like rock, and even

smells like rock, but it isn't rock! These lightweight hollow rock casts give the museum a very natural feel without the cost of real rock" (McKeever et al. 2008: 27).

22 Interview conducted September 30, 2011.

23 McKeever et al. 2008: 74.

24 See Diamond and Scotchmoor 2006: 25, "Inviting visitors to journey through time is a popular approach in natural history museum evolution exhibits."

25 See Forgan (1994) for a historical discussion of how science museums' built environment reflects contestations over knowledge production.

26 Throughout the eighteenth and early nineteenth centuries, exhaustive collections and systematic classifications of fossils were presented in support of divine wisdom and creation; even famous botanist Carl Linnaeus's taxonomic efforts could be harnessed in the pursuit of closer understandings of God's creation and plan. But, those same fossils could also be read as evidence of a thoroughly secularized understanding of natural selection and evolution. Charles Willson Peale's Museum in Philadelphia (1786) was generally considered the first natural history museum in the United States. Rather than display oddities and freaks of nature, Peale anchored his collection in academic and scholarly understandings—placing education above mere entertainment. Peale's fidelity to Linnaean classification systems led many collectors to deposit their fossil collections in his museum. Yet at the same time, he was fond of referring to his museum as a "House of God" (Schofield 1989: 37). This distinctively eighteenth-century brand of nature, truth, and divinity soon caused Peale's museum to fall out of favor with the general public, who came to prefer the new public museums created in Washington, DC, such as the Smithsonian, or distinct carnivals and sideshows.

27 Timeline exhibit caption in the entrance of Evolving Planet, recorded February 2017.

28 Lelièvre 2006.

29 The Field Museum and the Evolving Planet exhibit are used throughout the analysis for comparison since it is the largest and most well-known natural history museum geographically proximate to the Creation Museum. Fieldwork observations occurred from February 2016 to January 2017.

30 See Classen (2007) and Howes (2014) for a historical review of sensory museology.

31 See Findlen (1994) for a meticulous historical analysis of the transitions in curiosity cabinets during the sixteenth and seventeenth centuries in Italy.

32 See Bennett (1995, 1998) for how the shift toward a broader public demographic of museum visitors shaped expectations for displays of civility and comportment.

33 Historian and archaeologist Stephanie Moser (2003) notes this trend, "The introduction of more entertaining displays in the 1800s, particularly in natural history exhibitions, where large beasts were stuffed and featured in combat scenes, also attracted negative comments from scholars. Despite such resistance, by the end of the 19th century it was common for museums to create displays that looked like stage sets, and the men of science . . . to reluctantly accept that museums were

places where people came to be entertained. Thus, the current trend in museums to be more theatrical is a recent manifestation of a persisting theme, and while the pressure to become commercially viable is one reason for this increasing trend, also relevant is the increasing involvement of designers and 'visual professionals' in the display creation process. Although this had led to some positive developments (e.g., displays do not suffer from visual overload as much as they used to), many displays are now so slick and retail-like in their appearance that they have lost their distinctiveness" (16). See Barry (1998) for an account of how interactivity developed in contemporary museums across different cultural contexts.

34 Classen (2007) details how this prioritization occurred within the museum context throughout the eighteenth and nineteenth centuries (907). Hetherington (2002) contextualizes what it means to see by distinguishing between sight and "scopic"—how one knows what they might be seeing and makes sense of it in relation to others—in order to frame the significance of the historical shift when museums went from an orientation steeped in a concern for aesthetics or a picturesque setting to one that purported logic and chronology (187, 191–192).

35 Interview conducted April 20, 2012.

36 Interview conducted September 20, 2012.

37 Ironically, then, AiG indirectly draws upon a long line of work within the social sciences and philosophy that examines the moral, religious, and social foundations upon which science as an institution developed, i.e., how knowledge is constructed since scientific findings do not simply emerge from the natural world intact. See Golinski (2005) for a comprehensive historical review of constructivism as it relates to the sciences.

38 AiG discusses the origins of the dichotomy between historical and observational science in response to the following question from a reader, "As a scientist, I never encountered the terms 'historical' vs. 'observational' science before seeing them on your website." AiG replied, "The first recent major use of this concept, contrasting operational (observational) science with [human] origins (historical) science, was in *The Mystery of Life's Origin* (1984) by Charles Thaxton" (Lacey 2011).

39 An antagonistic view of the education system is deeply rooted in the creationist movement, which dates back to the Supreme Court cases in the 1960s where mandated prayer in the classroom and banning the teaching of evolution based on religious arguments were ruled unconstitutional; see *Abington School District v. Schempp* (1963) and *Epperson v. Arkansas* (1968) respectively. These decisions agitated many creationists; subsequently, Toumey (1994) suggested that the inclusion/exclusion of creationism in public school science curricula became an ultimate litmus test for movement success in the latter half of the twentieth century. Nonetheless, Binder's (2002) study found that even when creationists had political clout across the cases she analyzed, they were resoundingly unsuccessful in sustained influence and integration into the public school curricula, hence creationists' ongoing frustration (and increasingly active support of homeschooling).

40 Field Notes, March 11, 2017.

41 Classen 2007: 904.

42 The style of the Creation Museum's soundtrack is in keeping with broader trends in the evangelical music industry, if not aesthetically perceived as dated. See Marti (2017) for a review of Hillsong, one of the largest Christian music producers in the world where an emphasis on more contemporary rock music for worship services is distributed broadly. Yet AiG perceives Hillsong to be too mainstream, see Ham (2010).

43 See Levent and Pascual-Leone (2014), Kang and Schulte-Fortkamp (2016), and Klett (2014) for more on how soundscapes influence perceptions of the built environment.

44 McKeever et al. 2008: 82.

45 Field Notes, January 18, 2012.

46 Field Notes, March 22, 2012.

47 Interestingly, they did try to attend to these kind of aural conflation issues. As they note, "Many of the walls, like the one behind the Special Effects Theater and the wall between the bookstore and planetarium, required special sound proofing insulation to prevent the films from being heard through the walls" (McKeever et al. 2008: 97). But it appears the smaller videos were not as easily cordoned off.

48 Third Mass Extinction video, Field Museum, copyright 2006.

49 See MacDonald (1998) for a review of interactivity in museums and Conn (2006) for a more focused discussion of interactivity in science centers and museums.

50 Field Notes, March 10, 2017.

51 Interview conducted September 30, 2011.

52 Interview conducted September 30, 2011.

53 Witcomb 2006.

54 McKeever et al. 2008: 34.

55 Answers in Genesis 2008a: 22.

56 Fossilization Video, Field Museum, copyright 2006.

57 Classen 2007: 904.

58 See Murphy (2006) for a discussion of sensory engagement within institutionalized settings.

59 Text quoted from Stop #380 Confusion Room (Babel), audio tour. AiG acknowledges its own faith community's complicated past with race, colonization, and genocide. Yet AiG places much more emphasis on underscoring the prominence of Social Darwinism for justifying slavery, for instance, rather than pointing to the role of Christianity and slaveholders' readings of the Bible to support their claims as well. The latter is mentioned in various articles but not in the exhibit itself.

60 Yanni (2005) highlights how sometimes patrons even dined within the exhibits (135); see Cain (2013) for a detailed discussion of such an event held at the Crystal Palace Dinosaurs in London during the 1850s.

61 Ken Ham argues that climate change dates back to Noah's era and the Great Flood. He suggests that climate change is not new and therefore not driven by human consumption but rather original sin, see Abrams (2014).

62 Once AiG settled in Kentucky, the search for property dragged on from 1996 to 2001. In its *Behind the Scenes* book, AiG includes a detailed timeline that spans more than twelve pages in which it reviews step by step how it searched for property, how locations it pursued were opposed by local "secular humanist" groups, and the general obstacles it faced (McKeever et al. 2008: 10–22).

63 McKeever et al. 2008: 42.

64 Interview conducted September 30, 2011.

65 McKeever et al. 2008: 75.

66 McKeever et al. 2008: 66.

67 Often recounted within creationist circles, a prominent feature of Kurt Wise's biography is that he was a PhD student of Stephen Jay Gould at Harvard University. Gould was a renowned paleontologist and ardent critic of creationism. Gould was particularly active in public debates about creationism held at universities and media outlets throughout the second half of the twentieth century (Numbers 2006: 310).

68 Interview conducted December 14, 2012.

69 Interview conducted September 30, 2011.

70 Interview conducted September 30, 2011.

71 Interview conducted September 20, 2012.

4. "LUCY" UP CLOSE

1 Moser 2003: 16.

2 Capitalization and italics original.

3 Rothman 2015.

4 Dinosaurs and Fossil Evidence, Creation Museum Exhibit Text, parentheses original.

5 Snelling 2016.

6 Australian Museum 2015.

7 A retired Professor of Anatomy from Washington University School of Medicine in St. Louis, Menton gave talks and published materials with AiG about Lucy's anatomy over the years. This body of work, frequently titled, "Three Ways to Make an Ape Man," included a combination of historical approaches and contemporary interpretations of fossil evidence to question the shared evolutionary lineage between humans and primates.

8 Scott and Giusti 2006: 53.

9 Moser 2003.

10 MacDonald and Wiley 2012: 14.

11 Cladograms may be another way that organisms are related without the length of the branches holding as much significance for evolutionary mechanisms. See for further discussion the Understanding Evolution website, a collaboration between

the University of California Museum of Paleontology and the National Center for Science Education.

12 MacDonald and Wiley 2012: 26.

13 Moser 2003: 14.

14 MacDonald and Wiley 2012: 15.

15 Creation Museum's Primary Museum Document, p. 141.

16 "Science: The Lucy Link." *Time* January 29, 1979, Vol. 113, No. 5.

17 Spiegel et al. 2006: 73.

18 Diamond et al. 2012 cited in MacDonald and Wiley 2012: 15.

19 To, Tenenbaum, and Wormald 2016.

20 To et al. 2016: 378.

21 To et al. 2016; Spiegel et al. 2006.

22 Menton and Mitchell 2012.

23 "The Museum traces its roots back to a two-room wooden structure on Public Square that served as a meeting place for 26 young men interested in the natural sciences. Because the mounted birds and mammals occupied every corner of the building, it became known as the 'Ark.' The young men are called the 'Arkites'" (Cleveland Museum of Natural History website, accessed May 2018).

24 Mitchell 2013.

25 Field Museum website, www.fieldmuseum.org.

26 Evolving Planet Exhibit website, www.fieldmuseum.org.

27 Fieldwork from February to December 2017.

28 Mullen 2006.

29 Looy 2006.

30 Smithsonian website, https://naturalhistory.si.edu.

31 Named after a key funder, David H. Koch, who is a well-known philanthropist and political fund-raiser for politically conservative causes, the exhibit's opening had more controversy about the paucity of its treatment of climate change in relation to human evolution than conservative religious rancor (Kamen and Itkowitz 2015).

32 *Official Guide to the Smithsonian National Museum of Natural History*, revised edition. 2014.Washington, DC: Smithsonian Books.

33 Smithsonian website, https://naturalhistory.si.edu.

34 Ham 2010.

35 Site visits were conducted from February 2017 to December 2017.

36 Creation Museum interviews, online content; Cleveland Museum of Natural History email with staff, online content; Smithsonian National Natural History Museum curator interviews, online content, internal documents; Field Museum online interviews, content, archives.

37 Descriptions of inquirer categories and use of inquirer dictionaries. General Inquirer website, www.wjh.harvard.edu, retrieved January 2, 2015.

38 Three measures of assertion, positive claim, certainty (SureLw, Overstatement, Causal); three measures of doubt, uncertainty, or negation (If, Understatement, NotLw); three measures of neutral knowledge, claims (Academy, Perceive, Solve).

39 See Evans 2011, 2013; O'Brien and Noy 2015; Noy and O'Brien 2016. Roos 2016 examines how social scientists measure contested knowledge.

40 National Center for Science and Engineering Statistics 2016: 828.

41 Gallup Poll 2014.

42 Larson 2006.

43 Genesis 1:27, New King James Version.

44 Swift 2017.

45 Interestingly, there is a plaque in the lower level of the Creation Museum using a series of horses to argue that "Organisms change rapidly as the earth changes," but there is no mention of the infamous horse series and it is located in an offshoot area by the bathroom. See AiG's blog post on the horse fossil series.

46 Overall frequencies for Evidence (44 total): Cleveland Museum of Natural History (3), Creation Museum (21), Field Museum (9), Smithsonian National Museum of Natural History (11).

47 Proportion is based on the number of references to evidence divided by the total number of codes assigned across all categories.

48 Diamond and Scotchmoor 2006: 28.

49 All direct quotes of exhibit content are identified in relation to the respective museum and its human origins exhibit.

50 Ironically, the relative completeness of Lucy's fossil record is also frequently cited in the mainstream museums given the rareness and difficulty of such a discovery. But, given approximately less than a quarter of Lucy's fossils were directly involved in the 1970s discovery positions AiG's emphasis on the incompleteness of the fossil record as potentially plausible for a general visitor.

51 Anatomical features are all discussed in the exhibit, but the order has been adjusted to provide a side-by-side comparison. All boldface text in table 4.1 is by the author.

52 Moser 2003: 4. Other work supports this trend. See Carnall, Ashby, and Ross (2013) for how a museum management journal article about an intentionally controversial exhibit full of questions about conservation, the ethics of museum collections, the biological study of race, and humans' destruction of the natural world does not mention human origins as a similarly contentious issue.

53 For instance, after deriding the American Museum of Natural History for ending their human origins exhibit with video excerpts of scientists discussing the potential for compatibility between religion and science as sources of authority, philosopher Stephen Asma argued, "The Smithsonian, by contrast, seems to avoid this careful placating, sensitive tiptoeing, and accommodating consideration. Refreshingly, the David H. Koch Hall of Human Origin does not treat the visitor with kid gloves. The curators do not seem nervous about evangelical blowback. They don't waste time and space repeatedly reassuring visitors with plaques and videos about the dignity of everyone's diverse cultural beliefs (Asma 2011: 152).

54 Landau 2007.

55 Nine codes across three axes (positive, neutral, or negative claims) were identified as relevant for capturing tone in the GI dictionary. Since the analysis is keyword driven, phrases or sentences could be coded more than once.

56 GI codes SureLw, Overstatement, Causal.

57 GI codes If, Understatement, NotLw.

58 GI codes Academy, Perceive, Solve.

59 General Inquirer 2002.

60 Asma 2011; Moser 2003.

61 Manual codes.

62 The Smithsonian's interactive booth asks visitors, "What would you look like as an early human?" The booth photographs the person sitting in front of a multimedia screen and instructs, "Turn yourself into one of these eight species. Sahelanthropus tchadensis; Homo erectus; Homo floresiensis; Homo heidelbergensis; Homo neanderthalensis; Paranthropus boisei; Australopithecus africanus; Australopithecus afarensis." Yet there is no accompanying discussion as to how the images are constructed.

63 Scott and Giusti 2006: 62–63.

64 Interestingly, AiG's emphasis on artistic reconstruction finds some support in the literature. See Moser (2003) for more about ethno-racial representation in human origins exhibits: "Many museum visitors assume that the subject of human evolution does not have a contemporary political dimension because it is about extremely ancient specimens living in the very distant past. This is a false assumption, because displays about hominid ancestors have an influence on perceptions of racial difference and the links between contemporary populations and 'primitive' ancestors . . . One way of achieving this [correction] would be to show how historic images of ancestors that emphasized their primitive qualities (e.g. hairiness, hunched posture, nakedness) attributed them with many features of African people, and that the legacy of this practice lives on because such images continue to be reinforced in popular representations. Visitors should be encouraged to acknowledge this bias and challenge the associations that are still made between hominid ancestors and living populations. This could be done by alerting visitors to the fact that the skin colour chosen when depicting ancient ancestors has contemporary implications for people in the present" (10, 11).

65 Menton and Mitchell 2012.

66 Moser 2003: 11.

67 Scott and Giusti 2006: 65.

68 Hine and Medvecky 2015: 7.

69 Museum professionals, Mark Carnall, Jack Ashby, and Claire Ross (2013), provide the historical context, "The concept of trusting audiences and encouraging visitor participation in interpretation runs contrary to the traditional ideas of museum authority and communication" (66).

70 Implicit is the operative word here since the only reference I have seen in AiG materials in relation to this body of science studies work is the best-selling Thomas Kuhn text, *The Structure of Scientific Revolutions* (1962).

5. WHAT AUDIENCES THINK OF THE CREATION MUSEUM

1 See for historical context Lipsky (1968) and for more contemporary discussions of using media reach as a gauge for public influence see Gamson 2004; Koopmans 2004; Amenta et al. 2009; Andrews and Caren 2010.

2 Earl et al. 2004.

3 McCarthy and Zald 1977; Barker-Plummer 2002; Ortiz et al. 2005; Amenta et al. 2009.

4 McAdam et al. 1996; Oliver and Maney 2000; Earl et al. 2004; Rohlinger et al. 2012.

5 Oliver and Myers 1999; Oliver and Maney 2000; Koopmans 2004; see for review Earl et al. 2004.

6 Gans 1979; Gitlin 1980; Oliver and Myers 1999; Koopmans 2004.

7 Griswold 2004: 122.

8 Ferree 2003; Rohlinger et al. 2012.

9 Cultural resonance is analytically tricky to pin down since it may often be treated cyclically—something resonates because it taps into an issue for the audience, and in turn it works because it resonates for the audience. Cultural sociologists McDonnell, Bail, and Tavory (2017) point to a way out, "Our approach recasts resonance as an emergent process wherein the fit between a cultural message and its audience shifts over time . . . As people encounter cultural objects in specific situations, some of them crystallize into such a solution to a problem encountered in actors' lives. This solution can take different forms: it may crystallize a previously unarticulated experience, provide a novel way to approach a problem actors routinely encounter, or actually problematize something previously taken for granted" (2, 4).

10 For a discussion of social movement outcomes in relation to culture, see Earl 2000, 2004; Isaac 2008; Polletta 2008. More broadly, social and cultural change are often measured in terms of shifts in economic and political institutions. This neglects those who demand change that is not directed toward some economic or political injustice (Crane 1992: 95). In fact, the social movement literature has yet to take culture as seriously as it might. For foundational work establishing this renewed line of inquiry, see Polletta 2004; Van Dyke, Soule, and Taylor 2004; Armstrong and Bernstein 2008; Isaac 2009.

11 While issues of production and design have received a substantial amount of attention, reception has been relatively neglected; more emphasis has been placed on the creators/designers and the field in which their activity occurs. "Reception theory" developed mainly among scholars who were more interested in the cultural products themselves. Central lines of inquiry included: how cultural products were interpreted by audiences; how some objects (such as novels or television) carried multiple and contrasting meanings; and how social location like audiences' socioeconomic position influenced how they engaged with cultural goods (Bourdieu 1984, 1992; Crane 1992; Press 1994). But, as Isaac (2009) asserts,

rarely is the "production of culture" perspective connected to a social movement's efforts to change a specific institutional arena, which requires moving beyond the study of cultural products for consumption.

12 Berezin 1994; Stamatov 2002; Griswold 2004; Zubrzycki 2013; McDonnell 2016.

13 Clayman and Reisner 1998.

14 Social movement actors may use culture in principled ways (ideological commitments, beliefs, or shared values) and with instrumental methods (calculating, pragmatic) in order to be effective (Johnston and Klandermans 1995; Polletta 2004, 2008). This often occurs during "unsettled times" when institutions are perceived as having multiple, contradictory schemas, and ideological clarity is preferred by the public as opposed to the dissonance commonly accepted among the public during more settled periods of history (Swidler 1986, 1995; Griswold 2004; Isaac 2009; Wagner-Pacifici 2010; Bail 2012).

15 Research on innovative cultural and organizational forms is well established, but the study of the reception of alternative institutions like a museum produced by a social movement is much less common. Most work analyzing a new form—whether it be the appropriation of an existing community institution, the creation of a new clinic, or the adoption of a volunteer association's organizational structure—fails to focus on how that form is received outside the movement that produces it (Clemens 1993; Rao, Morrill, and Zald 2000; Davis et al. 2005). This inattention is particularly evident for alternative institutions such as social welfare agencies, free healthcare clinics, or churches, which are intended first and foremost to address the immediate needs of their communities. In these accounts, however, the physical and geographic sites were crucial for current and potential adherents to learn about the movement.

16 What shapes the immediate patterns of social movements' media attention are the documented patterns of bias (cultural, religious, and political) among media producers. To offset this bias, some social movement scholars draw on a variety of newspaper sources. Rather than draw only from mainstream news such as the *New York Times*, the goal is to capture how the content for mainstream audiences and for specialized audiences may differ. For instance, Rohlinger et al. (2012) found that political elites (such as the President) significantly increase media coverage in specialized, partisan media outlets by increasing attention to anti-abortion efforts, but there was no corresponding effect in mainstream news outlets. Banerjee (2013) found that negative coverage of the Tea Party in partisan media sources provided an opportunity for advocates to frame such negative coverage as evidence of liberal media bias. This coincides with right-wing efforts to build alternative media outlets as a counter to this perceived bias. See also Diamond 1995, Blee and Creasap 2010; Gross et al 2011; Worthen 2014.

17 By extending the focus beyond protest events, I minimize some of the larger concerns about social movement scholars' bias toward using newspaper data to construct protest event measures for dependent variables (Ortiz et al. 2005).

18 Using seven media sources, compared to the usual one or two, helps curb the influence of bias and increases reliability. I performed searches using Lexus Nexus Academic, Academic Search Premier, and each source's internal archives whenever available. For discussion of how media sources vary by geographic scope, see Oliver and Maney 2000; Andrews and Caren 2010. I follow Earl et al.'s (2004) suggestion to use both a triangulation of media sources and electronic archives (74).

19 While all articles were collected that met the search criteria, 311 articles (18.09%) did not warrant any subsequent coding. The final sample size was 1,719 articles.

20 "State of the News Media," Pew Research Center, www.pewresearch.org. While the *Los Angeles Times* was considered, restricted access to articles dating back to the 1990s made it untenable.

21 Groseclose and Milyo 2005.

22 "Who We Are," *Christianity Today*, www.christianitytoday.org.

23 Worthen 2014.

24 "About," *World*, www.worldmag.com.

25 See Kaden (2019) for additional background on the National Center for Science Education's connections to the creationist movement.

26 The NCSE's submission on the non-profit clearinghouse site: "The National Council for Science and the Environment," GuideStar, http://www.guidestar.org.

27 See www.sciencemag.org.

28 This difference could affect the type and range of coverage, see Ortiz et al. 2005.

29 During pre-testing, in order to yield valid results, I examined every available article within a given source and finalized the search criteria for the search terms and time period.

30 See Oliver and Maney (2000) for further discussion. I treated each sentence as the textual unit of analysis in the search for pre-defined codes (exact search terms to reduce ambiguity). For instance, the code name Answers in Genesis was used for any reference to the organization using terms "AiG"; "Answers in Genesis"; "Answers." I reviewed all articles that resulted from the sampling strategy, and manually removed false positives. Duplicates, defined as identical content on the same day of publication in the same source (e.g., morning and evening editions), were common, and in these cases the first instance was accepted, while subsequent duplicates were thrown out.

31 Pre-testing indicated that a small number of articles used some search terms repeatedly within the same article (often quite frequently).

32 Rather than use the dataset to capture only media attention to protest events (a common approach in much of the social movements' literature), I analyze data on a range of routine events over time (Rohlinger et al. 2012).

33 Relying on previous literature on creationism to determine the types of contexts, I used construct validity to ensure that the output from this coding structure would capture what I intended.

34 Sarah Eekhoff Zylstra, "Ken Ham's Enormous Ark Park Open for Business," *Christianity Today*, July 7, 2016, www.christianitytoday.com.

35 *World*, October 10, 2008.

36 Oliver and Maney (2000) found that while disruptive protests (e.g., marches, rallies, pickets) received more coverage, non-protest forms (e.g., ceremonies, speeches) were more often covered if controversial issues were addressed in those events (482, 498).

37 For more about the "tent strategy," see Numbers (2006: 380); for more about the "wedge strategy," see Forrest and Gross (2004) and Kaden (2019).

38 *Christianity Today. Headlines.* July 2007, www.christianitytoday.com.

39 Oliver and Myers 1999; Earl et al. 2004; Amenta et al. 2009; Andrews and Caren 2010.

40 For instance, most search engines began in 1994/1995 and there was a dramatic jump in the number of websites from 1996 (approximately 250,000 sites) to 1997 (over a million sites). "Total Number of Websites," Internet Live Stats, www.internetlivestats.com.

41 Karl Giberson and Darrel Falk, "We Believe in Evolution," *USA Today*, August 10, 2009, www.usatoday.com.

42 Oliver and Maney 2000; Earl et al. 2004; Amenta et al. 2009.

43 See Rohlinger and Earl (2017) for an overview. AiG's continued focus on digital activism through their website and social media accounts is in keeping with Schradie's (2019) work that underscores the amount of energy conservative right-wing movements dedicated to using the internet as a platform for their own ideas to circulate since the mid-2000s. Schradie finds that hierarchical groups with a lot of resources (monetary and volunteers) are most successful in doing so, like AiG.

44 "Traffic Overview," SimilarWeb, March 29, 2019, www.similarweb.com.

45 Interview conducted September 30, 2011.

46 Lewandowsky et al. 2015; Castro and Andrews 2018; Koltsova and Shcherbak 2015.

47 Issues with attendance estimates include that children are free (under the age of six typically) and others may have lifetime passes. On average, attendance tends to be approximately 300,000 people per year and this remains relatively steady throughout its operations (Westerman 2016).

48 A classic reception studies approach would survey museum-goers focused on visitor feedback capturing their immediate impressions. While possible to collect during my on-site fieldwork, there were limitations in terms of movement dynamics, and methodologically. I had concerns about the autonomy of the data collection process—would my access be revoked at certain points or would the data collected require pre-approval before I analyzed and published it. But more important, the analytical limitations ultimately proved this approach unviable. The overall potential bias in museum visitors' response given the positioning of the museum and mixed support for immediate survey recall led me to look for ways that would allow respondents to have time to consider what they ultimately found noteworthy rather than only prioritizing their immediate reaction. A newer approach could be using Twitter, where I would analyze related hashtags associated with AiG and the Creation Museum, but there are technical and conceptual

drawbacks as well. Twitter officially began in 2006; it did not pick up broad support until later in 2007/2008, so coverage during the target time period is not consistent and the restricted amount of content per tweet made this less compelling. In addition, Twitter's demographics are skewed. Some 24% of online adults used Twitter in January 2018, and it is particularly popular among those under age thirty and the college-educated. Since a goal of this chapter is to unpack what audiences think, my aim is to maximize the reach and span of the audiences captured (Pew Social Media Fact Sheet).

49 In order to minimize ethical concerns about using data from personal blogs, I only searched blog posts published to be open to the public, and I cited each blog post by the title and date it was posted rather than the blog itself, which would be more readily identifiable.

50 The final search term with the least amount of noise was "creation museum" from January 1, 2005 to December 31, 2018 using the site: search limiter. My research assistant sorted through links and created a database of all the posts; two coders determined the relevance to the Creation Museum and AiG, specifically. The unit of analysis is individual blog post entry. Admittedly, there is difficulty in acquiring an exhaustive dataset. A certain degree of unexplained errors is built into the process since, despite the best efforts to properly define search conditions, wading through unknown proprietary Google algorithms sometimes produced search results that varied and it was difficult to know why. Our solution was to document the time of day and day of the week during which we performed these searches, and we performed them within a single week; hence, whatever might be operating in the background would be presumably the same. That is, we tried to narrow our search rather than collect blog posts over a long period, thereby increasing the chances that Google's search algorithms were updated, altered, or otherwise different during multiple data collection trials.

51 The following blog hosting sites were examined: wordpress.com, blogger.com, tumblr.com, squarespace.com, plus.goggle.com, medium.com, hubpages.com, joomla.com, livejournal.com, typepad.com, weebly.com, drupal.org, squidoo.com, blog.com, sett.com, and.blog. In addition, I studied one focused topical blog: freethoughtsblog.com. {AT: Should the sites listed in this note be styled as url?}

52 I invalidated any posts associated with a news media organization, e.g., CNN religion blog, or other formal organizations with a paid staff. The focus is on individuals maintaining their own personal blog sites or collectively held blog sites, but without professional staff or pay wall content (Karpf 2012).

53 While the search ranged from 2005 to 2018, no blog posts were published in 2005 or 2006.

54 "The Lowdown on the Creation," blog post, July 3, 2012, https://shellsstory.wordpress.com.

55 "The Creation Museum—A Controversial Attraction in Kentucky," blog post, April 19, 2012, http://www.odditycentral.com.

56 "Creating a Truth," blog post, August 6, 2007, https://thesmartset.com.

57 "Road Trip #13," blog post, August 11, 2016, https://pictinpa.wordpress.com.

58 "Paleontologists Visit the Answers in Genesis Museum," blog post, July 2, 2009, https://geochristian.com.

59 "Creating a Truth," blog post, August 6, 2007, https://thesmartset.com.

60 "Prepare to Believe," blog post, July 10, 2013, https://journal.davidbyrne.com.

61 "An Old-Earth Christian at the Creation Museum Part 1," blog post, August 17, 2016, https://geochristian.com.

62 "CreoZerg! PZ Myers and 285 Atheists Visit Creation Museum," blog post, August 7, 2009, https://struckbyenlightning.wordpress.com.

63 "The Universal Never-Science Museum Tour Map," blog post, March 25, 2016, http://www.whenyouworkatamuseum.com.

64 Ibid.

CONCLUSION

1 American Institute of Physics 2017; Troyan 2016.

2 Funk 2014.

3 And increasingly, the political polarization that continues to characterize the US electoral landscape suggests that both the Creation Museum and MOTB's public narrative about racial unity papers over a mobilized white base of evangelicals; as sociologist Ryan Jerome LeCount outlines, "What it means to identify with the liberal or conservative 'team' for U.S. Whites is increasingly bound up with one's racial politics. Even after considering economic measures, political ideology is increasingly driven by racial resentment in the modern United States" (LeCount 2018).

4 Gordon 2017; Saletan 2018.

5 McGlone 2019.

6 Gauchat 2012; O'Brien and Noy 2015; Scheitle 2018.

7 Numbers 2006; Worthen 2014.

8 For instance, adherents of this ideology use the alleged decline of religiosity in public life to justify their vigilant stance against "secular humanism." Secular humanism is a moral framework in which the centrality of humans displaces the importance of the supernatural. With origins in the mid-twentieth century, secular humanism was constructed largely by creationists rather than advocated for by self-identified humanist groups who focus more than anything else on the separation of Church and State during federal court cases concerning the First Amendment, see Toumey 1994: 78–81; Lienesch 2007.

9 Tooley and Milliner 2017.

10 Tooley and Milliner 2017.

11 Coppedge 2017.

12 The 2011 IRS 990 form with this language is available through ProPublica Non-profit Explorer, "Museum of the Bible, Inc."

13 Moss and Baden 2017.

14 Stewart 2018.

15 Stewart 2018.

16 Jones 2017.

17 "About Us," Museum of the Bible, December 1, 2019, www.museumofthebible.org.

18 Amos 2018.

19 Capitol Ministries, December 1, 2019, https://capmin.org/.

20 Emphasis in the original. AiG even offered potential readers complimentary tickets to MOTB, along with tickets to the Creation Museum and the Ark Encounter, as part of a publicity campaign for Ham's new book, *Gospel Reset*, see Linville 2019: 268.

21 See Linville (2019) for an extended analysis of the ideological similarities displayed in museum exhibits between the Creation Museum and MOTB.

22 Goodstein 2005.

23 Forrest and Gross 2004.

24 Meyer 2006; Discovery Institute (n.d. page 4) is not dated, but presumably is from the mid-2000s given its framing of the present discussion and the "recent events" that occurred in 2005.

25 Discovery Institute (n.d. page 2).

26 Funk 2019.

27 National Center for Education Statistics 2018; Ray 2018.

28 Dreifus 2013.

REFERENCES

Abrams, Lindsay. 2014. "Creationist Ken Ham 'Explains Climate Change: Earth Is Just 'Settling Down' After the Great Flood." *Salon*, November 24, www.salon.com.

Alexander, Victoria D. 1996. "Pictures at an Exhibition: Conflicting Pressures in Museums and the Display of Art." *American Journal of Sociology* 101:797–839.

Allison-Bunnell, Steven W. 1998. "Making Nature 'Real' Again: Natural History Exhibits and Public Rhetorics of Science at the Smithsonian Institution in the Early 1960s." Pp. 77–97 in *The Politics of Display: Museums, Science, and Culture*, edited by S. Macdonald. New York: Routledge.

Amenta, Edwin, Neal Caren, Sheera Joy Olasky, and James E. Stobaugh. 2009. "All the Movements Fit to Print: Who, What, When, Where, and Why SMO Families Appeared in the New York Times in the Twentieth Century." *American Sociological Review* 74:636–656.

American Alliance of Museums. 2009. *2009 Museum Financial Information*. Arlington, VA: American Alliance of Museums.

American Alliance of Museums. n.d. "Statistics." www.aam-us.org.

American Association for the Advancement of Science. 1980. "Republican Candidate Picks Fight with Darwin." *Science* 209:1214.

American Institute of Physics. 2017. "President Obama Leaves Broad Legacy for Science and Technology Policy." *FYI*, January 24, www.aip.org.

Amos, Owen. 2018. "Inside the White House Bible Study Group." *BBC News,* April 8, Washington DC, www.bbc.com.

Andrews, Kenneth T. and Michael Biggs. 2006. "The Dynamics of Protest Diffusion: Movement Organizations, Social Networks, and News Media in the 1960 Sit-Ins." *American Sociological Review* 71:752–777.

Andrews, Kenneth T. and Neal Caren. 2010. "Making the News: Movement Organizations, Media Attention, and the Public Agenda." *American Sociological Review* 75:841–866.

Answers in Genesis. n.d. "Dragon Legends," https://answersingenesis.org.

———. 2007. *Men in White: A Creation Museum Special Effects Theater Show*. Creation Museum Film.

———. 2008a. *Creation Museum: Prepare to Believe*. Museum Souvenir Guide.

———. 2008b. *Journey through the Creation Museum*. Green Forest, AR: Master Books.

———. 2009. "Spring Is on the Way." Answers in Genesis Blog, March 13, https://answersingenesis.org.

———. 2010. "Slaying the Dragon Myth." *Answers in Genesis Blog*, December 27, https://answersingenesis.org.

———. 2012. Collections Management Policy. Internal Document.

———. 2014. *Enhanced Tour*, May, https://creationmuseum.org.

AP-NORC. 2015. "Confidence in Institutions: Trends in Americans' Attitudes toward Government, Media, and Business." *AP-NORC*, www.apnorc.org.

Armstrong, Elizabeth A. 2002. *Forging Gay Identities: Organizing Sexuality in San Francisco, 1950–1994*. Chicago: University of Chicago Press.

———. 2005. "From Struggle to Settlement: The Crystallization of a Field of Lesbian/ Gay Organizations in San Francisco, 1969–1973." Pp. 161–188 in *Social Movements and Organization Theory*, edited by G. F. Davis, R. W. Scott, D. McAdam, and M. N. Zald. New York: Cambridge University Press.

Armstrong, Elizabeth A. and Suzanna M. Crage. 2006. "Movements and Memory: The Making of the Stonewall Myth." *American Sociological Review* 71:724–751.

Armstrong, Elizabeth and Mary Bernstein. 2008. "Culture, Power, and Institutions: A Multi-Institutional Politics Approach to Social Movements." *Social Theory* 26:74–99.

Asma, Stephen T. 2007. "Solomon's House: The Deeper Agenda of the New Creation Museum in Kentucky." *Skeptic*, May 23, www.skeptic.com.

———. 2011. "Risen Apes and Fallen Angels: The New Museology of Human Origins." *Curator: The Museum Journal* 54:141–163.

Association of Science-Technology Center. 2013. 2013 Science Center and Museum Statistics, www.astc.org.

Attridge, Harold W., Ronald L. Numbers, Kenneth R. Miller, and Keith S. Thomson. 2009. *The Religion and Science Debate: Why Does It Continue?* New Haven, CT: Yale University Press.

Autry, Robyn. 2013. "The Political Economy of Memory: The Challenges of Representing National Conflict at 'Identity Driven' Museums." *Theory and Society* 42:57–80.

Bail, Christopher A. 2012. "The Fringe Effect: Civil Society Organizations and the Evolution of Media Discourse about Islam since the September 11th Attacks." *American Sociological Review* 77:855–879.

Balser, Deborah B. 1997. "The Impact of Environmental Factors on Factionalism and Schism in Social Movement Organizations." *Social Forces* 76:199–228.

Banerjee, Tarun. 2013. "Media, Movements, and Mobilization: Tea Party Protests in the United States, 2009–2010." Pp. 39–75 in *Research in Social Movements, Conflicts and Change*, vol. 36, edited by P. G. Coy. Bingley, UK: Emerald Publishing.

Barker-Plummer, Bernadette. 2002. "Producing Public Voice: Resource Mobilization and Media Access in the National Organization for Women." *Journalism & Mass Communication Quarterly* 79:188–205.

Barry, Andrew. 1998. "On Interactivity: Consumers, Citizens, and Culture." Pp. 98–117 in *The Politics of Display: Museums, Science, Culture*, edited by S. Macdonald. New York: Routledge.

Barton, Bernadette. 2012. "'Prepare to Believe': The Creation Museum." Pp. 151–172 in *Pray the Gay Away: The Extraordinary Lives of Bible Belt Gays.* New York: New York University Press.

Beit-Hallahmi, Benjamin. 2015. "Explaining the Secularity of Academics: Historical Questions and Psychological Findings." *Science, Religion and Culture* 2:104–119.

Benford, Robert D. and David A. Snow. 2000. "Framing Processes and Social Movements: An Overview and Assessment." *Annual Review of Sociology* 26:11–39.

Bennett, Tony. 1995. *The Birth of the Museum: History, Theory, Politics.* New York: Routledge.

———. 1998. "Speaking to the Eyes: Museums, Legibility, and the Social Order." Pp. 25–35 in *The Politics of Display: Museums, Science, Culture,* edited by S. Macdonald. New York: Routledge.

Berezin, Mabel. 1994. "Cultural Form and Political Meaning: State-Subsidized Theater, Ideology, and the Language of Style in Fascist Italy." *American Journal of Sociology* 99:1237–1286.

Biagioli, Mario. 1995. "Confabulating Jurassic Science." Pp. 399–431 in *Technoscientific Imaginaries: Conversations, Profiles, and Memoirs,* edited by G. E. Marcus. Chicago: University of Chicago Press.

Bielo, James S. 2018. *Ark Encounter: The Making of a Creationist Theme Park.* New York: New York University Press.

Binder, Amy. 2002. *Contentious Curricula: Afrocentrism and Creationism in American Public Schools.* Princeton, NJ: Princeton University Press.

———. 2007. "Gathering Intelligence on Intelligent Design: Where Did It Come from, Where Is It Going, and How Do (and Should) Progressive Coalitions Manage It?" *American Journal of Education* 113:549–576.

Blau, Judith R. 1991. "The Disjunctive History of U.S. Museums, 1869–1980." *Social Forces* 70:87–105.

Blee, Kathleen M. 2002. *Inside Organized Racism: Women and Men in the Hate Movement.* Berkeley: University of California Press.

Blee, Kathleen M. and Kimberly A. Creasap. 2010. "Conservative and Right-Wing Movements." *Annual Review of Sociology* 36:269–286.

Bordt, Rebecca L. 1997. "How Alternative Ideas Become Institutions: The Case of Feminist Collectives." *Nonprofit and Voluntary Sector Quarterly* 26:132–155.

Bourdieu, Pierre. 1984. *Distinction: A Social Critique of the Judgment of Taste.* Cambridge, MA: Harvard University Press.

———. 1992. *The Rules of Art: Genesis and Structure of the Literary Field.* Stanford, CA: Stanford University Press.

Brenneman, Robert and Brian J. Miller. 2016. "When Bricks Matter: Four Arguments for the Sociological Study of Religious Buildings." *Sociology of Religion* 77:82–101.

Breyman, Steve, Nancy Campbell, Virginia Eubanks, and Abby Kinchy. 2016. "Chapter 10: STS and Social Movements: Pasts and Futures." Pp. 289–317 in *The Handbook of Science and Technology Studies,* edited by U. Felt, R. Fouché, C. A. Miller, and L. Smith-Doerr.

Browne, Janet. 2003. "Noah's Flood, the Ark, and the Shaping of Early Modern Natural History." Pp. 111–138 in *When Science and Christianity Meet*, edited by R. L. Numbers and D. C. Lindberg. Chicago: University of Chicago Press.

Butler, Ella. 2010. "God Is in the Data: Epistemologies of Knowledge at the Creation Museum." *Ethnos* 75:229–251.

Caiani, Manuela, Donatella Della Porta, and Claudius Wagemann. 2012. *Mobilizing on the Extreme Right: Germany, Italy, and the United States*. New York: Oxford University Press.

Cain, Joe. 2013. "Dinner in the Iguanodon." *Friends of Crystal Palace Dinosaurs* Blogs. July 21, http://cpdinosaurs.org.

Cameron, Fiona. 2007. "Moral Lessons and Reforming Agendas: History Museums, Science Museums, Contentious Topics and Contemporary Societies." Pp. 330–342 in *Museum Revolutions: How Museums Change and Are Changed.*, edited by Simon, Knell, S. MacLeod, and S. Watson. New York: Routledge.

Carey, Bjorn. 2010. "If Evolution Had Taken a Different Turn, Could Dragons Have Existed?" *Popular Science*, www.popsci.com.

Carnall, Mark, Jack Ashby, and Claire Ross. 2013. "Natural History Museums as Provocateurs for Dialogue and Debate." *Museum Management and Curatorship* 28:55–71.

Casanova, Jose. 1994. *Public Religions in the Modern World*. Chicago: University of Chicago Press.

Castro, Aimee and Gavin Andrews. 2018. "Nursing Lives in the Blogosphere: A Thematic Analysis of Anonymous Online Nursing Narratives." *Journal of Advanced Nursing* 74: 329–338.

Caudill, Edward. 2010. "Intelligently Designed: Creationism's News Appeal." *Journalism & Mass Communication Quarterly* 87:84–99.

Classen, Constance. 2007. "Museum Manners: The Sensory Life of the Early Museum." *Journal of Social History* 40(4):895–914.

Clayman, Steven E. and Ann Reisner. 1998. "Gatekeeping in Action: Editorial Conferences and Assessments of Newsworthiness." *American Sociological Review* 2:178–199.

Clemens, Elisabeth S. 1993. "Organizational Repertoires and Institutional Change: Women's Groups and the Transformation of US Politics, 1890–1920." *American Journal of Sociology* 98:755–798.

———. 2005. "Two Kinds of Stuff: The Current Encounter of Social Movements and Organizations." Pp. 351–366 in *Social Movements and Organization Theory*, edited by G. F. Davis, D. McAdam, W. R. Scott, and M. N. Zald. New York: Cambridge University Press.

Clemens, Elisabeth S. and James M. Cook. 1999. "Politics and Institutionalism: Explaining Durability and Change." *Annual Review of Sociology* 25:441–466.

Conn, Steven. 1998. *Museums and American Intellectual Life, 1876–1926*. Chicago: University of Chicago Press.

———. 2006. "Science Museums and the Culture Wars." Pp. 494–508 in *A Companion to Museum Studies*, edited by S. Macdonald. Malden, MA: Blackwell.

———. 2010. *Do Museums Still Need Objects?* Philadelphia: University of Pennsylvania Press.

Cooper, Karen C. 2008. *Spirited Encounters: American Indians Protest Museum Policies and Practices.* Lanham, MD: Altamira Press.

Coppedge, David F. 2017. "Museum of the Bible Opens: Biased Reporters Find Fault." *Creation Evolution Headlines*, November 18, https://crev.info.

Crane, Diana. 1992. *The Production of Culture: Media and the Urban Arts.* Newbury Park, CA: Sage.

Davenport, Christian. 2007. "State Repression and Political Order." *Annual Review of Political Science* 10:1–23.

Davis, Gerald F., Doug McAdam, Richard W. Scott, and Mayer N. Zald, eds. 2005. *Social Movements and Organization Theory.* Cambridge, UK: Cambridge University Press.

Davis, Nancy J. and Robert V. Robinson. 2012. *Claiming Society for God: Religious Movements and Social Welfare in Egypt, Israel, Italy, and the United States.* Bloomington: Indiana University Press.

de Certeau, Michel. 1984. *The Practice of Everyday Life.* Trans. S. Randall. Berkeley: University of California Press.

DeNora, Tia. 2000. *Music in Everyday Life.* New York: Cambridge University Press.

Desilver, Drew. 2017. "U.S. Students' Academic Achievement Still Lags that of Their Peers in Many Other Countries." *Pew Research Center*, February 15, http://pewrsr.ch/.

De Vaujany, François-Xavier and Emmanuelle Vaast. 2013. "If These Walls Could Talk: The Mutual Construction of Organizational Space and Legitimacy." *Organization Science* 25:713–731.

Diamond, Judy and Judy Scotchmoor. 2006. "Exhibiting Evolution." *Museums & Social Issues* 1:21–48.

Diamond, Sara. 1995. *Roads to Dominion: Right-wing Movements and Political Power in the United States.* New York: Guilford Press.

Discovery Institute. 1999. "The Wedge." *Center for the Renewal of Science & Culture.*

Discovery Institute. n.d. "The 'Wedge Document': 'So What?'" www.discovery.org/id/.

DiMaggio, Paul. 1991. "Constructing an Organizational Field as a Professional Project: U.S. Art Museums, 1920–1940." Pp. 267–292 in *The New Institutionalism in Organizational Analysis*, edited by W. Powell and P. DiMaggio. Chicago: University of Chicago Press.

Dominguez Rubio, Fernando. 2014. "Preserving the Unpreservable: Docile and Unruly Objects at MOMA." *Theory and Society* 43:617–645.

Dreifus, Claudia. 2013. "Ideas for Improving Science Education in the U.S." *New York Times*, September 2, www.nytimes.com.

Duncan, Otis D. and Claudia Geist. 2004. "The Creationists: How Many, Who, and Where?" *Reports of the National Center for Science Education* 24:26–32.

Durkheim, Emile. 1995[1912]. *Elementary Forms of the Religious Life.* New York: Free Press.

Earl, Jennifer. 2000. "Methods, Movements, and Outcomes: Methodological Difficulties in the Study of Extra-Movement Outcomes." Pp. 3–25 in *Research in Social Movements, Conflicts and Change Methods, Movements, and Outcomes*. Greenwich, CT: JAI Press.

———. 2004. "The Cultural Consequences of Social Movements." Pp. 508–530 in *The Blackwell Companion to Social Movements*, edited by D. A. Snow, S. Soule, and H. Kriesi. Malden, MA: Blackwell.

———. 2011. "Political Repression: Iron Fists, Velvet Gloves, and Diffuse Control." *Annual Review of Sociology* 37:261–284.

Earl, Jennifer, Andrew Martin, John D. McCarthy, and Sarah A. Soule. 2004. "The Use of Newspaper Data in the Study of Collective Action." *Annual Review of Sociology* 30:65–80.

Earl, Jennifer and Katrina Kimport. 2011. *Digitally Enabled Social Change: Activism in the Internet Age*. Cambridge, MA: MIT Press.

Earl, Jennifer, Katrina Kimport, Greg Prieto, Carly Rush, and Kimberly Reynoso. 2010. "Changing the World One Webpage at a Time: Conceptualizing and Explaining Internet Activism." *Mobilization* 15:425–446.

Ecklund, Elaine H. 2010. *Science Vs. Religion: What Scientists Really Think*. New York: Oxford University Press.

Ecklund, Elaine H. and Elizabeth Long. 2011. "Scientists and Spirituality." *Sociology of Religion* 72(3):253–274.

Ecklund, Elaine H., Jerry Z. Park, and Katherine L. Sorrell. 2011. "Scientists Negotiate Boundaries between Religion and Science." *Journal for the Scientific Study of Religion* 50(3):552–569.

Ecklund, Elaine H. and Christopher P. Scheitle. 2007. "Religion among Academic Scientists: Distinctions, Disciplines, and Demographics." *Social Problems* 54:289–307.

Edgell, Penny. 2012. "A Cultural Sociology of Religion: New Directions." *Annual Review of Sociology* 38:247–265.

Epstein, Steven. 1996. *Impure Science: AIDS, Activism, and the Politics of Knowledge*. Oakland: University of California Press.

———. 2007. *Inclusion: The Politics of Difference in Medical Research*. Chicago: University of Chicago Press.

———. 2008. "Culture and Science/Technology: Rethinking Knowledge, Power, Materiality, and Nature." *Annals of the American Academy of Political and Social Science* 619:165–182.

Evangelical Council for Financial Accountability. 2017. "Answers in Genesis," www.ecfa.org.

Evans, John H. 2011. "Epistemological and Moral Conflict between Religion and Science." *Journal for the Scientific Study of Religion* 50:707–727.

———. 2013. "The Growing Social and Moral Conflict between Conservative Protestantism and Science." *Journal for the Scientific Study of Religion* 52(2):368–385.

Eve, Raymond A. and Francis B. Harrold. 1990. *The Creationist Movement in Modern America*. Boston: Twayne Publishers.

Falk, Dan. 2016. "A Debate Over the Physics of Time." *Quanta Magazine*, July 19, www .quantamagazine.org.

Ferree, Myra Marx. 2003. "Resonance and Radicalism: Feminist Framing in the Abortion Debates of the United States and Germany." *American Journal of Sociology* 109:304–344.

Ferree, Myra Marx, William A. Gamson, Jurgen Gerhards, and Dieter Rucht. 2002. *Shaping Abortion Discourse: Democracy and the Public Sphere in Germany and the United States*. New York: Cambridge University Press.

Findlen, Paula. 1994. *Possessing Nature: Museums, Collecting, and Scientific Culture in Early Modern Italy*. Berkeley: University of California Press.

Foote, Michael and Arnold L. Miller. 2017. "David M. Raup: Biographical Memoirs." National Academy of Sciences, www.nasonline.org.

Forgan, Sophie. 1994. "The Architecture of Display: Museums, Universities and Objects in Nineteenth-Century Britain." *History of Science* 32:139–162.

———. 2005. "Building the Museum: Knowledge, Conflict, and the Power of Place." *Isis* 96:572–585.

Forrest, Barbara and Paul R. Gross. 2004. *Creationism's Trojan Horse: The Wedge of Intelligent Design*. New York: Oxford University Press.

Foucault, Michel. 1972. *The Archaeology of Knowledge and the Discourse on Language*. New York: Pantheon Books.

Freeman, Jo. 1983. *Social Movements of the Sixties and Seventies*. Boston, MA: Addison-Wesley Longman Ltd.

Frickel, Scott and Neil Gross. 2005. "A General Theory of Scientific/Intellectual Movements." *American Sociological Review* 70:204–232.

Frickel, Scott and Kelly Moore. 2006. *The New Political Sociology of Science: Institutions, Networks, and Power*. Madison: University of Wisconsin Press.

Friedland, Roger and Robert R. Alford. 1991. "Bringing Society Back In: Symbols, Practices and Institutional Contradictions." Pp. 232–263 in *The New Institutionalism in Organizational Analysis*, edited by W. W. Powell and P. J. DiMaggio. Chicago: University of Chicago Press.

Funk, Cary. 2014. "Republicans' Views on Evolution." *Pew Research Center*, January 3, www.pewresearch.org.

Funk, Cary. 2019. "How Highly Religious Americans View Evolution Depends on How They're Asked about It." *Pew Research Center*, February 6, www.pewresearch.org.

Funk, Cary, Jeffrey Gottfried, and Amy Mitchell. 2017. "Science News and Information Today: A Majority of Americans Rely on General Outlets for Science News but More Say Specialty Sources Get the Facts Right about Science." *Pew Research Center*, September 20, www.journalism.org.

Gallup Poll. 2014. "Evolution, Creationism, Intelligent Design," https://news.gallup .com.

Gamson, Williams A. 1998. "Social Movements and Cultural Change." Pp. 57–77 in *From Contention to Democracy*, edited by Marco G. Giugni. Lanham, MD: Rowman & Littlefield.

———. 2004. "Bystanders, Public Opinion, and the Media." Pp. 242–261 in *The Black-well Companion to Social Movements*, edited by D. A. Snow, S. A. Soule, and H. Kriesi. Malden, MA: Blackwell.

Gans, Herbert J. 1979. *Deciding What's News: A Study of CBS Evening News, NBC Nightly News, Newsweek, and Time*. Chicago, IL: Northwestern University Press.

Ganz, Marshall. 2000. "Resources and Resourcefulness: Strategic Capacity in the Unionization of California Agriculture, 1959–1966." *American Journal of Sociology* 105:1003–1062.

———. 2004. "Why David Sometimes Wins: Strategic Capacity in Social Movements." Pp. 177–200 in *Rethinking Social Movements: Structure, Meaning, and Emotion*, edited by J. Goodwin and J. M. Jasper. Lanham, MD: Rowman & Littlefield.

Gauchat, Gordon. 2011. "The Cultural Authority of Science: Public Trust and Acceptance of Organized Science." *Public Understanding of Science (Bristol, England)* 20(6):751–770.

———. 2012. "Politicization of Science in the Public Sphere a Study of Public Trust in the United States, 1974 to 2010." *American Sociological Review* 77(2):167–187.

———. 2015. "The Political Context of Science in the United States: Public Acceptance of Evidence-Based Policy and Science Funding." *Social Forces* 94:723–746.

Geertz, Clifford. 1973 [1964]. *The Interpretation of Cultures*. New York: Basic Books.

General Inquirer. n.d. www.wjh.harvard.edu.

Gerring, John. 1997. "Ideology: A Definitional Analysis." *Political Research Quarterly* 50:957–994.

Ghaziani, Amin and Delia Baldassarri. 2011. "Cultural Anchors and the Organization of Differences." *American Sociological Review* 76:179–206.

Gieryn, Thomas F. 1999. *Cultural Boundaries of Science: Credibility on the Line*. Chicago: University of Chicago Press.

———. 2000. "A Space for Place in Sociology." *Annual Review of Sociology* 26:463–496.

———. 2001. "Can Museums Lie?" Museums and Science: Exposing the Boundaries, American Anthropological Association Annual Meeting, Washington, DC.

———. 2002. "What Buildings Do." *Theory and Society* 31:35–74.

———. 2008. "Laboratory Design for Post-Fordist Science." *ISIS* 99:796–802.

Gieryn, Thomas F., George M. Bevins, and Stephen C. Zehr. 1985. "Professionalization of American Scientists: Public Science in the Creation/Evolution Trials." *American Sociological Review* 50:392–409.

Gishlick, Alan. 2006. "Baraminology." *National Center for Science Education* 26(4):17–21.

Gitlin, Todd. 1980. *The Whole World Is Watching: Mass Media in the Making and Un-making of the New Left*. Berkeley: University of California Press.

Golinski, Jan. 2005 [1998]. *Making Natural Knowledge: Constructivism and the History of Science, with a New Preface*. Chicago: University of Chicago Press.

Goodstein, Laurie. 2005. "Judge Rejects Teaching Intelligent Design" *New York Times*, December 21.

———. 2018. "Billy Graham Warned Against Embracing a President. His Son Has Gone another Way." *New York Times*, February 26, www.nytimes.com.

Goodwin, Jeff and Jasper M. Jasper. 2004. *Rethinking Social Movements: Structure, Meaning, and Emotion.* Lanham, MD: Rowman & Littlefield.

Gordon, James S. 2017. "Does the 'Cyrus Prophecy' Help Explain Evangelical Support for Donald Trump?." *The Guardian*, March 23, Opinion. www.theguardian.com.

Green, Emma. 2017. "White Evangelicals Believe They Face More Discrimination Than Muslims: A New Study Suggests Different Groups of Americans See Their Country in Radically Divergent Ways." *The Atlantic*, March 10.

Greenland, Fiona. 2019. "Material Culture and the Problem of Agency." *American Journal of Cultural Sociology* 7:412–420.

Griswold, Wendy. 2004. *Cultures and Society in a Changing World*, 4th edition. New York: Sage.

Griswold, Wendy, Gemma Mangione, and Terence E. McDonnell. 2013. "Objects, Words, and Bodies in Space: Bringing Materiality into Cultural Analysis." *Qualitative Sociology* 36:343–364.

Groseclose, Tim and Jeffrey Milyo. 2005. "A Measure of Media Bias." *Quarterly Journal of Economics* 120:1191–1237.

Gross, Neil, Thomas Medvetz, and Rupert Russell. 2011. "The Contemporary American Conservative Movement." *Annual Review of Sociology* 37:325–354.

Gross, Neil and Solon Simmons. 2009. "The Religiosity of American College and University Professors." *Sociology of Religion* 70: 101–129.

Guidestar. 2013. Answers in Genesis Report. www.guidestar.org.

Ham, Ken. 2007. "Media Blitz on the Creation Museum." Answers in Genesis, Blog, https://answersingenesis.org/blogs.

———. 2010. "A Sad Day for the Assemblies of God Denomination." Answers in Genesis, Blog. https://answersingenesis.org/blogs.

———. 2014. "More Awards for Answers Magazine." Answers in Genesis, blog, https://answersingenesis.org/blogs.

Henke, Christopher and Thomas F. Gieryn. 2008. "Sites of Scientific Practice: The Enduring Importance of Place." Pp. 353–376 in *The Handbook of Science and Technology Studies*, edited by E. Hackett, O. Amsterdamska, M. Lynch, and J. Wajcman. Cambridge, MA: MIT Press.

Hetherington, Kevin. 2002. "The Unsightly: Touching the Parthenon Frieze." *Theory, Culture & Society* 19:187–205.

Hine, Amelia and Fabien Medvecky. 2015. "Unfinished Science in Museums: A Push for Critical Science Literacy." *Journal of Science Communication* 14:1–14.

Hirschkind, Charles. 2006. *The Ethical Soundscape: Cassette Sermons and Islamic Counterpublics.* New York: Columbia University Press.

Hodge, Bodie. 2010. "Was the Forbidden Fruit an Apple? How Did Eve Know It Was Edible?" Answers in Genesis Blog, June 29, https://answersingenesis.org.

Howes, David. 2014. "Introduction to Sensory Museology." *The Senses & Society* 9(3):259–267.

Isaac, Larry. 2008. "Movement of Movements: Culture Moves in the Long Civil Rights Struggle." *Social Forces* 87:33–63.

———. 2009. "Movements, Aesthetics, and Markets in Literary Change: Making the American Labor Problem Novel." *American Sociological Review* 74(6):938–965.

Jansen, Robert S. 2008. "Jurassic Technology? Sustaining Presumptions of Intersubjectivity in a Disruptive Environment." *Theory and Society* 37:127–159.

Johnston, Hank and Bert Klandermans. 1995. *Social Movements and Culture*. Minneapolis: University of Minnesota Press.

Jones, Martyn W. 2017. "Inside the Museum of the Bible." *Christianity Today*, October 20, www.christianitytoday.com.

Jost, John T., Christopher M. Federico, and Jaime L. Napier. 2009. "Political Ideology: Its Structure, Functions, and Elective Affinities." *Annual Review of Psychology* 60:307–337.

Kaden, Tom. 2019. *Creationism and Anti-Creationism in the United States: A Sociology of Conflict*. Basel, Switzerland: Springer International.

Kamen, Al and Colby Itkowitz. 2015. "A Fight at the Museum: When Fossil Fuels Fuel Fossils." *Washington Post*, March 25, A19.

Kang, Jian and Brigitte Schulte-Fortkamp. 2016. *Soundscape and the Built Environment*. Boca Raton, FL: CRC Press.

Karpf, David. 2012. "Social Science Research Methods in Internet Time." *Information, Communication & Society* 15:639–661.

Keane, Webb. 2003. "Semiotics and the Social Analysis of Material Things." *Language and Communication* 23:409–425.

Kelly, Casey R. and Kristen E. Hoerl. 2012. "Genesis in Hyperreality: Legitimizing Disingenuous Controversy at the Creation Museum." *Argumentation and Advocacy* 48(3):123–141.

Kilde, Jeanne H. 2002. *When Church Became Theatre: The Transformation of Evangelical Architecture and Worship in Nineteenth-Century America*. New York: Oxford University Press.

———. 2006. "Reading Megachurches: Investigating the Religious and Cultural Work of Church Architecture." Pp. 225–247 in *American Sanctuary: Understanding Sacred Spaces*, edited by L. P. Nelson. Bloomington: Indiana University Press.

Klein, Jurgen. 2012. "Francis Bacon." *Stanford Encyclopedia of Philosophy*, https://plato.stanford.edu.

Klett, Joseph. 2014. "Sound on Sound Situating Interaction in Sonic Object Settings." *Sociological Theory* 32:147–161.

Knell, Simon J., Suzanne Macleod, and Shelia E. R. Watson. 2007. *Museum Revolutions: How Museums Change and Are Changed*. New York: Routledge.

Kniss, Fred and Gene Burns. 2004. "Religious Movements." Pp. 694–715 in *The Blackwell Companion to Social Movements*, edited by D. A. Snow, S. A. Soule, and H. Kriesi. Malden, MA: Blackwell.

Knorr-Cetina, Karin. 1992. "The Couch, the Cathedral, and the Laboratory: On the Relationship between Experiment and Laboratory Science." Pp. 113–138 in *Science as Practice and Culture*, edited by A. Pickering. Chicago: University of Chicago Press.

———. 1997. "Sociality with Objects: Social Relations in Postsocial Knowledge Societies." *Theory, Culture & Society* 14:1–30.

———. 1999. *Epistemic Cultures: How the Sciences Make Knowledge*. Cambridge, MA: Harvard University Press.

Kohler, Robert E. 2002. *Landscapes and Labscapes: Exploring the Lab-Field Border in Biology*. Chicago: University of Chicago Press.

Koltsova, Olessia and Andrey Shcherbak. 2015. "'LiveJournal Libra!': The Political Blogosphere and Voting Preferences in Russia in 2011–2012." *New Media & Society* 17(10):1715–1732.

Konieczny, Mary E. and Megan C. Rogers. 2016. "Religion, Secular Humanism, and Atheism: Multi-Institutional Politics and the USAFA Cadets' Freethinkers Group." *Journal for the Scientific Study of Religion* 55(4):821–838.

Koopmans, Ruud. 2004. "Movements and Media: Selection Processes and Evolutionary Dynamics in the Public Sphere." *Theory & Society* 33:367–391.

Krieger, Zvika. 2007. "Exhibition Game: Hezbollah's Creepy New Museum." *New Republic*, August 26, https://newrepublic.com.

Kuhn, Thomas S. 1962. *The Structure of Scientific Revolutions*. Chicago: University of Chicago Press.

Lacey, Troy. 2011. "Deceitful or Distinguishable Terms—Historical and Observational Science." Answers in Genesis Blog, June 10, https://answersingenesis.org.

Landau, Elizabeth. 2007. "Science Museums Adapt in Struggle against Creationist Revisionism." *Scientific American*, July 12, www.scientificamerican.com.

Larson, Edward J. 2003. *Trial and Error: The American Controversy over Creation and Evolution*. New York: Oxford University Press.

———. 2006. *Summer for the Gods: The Scopes Trial and America's Continuing Debate over Science and Religion*. New York: Basic Books.

Latour, Bruno. 1983. "Give Me a Laboratory and I Will Raise the World." Pp. 141–170 in *Science Observed: Perspectives on the Social Study of Science*, edited by K. Knorr-Cetina and M. J. Mulkay. Beverly Hills, CA: Sage.

Leahy, Michael P. 2007. "The Trouble with Fred and Wilma." *Los Angeles Times*, June 12, Opinion, http://www.latimes.com.

LeCount, Ryan Jerome. 2018. "Visualizing the Increasing Effect of Racial Resentment on Political Ideology among Whites, 1986 to 2016." *Socius* 4.

Lelievre, Michelle A. 2006. "Evolving Planet: Constructing the Culture of Science Chicago's Field Museum." *Anthropologica* 48:293–296.

Letzter, Rafi. 2016. "Here's Why So Many Smart People Don't Believe in Evolution." *Business Insider*, September 15, www.businessinsider.com.

Levent, Nina and Pascual-Leone, Alvaro, eds. 2014. *The Multisensory Museum: Cross-Disciplinary Perspectives on Touch, Sound, Smell, Memory, and Space*. Lanham, MD: Rowman & Littlefield.

Lewandowsky, Stephan, Klaus Oberauer, Scott Brophy, Elisabeth A. Lloyd, and Michael Marriott. 2015. "Recurrent Fury: Conspiratorial Discourse in the Blogosphere Triggered by Research on the Role of Conspiracist Ideation in Climate Denial." *Journal of Social and Political Psychology* 3:142–178.

Lienesch, Michael. 2007. *In the Beginning: Fundamentalism, the Scopes Trial, and the Making of the Antievolution Movement*. Chapel Hill: University of North Carolina Press.

Lindekilde, Lasse E. 2008. "In the Name of the Prophet? Danish Muslim Mobilization During the Muhammad Caricatures Controversy." *Mobilization* 13:219–238.

Linville, James R. 2019. "The Creationist Museum of the Bible." Pp. 257–73 in *The Museum of the Bible: A Critical Introduction*, edited by J. Hicks-Keeton and C. Concannon. Lanham, MD: Lexington Books.

Lipsky, Michael. 1968. "Protest as a Political Resource." *American Political Science Review* 62:1144–1158.

Livingstone, David N. 2003. *Putting Science in Its Place: Geographies of Scientific Knowledge*. Chicago: University of Chicago Press.

Loonsbury, Michael and Marc J. Ventresca. 2002. *Social Structure and Organizations Revisited*. Oxford, UK: Elsevier Science.

Looy, Mark. 2006. "A Field Trip to an Evolving Planet." Answers in Genesis, March 13, www.answersingenesis.org.

Loveland, Anne C. and Otis B. Wheeler. 2003. *From Meetinghouse to Megachurch: A Material and Cultural History*. Columbia: University of Missouri Press.

Lynch, John. 2013. "'Prepare to Believe': The Creation Museum as Embodied Conversion Narrative." *Rhetoric & Public Affairs* 16(1):1–27.

MacDonald, Sharon. 1998. "Exhibitions of Power and Powers of Exhibition: An Introduction to the Politics of Display." Pp. 1–24 in *The Politics of Display: Museums, Science, Culture*, edited by S. MacDonald. New York: Routledge.

———. 2006. "Collecting Practices." Pp. 81–97 in *A Companion to Museum Studies*, edited by S. Macdonald. Malden, MA: Blackwell.

MacDonald, Teresa and E. O. Wiley. 2012. "Communicating Phylogeny: Evolutionary Tree Diagrams in Museums." *Evolution Education Outreach* 5:28.

MacFadden, Bruce J., Luz Helena Oviedo, Grace M. Seymour, and Shari Ellis. 2012. "Fossil Horses, Orthogenesis, and Communicating Evolution in Museums." *Evolution Education Outreach* 5:29–37.

Mangione, Gemma. 2016. "Making Sense of Things: Constructing Aesthetic Experience in Museum Gardens and Galleries." *Museum & Society* 14(1):33–51.

Marsden, George M. 1980. *Fundamentalism and American Culture: The Shaping of Twentieth-Century Evangelicalism 1870–1925*. New York: Oxford University Press.

Marti, Gerardo. 2017. "The Global Phenomenon of Hillsong Church: An Initial Assessment." *Sociology of Religion* 78(4):377–386.

McAdam, Doug, John D. McCarthy, and Mayer N. Zald. 1996. *Comparative Perspectives on Social Movements: Political Opportunities, Mobilizing Structures, and Cultural Framings*. New York: Cambridge University Press.

McCarthy, John D. and Mayer N. Zald. 1977. "Resource Mobilization and Social Movements: A Partial Theory." *American Journal of Sociology* 82:1212–1241.

McDonnell, Terence E. 2010. "Cultural Objects as Objects: Materiality, Urban Space, and the Interpretation of AIDS Campaigns in Accra, Ghana." *American Journal of Sociology* 115:1800–1852.

———. 2016. *Best Laid Plans: Cultural Entropy and the Unraveling of AIDS Media Campaigns.* Chicago: University of Chicago Pres.

McDonnell, Terence E., Christopher A. Bail, and Iddo Tavory. 2017. "A Theory of Resonance." *Sociological Theory* 35(1):1–14.

McGlone, Peggy. 2019. "The Museum of the Bible Expands Programming to Attract More Repeat Visitors." *Washington Post*, November 6.

McKeever, Stacia, Gary Vaterlaus, and Diane King. 2008. *The Creation Museum: Behind the Scenes.* Hebron, KY: Answers in Genesis–USA.

McVeigh, Rory. 2009. *The Rise of the Ku Klux Klan: Right-Wing Movements and National Politics.* Minneapolis: University of Minnesota Press.

Medvetz, Thomas. 2012. *Think Tanks in America.* Chicago: University of Chicago Press.

Menton, David and Elizabeth Mitchell. 2012. "A Look at Lucy's Legacy." *Answers in Depth*, June 6, https://answersingenesis.org.

Meyer, Birgit. 2010. "Aesthetics of Persuasion: Global Christianity and Pentecostalism's Sensational Forms." *South Atlantic Quarterly* 109:741–763.

Meyer, David S. and Eulalie Laschever. 2016. "Social Movements and the Institutionalization of Dissent in America." in *The Oxford Handbook of American Political Development, Oxford Handbooks Online*, edited by R. Valelly, S. Mettler, and R. Lieberman.

Meyer, Stephen C. 2006. "Intelligent Design Is Not Creationism." *Telegraph*, January 28, www.telegraph.co.uk.

Michels, Robert. 1962 [1911]. *Political Parties: A Sociological Study of the Oligarchical Tendencies of Modern Democracy.* New York: Free Press.

Mitchell, Amy, Jeffrey Gottfried, Jocelyn Kiley, and Katerina E. Matsa. 2014. "Section 1: Media Sources: Distinct Favorites Emerge on the Left and Right." *Pew Research Center*, October 21, www.journalism.org.

Mitchell, Elizabeth. 2013. "Lucy Makeover Shouts a Dangerously Deceptive Message About Our Supposed Ancestors." Answers in Genesis, October 5, www.answersingenesis.org.

Moore, John N. and Harold S. Slusher. 1970. *Biology: A Search for Order in Complexity.* Grand Rapids, MI: Zondervan.

Moore, Kelly. 2008. *Disrupting Science: Social Movements, American Scientists and Politics of the Military, 1945–75.* Princeton, NJ: Princeton University Press.

Moran, Jeffrey P. 2012. *American Genesis: The Antievolution Controversies from Scopes to Creation Science.* New York: Oxford University Press.

Morello-Frosch, Rachel, Stephen Zavestoski, Phil Brown, Rebecca Gasior, Sabrina McCormick, and Brian Mayer. 2006. "Embodied Health Movements: Responses to a Scientized World." Pp. 244–271 in *The New Political Sociology of Science.*

"Embodied Health Movements: Responses to a Scientized World." Madison: University of Wisconsin Press.

Morris, Aldon D. 1984. *The Origins of the Civil Rights Movement: Black Communities Organizing for Change.* New York: Free Press.

Morris, Henry M. 2010 [1988]. "Is Creationism Important in Education?" Answers in Genesis Blog, https://answersingenesis.org.

Moser, Stephanie. 2003. "Representing Archaeological Knowledge in Museums: Exhibiting Human Origins and Strategies for Change." *Public Archaeology* 3:3–20.

Moss, Candida and Joel S. Baden. 2017. "Just What Is the Museum of the Bible Trying to Do?" *Politico*, October 15, www.politico.com.

Mukerji, Chandra. 1994. "Toward a Sociology of Material Culture: Science Studies, Cultural Studies and the Meanings of Things." Pp. 143–162 in *The Sociology of Culture: Emerging Theoretical Perspectives*, edited by D. Crane. Cambridge, MA: Blackwell.

Mullen, William. 2006. "Field Exhibit Out to Show We've Come a Long Way." *Chicago Tribune*, March 7.

Murphy, Michelle. 2006. *Sick Building Syndrome and the Problem of Uncertainty: Environmental Politics, Technoscience, and Women Workers.* Durham, NC: Duke University Press.

National Center for Science and Engineering Statistics. 2016. *National Science Board: Science and Engineering Indicators.* Arlington, VA: National Science Foundation.

National Center for Education Statistics. 2018. *The Condition of Education: Private School Enrollment.* Washington, DC: Institute of Education Sciences.

Natural History Museum Archives London. n.d. Retrieved October 24, 2017, www.nhm.ac.uk.

Nelkin, Dorothy. 1977. *Science Textbook Controversies and the Politics of Equal Time.* Cambridge, MA: MIT Press.

Nelson, Alondra. 2013. *Body and Soul: The Black Panther Party and the Fight Against Medical Discrimination.* Minneapolis: University of Minnesota Press.

Noy, Shiri and Timothy O'Brien. 2016. "A Nation Divided: Science, Religion, and Public Opinion in the United States." *Socius* 2:1–15.

Numbers, Ronald L. 2006. *The Creationists: From Scientific Creationism to Intelligent Design.* Cambridge, MA: Harvard University Press.

Numbers, Ronald L. and T. Joe Wiley. 2015. "Baptizing Dinosaurs: How Once-Suspect Evidence of Evolution Came to Support the Biblical Narrative." *Spectrum: Journal of the Association of Adventist Forums* 43(1):57–68.

O'Brien, Timothy and Shiri Noy. 2015. "Traditional, Modern, and Post-Secular Perspectives on Science and Religion in the United States." *American Sociological Review* 80:92–115.

Oliver, Pamela E. and Hank Johnston. 2000. "What a Good Idea! Ideologies and Frames in Social Movement Research." *Mobilization* 5:37–54.

Oliver, Pamela E. and Gregory M. Maney. 2000. "Political Processes and Local News-paper Coverage of Protest Events: From Selection Bias to Triadic Interactions." *American Journal of Sociology* 106:463–505.

Oliver, Pamela E. and Daniel J. Myers. 1999. "How Events Enter the Public Sphere: Conflict, Location, and Sponsorship in Local Newspaper Coverage of Public Events." *American Journal of Sociology* 105:38–87.

O'Neill, Mark. 2004. "Enlightenment Museums: Universal or Merely Global?" *Museums & Society* 2(3):190–202.

Ophir, Adi and Steven Shapin. 1991. "The Place of Knowledge: A Methodological Sur-vey." *Science in Context* 4:3–22.

Opinion, Editorial. 2007. "Yabba-Dabba Science: The Bedrock Truth Is that the Creation Museum May Be a Gay Old Time, But It's Not a Page Out of History." *Los Angeles Times*, May 24, http://articles.latimes.com.

Ortiz, David G., Daniel J. Myers, Eugene N. Walls, and Maria-Elena D. Diaz. 2005. "Where Do We Stand with Newspaper Data?" *Mobilization: An International Quar-terly* 10:397–419.

Pachucki, Mark C. 2012. "Classifying Quality: Cognition, Interaction, and Status Ap-praisal of Art Museums." *Poetics* 40:67–90.

Pattillo-McCoy, Mary. 1998. "Church Culture as a Strategy of Action in the Black Com-munity." *American Sociological Review* 63(6):767–784.

Pew Research Center. 2015. *U.S. Public Becoming Less Religious: Modest Drop in Overall Rates of Belief and Practice, but Religiously Affiliated Americans Are as Observant as Before*. Washington, DC: Pew Research Center.

Phelps, Daniel. 2008. "The Anti-Museum: An Overview and Review of the Answers in Genesis Creation 'Museum.'" *National Center for Science Education*, April.

Piven, Frances F. and Richard A. Cloward. 1977. *Poor People's Movements: Why They Succeed, How They Fail*. New York: Pantheon Books.

Platt, Gerald M. and Rhys H. Williams. 2002. "Ideological Language and Social Movement Mobilization: A Sociolinguistic Analysis of Segregationists' Ideologies." *Sociological Theory* 20(3): 328–359.

Polletta, Francesca. 1999. "'Free Spaces' in Collective Action." *Theory and Society* 28:1–38.

———. 2004. "Culture Is Not Just in Your Head." Pp. 97–110 in *Rethinking Social Move-ments: Structure, Meaning, and Emotion*, edited by J. Goodwin and J. M. Jasper. Lanham, MD: Rowman & Littlefield.

———. 2008. "Culture and Movements." *Annals of the American Academy of Political and Social Science* 619(1):78–96.

Polletta, Francesca and James M. Jasper. 2001. "Collective Identity and Social Move-ments." *Annual Review of Sociology* 27:283–305.

Polletta, Francesca and Kelsy Kretschmer. 2013. "Free Spaces." Pp. 477–480 in *The Wiley-Blackwell Encyclopedia of Social and Political Movements*, edited by D. A. Snow, D. Della Porta, B. Klandermans, and D. McAdam. Hoboken, NJ: Wiley.

Press, Andrea L. 1994. "The Sociology of Cultural Reception: Notes Toward an Emerging Paradigm." Pp. 221–245 in *The Sociology of Culture*, edited by D. Crane. Cambridge, MA: Blackwell.

Price, George McCready. 1923. *The New Geology*. Oakland, CA: Pacific Press Publishing Association.

Ramm, Bernard. 1954. *Christian View of Science and Scripture*. Grand Rapids, MI: Wm. B. Eerdmans Publishing.

Rao, Hayagreeva and Sunasir Dutta. 2012. "Free Spaces as Organizational Weapons of the Weak: Religious Festivals and Regimental Mutinies in the 1857 Bengal Native Army." *Administrative Science Quarterly* 57(4):625–668.

Rao, Hayagreeva, Calvin Morrill, and Mayer Zald. 2000. "Power Plays: How Social Movements and Collective Action Create New Organizational Forms." *Research in Organizational Behaviour* 22:239–282.

Ray, Brian D. 2018. "Homeschooling Growing: Multiple Data Points Show Increase 2012 to

2016 and Later." *National Home Education Research Institute*, www.nheri.org.

Redfern, Martin. 2007. "Creationist Museum Challenges Evolution." *BBC News*, April 14. http://news.bbc.co.uk.

Rohlinger, Deana A. and Jennifer Earl. 2017. "The Past, Present, and Future of Media and Social Movements Studies: Introduction to the Special Issue on Media and Social Movements." Pp. 1–20 in *Social Movements and Media,* Vol. 14, "The Past, Present, and Future of Media and Social Movements Studies: Introduction to the Special Issue on Media and Social Movements." Bingley, UK: Emerald Publishing.

Rohlinger, Deana A., Ben Kail, Miles Taylor, and Sarrah Conn. 2012. "Outside the Mainstream: Social Movement Organization Media Coverage in Mainstream and Partisan News Outlets." Pp. 51–80 in *Media, Movements, and Political Change: Research in Social Movements, Conflicts and Change*, Vol. 33, edited by J. Earl and D. A. Rohlinger. Bingley, UK: Emerald Publishing.

Rojas, Fabio. 2007. *From Black Power to Black Studies: How a Radical Social Movement Became an Academic Discipline*. Baltimore, MD: John Hopkins University Press.

Roos, J. Micah. 2014. "Measuring Science or Religion? A Measurement Analysis of the National Science Foundation Sponsored Science Literacy Scale 2006–2010." *Public Understanding of Science* 23:797–813.

———. 2016. "Alternately Contested: A Measurement Analysis of Alternately Worded Items in the National Science Foundation Science Literacy Scale." *Socius: Sociological Research for a Dynamic World*, 2. http://journals.sagepub.com.

Rose-Greenland, Fiona. 2016. "Color Perception in Sociology: Materiality and Authenticity at the Gods in Color Show." *Sociological Theory* 34(2):81–105.

Rosenhouse, Jason. 2012. *Among the Creationists: Dispatches from the Anti-Evolutionist Front Line*. New York: Oxford University Press.

Roth, Matthew W. 2002. "The Museum of Jurassic Technology: Culver City, California." *Technology and Culture* 43:102–109.

Rothman, Lily. 2015. "How Lucy the Australopithecus Changed the Way We Understand Human Evolution." *TIME*, November 24, http://time.com.

Rothstein, Edward. 2007. "Adam and Eve in the Land of the Dinosaurs." *New York Times*, May 24, Petersburg, KY.

Rydgren, Jens. 2007. "The Sociology of the Radical Right." *Annual Review of Sociology* 33:241–262.

Saletan, William. 2018. "Never Trumpers for Trump: How Trump's Conservative Critics Became Wingmen for the President's Supporters." *Slate*, November 29, Politics, https://slate.com.

Scheitle, Christopher P. 2018. "Politics and the Perceived Boundaries of Science: Activism, Sociology, and Scientific Legitimacy." *Socius* 4.

Scheitle, Christopher P. and Elaine H. Ecklund. 2015. "The Influence of Science Popularizers on the Public's View of Religion and Science: An Experimental Assessment." *Public Understanding of Science (Bristol, England)* 26(1):25–39.

Schofield, Robert E. 1989. "The Science Education of an Enlightened Entrepreneur: Charles Willson Peale and His Philadelphia Museum, 1784–1827." *American Studies* 30:21–40.

Schradie, Jen. 2019. *The Revolution That Wasn't: How Digital Activism Favors Conservatives.* Cambridge, MA: Harvard University Press.

Schudson, Michael. 1989. "How Culture Works: Perspectives from Media Studies on the Efficacy of Symbols." *Theory and Society* 18:153–180.

Scott, Monique and Ellen Giusti. 2006. "Designing Human Evolution Exhibitions. Insights from Exhibitions and Audiences." *Museums & Social Issues* 1:49–68.

Scully, Maureen and Amy Segal. 2002. "Passion with an Umbrella: Grassroots Activists in the Workplace." Pp. 127–170 in *Research in the Sociology of Organizations*, edited by M. J. Ventresca and M. Loonsbury. Oxford, UK: JAI Press.

Seib, Gerald F. 2016. "Donald Trump's Challenge: Passing the Plausibility Test." *Wall Street Journal*, August 15, www.wsj.com.

Sewell, William H., Jr. 2005. *Logics of History: Social Theory and Social Transformation.* Chicago: University of Chicago Press.

Shapin, Steven. 1994. *A Social History of Truth: Civility and Science in Seventeenth-Century England.* Chicago: University of Chicago Press.

Shermer, Michael. 2005. "The Fossil Fallacy: Creationists' Demand for Fossils that Represent 'Missing Links' Reveals a Deep Misunderstanding of Science." *Scientific American*, March 1, www.scientificamerican.com.

Slack, Gordy. 2007. "Inside the Creation Museum: Adam and Eve Frolic Amid the Dinosaurs in the New $27 Million Museum that Demonstrates Darwin Has Nothing on the Book of Genesis." *Salon*, May 31.

Slevin, Peter. 2007. "A Monument to Creation." *Washington Post*, May 21.

Smith, Christian. 2003. *The Secular Revolution: Power, Interests, and Conflict in the Secularization of American Public Life.* Berkeley: University of California Press.

Smith, Gregory A. and Jessica Martínez. 2016. "How the Faithful Voted: A Preliminary 2016 Analysis." *Pew Research Center*, November 9, www.pewresearch.org.

Snelling, Andrew A. 2016. "Misunderstood Messengers from Space: Planetary Geology." *Answers in Genesis*, April 1, www.answersingenesis.org.

Snow, David A. and Robert D. Benford. 1988. "Ideology, Frame Resonance, and Participant Mobilization." Pp. 197–218 in *International Social Movement Research: From Structure to Action*. Greenwich, CT: JAI Press.

Somers, Margaret R. 2008. "Fear and Loathing of the Public Sphere: How to Unthink a Knowledge Culture by Narrating and Denaturalizing Anglo-American Citizenship Theory." Pp. 254–288 in *Genealogies of Citizenship: Markets, Statelessness, and the Right to Have Rights*. New York: Cambridge University Press.

Soule, Sarah A. and Brayden G. King. 2008. "Competition and Resource Partitioning in Three Social Movement Industries." *American Journal of Sociology* 113:1568–1610.

Spiegel, Amy, Margaret Evans, Wendy Gram, and Judy Diamond. 2006. "Museum Visitors' Understanding of Evolution." *Museums & Social Issues* 1:69–86.

Staggenborg, Suzanne. 2001. "Beyond Culture Versus Politics: A Case Study of a Local Women's Movement." *Gender and Society* 15(4):507–530.

Stamatov, Peter. 2002. "Interpretive Activism and the Political Uses of Verdi's Operas in the 1840s." *American Sociological Review* 67:345–366.

Stewart, Katherine. 2018. "The Museum of the Bible Is a Safe Space for Christian Nationalists." *New York Times*, January 6, www.nytimes.com.

Stirrat, Michael and R. E. Cornwell. 2013. "Eminent Scientists Reject the Supernatural: A Survey of the Fellows of the Royal Society." *Evolution: Education and Outreach* 6(1):33.

Stoltz, Dustin S. and Marshall A. Taylor. 2017. "Paying with Change: The Purposeful Enunciation of Material Culture." *Poetics* 64:26–39.

Stryker, Robin. 1996. "Beyond History Versus Theory: Strategic Narrative and Sociological Explanation." *Sociological Methods Research* 24:304–352.

Swidler, Ann. 1986. "Culture in Action: Symbols and Strategies." *American Sociological Review* 51:273–286.

———. 1995. "Cultural Power and Social Movements." Pp. 25–40 in *Social Movements and Culture*, vol. 4, edited by H. Johnston and B. Klandermans. Minneapolis: University of Minnesota Press.

Swift, Art. 2017. "In US, Belief in Creationist View of Humans at New Low." *Gallup Poll Report*, www.gallup.com.

Tarrow, Sidney. 1998. *Power in Movement: Social Movements and Contentious Politics*. New York: Cambridge University Press.

Taylor, Verta. 1989. "Social Movement Continuity: The Women's Movement in Abeyance." *American Sociological Review* 54:761–775.

Taylor, Verta, Katrina Kimport, Nella Van Dyke, and Ellen Ann Andersen. 2009. "Culture and Mobilization: Tactical Repertoires, Same-Sex Weddings, and the Impact on Gay Activism." *American Sociological Review* 74:865–890.

Taylor, Verta and Nella Van Dyke. 2004. "Tactical Repertoires of Social Movements." Pp. 262–293 in *The Blackwell Companion to Social Movements*. Malden, MA: Blackwell.

Taylor, Verta and Nancy Whittier. 1995. "Analytical Approaches to Social Movement Culture: The Culture of the Women's Movement." Pp. 163–187 in *Social Movements and Culture*, edited by H. Johnston and B. Klandermans. Minneapolis: University of Minnesota Press.

Thorpe, Ann. 2014. "Applying Protest Event Analysis to Architecture and Design." *Social Movement Studies: Journal of Social, Cultural and Political Protest* 13:275–295.

Tilly, Charles. 1978. *From Mobilization to Revolution*. New York: McGraw-Hill.

Tlili, Anwar, Sharon Gewirtz and Alan Cribb. 2007. "New Labour's Socially Responsible Museum." *Policy Studies* 28(3):269–289.

To, Cheryl, Harriet R. Tenenbaum, and Daniel Wormald. 2016. "What Do Parents and Children Talk About at a Natural History Museum?" *Curator: The Museum Journal* 59:369–385.

Tooley, Christa B. and Matthew J. Milliner. 2017. "The Ark vs. Covenant: The Dramatic Contrast between the Creation Museum and the Museum of the Bible." *Washington Post*, November 20.

Toumey, Christopher P. 1994. *God's Own Scientists: Creationists in a Secular World*. New Brunswick, NJ: Rutgers University Press.

Trollinger, Susan L. and William Vance Trollinger Jr. 2016. *Righting America at the Creation Museum*. Baltimore, MD: Johns Hopkins University Press.

Troyan, Mary. 2016. "Congress Passes Bill to Protect Non-Believers for First Time." *USA Today*, December 21, www.usatoday.com.

Van Dyke, Nella, Sarah A. Soule, and Verta A. Taylor. 2004. "The Targets of Social Movements: Beyond a Focus on the State." *Research in Social Movements, Conflicts and Change* 25:27–51.

Vasi, Ion Bogdan and Chan S. Suh. 2016. "Online Activities, Spatial Proximity, and the Diffusion of the Occupy Wall Street Movement in the United States." *Mobilization* 21:139–154.

Wagner-Pacifici, Robin. 1996. "Memories in the Making: The Shapes of Things That Went." *Qualitative Sociology* 19:301–321.

———. 2010. "The Cultural Sociological Experience of Cultural Objects." Pp. 110–118 in *Handbook of Cultural Sociology*, edited by J. R. Hall, Laura Grindstaff, and Ming-Cheng Lo. London: Routledge.

Wagner-Pacifici, Robin and Barry Schwartz. 1991. "The Vietnam Veterans Memorial: Commemorating a Difficult Past." *American Journal of Sociology* 97:376–420.

Walker, Edward T., Andrew W. Martin, and John D. McCarthy. 2008. "Confronting the State, the Corporation, and the Academy: The Influence of Institutional Targets on Social Movement Repertoires." *American Journal of Sociology* 114(1):35–76.

Weber, Max. 1978. *Economy and Society: An Outline of Interpretive Sociology, Volume I*. Berkeley: University of California Press.

———. 2001 [1905]. *The Protestant Ethic and The Spirit of Capitalism*. Los Angeles, CA: Roxbury.

Weschler, Lawrence. 1995. *Mr. Wilson's Cabinet of Wonder: Pronged Ants, Horned Humans, Mice on Toast, and Other Marvels of Jurassic Technology.* New York: Random House.

Westerman, Ashley. 2016. "Life-Size Noah's Ark to Open Amid a Flood of Skepticism." *NPR*, July 5, Morning Edition, www.npr.org.

Whitcomb, John C. and Henry M. Morris. 1961. *The Genesis Flood: The Biblical Record and Its Scientific Implications.* Phillipsburg, NJ: Presbyterian & Reformed Publishing.

Williams, Rhys H. 2004. "The Cultural Contexts of Collective Action: Constraints, Opportunities, and the Symbolic Life of Social Movements." Pp. 91–115 in *The Blackwell Companion to Social Movements.* Malden, MA: Blackwell.

Wilson, John. 1973. *Introduction to Social Movements.* New York: Basic Books.

Witcomb, Andrea. 2006. "Interactivity: Thinking Beyond." Pp. 353–361 in *A Companion to Museum Studies*, edited by S. MacDonald. Malden, MA: Blackwell.

Worthen, Molly. 2014. *Apostles of Reason: The Crisis of Authority in American Evangelicalism.* New York: Oxford University Press.

Yanni, Carla. 2005 [1999]. *Nature's Museums: Victorian Science and the Architecture of Display.* New York: Princeton Architectural Press.

———. 2014. "Development and Display: Progressive Evolution in British Victorian Architecture and Architectural Theory." Pp. 227–260 in *Evolution and Victorian Culture*, edited by B. Lightman and B. Zon. New York: Cambridge University Press.

Zald, Mayer and John D. McCarthy. 1980. "Social Movement Industries: Competition and Cooperation among Movement Organizations." Pp. 1–20 in *Research in Social Movements, Conflicts and Change, Volume III.* Didcot, UK: Taylor and Francis.

Zolberg, Vera L. 1996. "Museums as Contested Sites of Remembrance." Pp. 69–82 in *Theorizing Museums: Representing Identity and Diversity in a Changing World*, edited by S. MacDonald and G. Fyfe. Cambridge, MA: Blackwell Publishers/Sociological Review.

———. 1998. "Contested Remembrance: The Hiroshima Exhibit Controversy." *Theory and Society* 27:565–590.

Zubrzycki, Geneviève. 2011. "History and the National Sensorium: Making Sense of Polish Mythology." *Qualitative Sociology* 34:21–57.

———. 2013. "Aesthetic Revolt and the Remaking of National Identity in Quebec, 1960–1969." *Theory and Society* 42(5):423–475.

———, ed. 2017. *National Matters: Materiality, Culture, and Nationalism.* Redwood City, CA: Stanford University Press.

INDEX

American Association for the Advancement of Science (AAAS), 70, 170, 172–73, 212n19

American Humanist Association, 80

American Museum of Natural History 94, 132, 235n53

American Scientific Affiliation (ASA) 66–71, 73, 87, 222n14, 222nn17, 18, 223n29, 225n59

Answers in Genesis (AiG) 2–5, 17–19, 22, 53–62, 78–88. See also *Answers*; *Answers Research Journal*

Answers (lay audience magazine), 61

Answers Research Journal, 61, 217n3, 218n4

apologetics 61, 178, 187, 201, 204, 210

Arab Spring, 195, 215n52

Ark Encounter, 8, 114, 118, 176–77, 183, 185, 189, 192, 195–96, 201, 210, 212n27, 243n20

Atheist, 58, 176, 185–87. *See also* American Humanist Association

audience reception studies, 92, 166–69, 173, 182, 237n11, 238n15, 240n48

Bacon, Francis, 38, 223n30; Baconian, 70, 222n15

Biblical interpretation, literal, 2, 4, 26, 35, 38, 67–68, 92, 96, 161, 187, 222n15; biblical inerrancy, 37, 40

Biological Sciences Curriculum Study (BSCS), 69–70, 223nn23, 24

BioLogos, 180–81

Black Lives Matter, 195

Black Panther Party, 11

Bryan, William Jennings, 67

built environment, 13, 20, 88, 91–92, 94, 126, 195, 204, 215n50, 228n10, 229n13n19, 230n25, 232n43; architecture, 4, 91, 94, 229n20

Capitol Ministries, 200, 243n19; Ralph Drollinger, 200–201

Carter, President Jimmy, 6

Christian Heritage College (CHC), 72–74, 77, 79, 82, 85, 175, 225n56

Civil Rights Movement, 8, 11–12, 224n39; Black churches and, 11–12, 214n43, 223n37

Cleveland Museum of Natural History, 135–36, 148, 149, 152, 155–56, 160–61, 234n23, 234n36, 235n46

collective identity, 11, 64, 69, 74, 76, 80, 83

Creation (Autralian magazine), 79

Creation Research Society (CRS) 5–6, 66, 68–74, 76–78, 80, 87–88, 222n18, 225n53

Creation Research Society Quarterly Journal, 68

Creation Science Ministries (CSM) 79, 226n63

creationist movement, 2, 5–8, 19, 39, 60–62, 178–82, 202–3, 212n25, 224n45, 231n39, 239n25; history of, *see* Chapter 2

cultural authority, 4, 10, 15, 19, 62–63, 90–91, 143, 214n50

cultural change, 13, 88, 167–68, 192, 216n69, 237n10

ABOUT THE AUTHOR

Kathleen C. Oberlin is a researcher based in Chicago. Formerly, she was an Assistant Professor in the Department of Sociology at Grinnell College. She received a PhD in sociology from Indiana University. Her work has been funded by the National Science Foundation and Social Science Research Council, among others.

Lightning Source UK Ltd.
Milton Keynes UK
UKHW012101081120
372905UK00015B/223

9 781479 805709